A World of Change

A World of Change

my life in the global women's rights movement

Anne S Walker

ARCADIA

© Anne S Walker 2018

First published 2018 by ARCADIA

the general books' imprint of

Australian Scholarly Publishing Pty Ltd

7 Lt Lothian St Nth, North Melbourne, Vic 3051

Tel: 03 9329 6963 / Fax: 03 9329 5452

enquiry@scholarly.info / www.scholarly.info

ISBN 978-1-925588-63-7

ALL RIGHTS RESERVED

Cover design: Wayne Saunders

Cover image: Anne S Walker

Contents

Preface vii

Part One
1. Melbourne, early years...3
2. Teacher training college and teaching experience........29
3. Sailing away in search of the world 37
4. Fiji: a decade that changed everything 61
5. USA: a chance to work
   with global women activists 87
6. Postgraduate studies and a new career 104
7. Mexico 1975: International Women's
   Year Conference and Tribune 113
8. International Women's
   Tribune Centre, New York 122
9. 'The Invisible Work of IWTC' 142
10. All roads lead to Beijing 173
11. The years after Beijing 1995 for IWTC 180
12. New York under attack: 11 September 2001 199
13. IWTC and the years after 9/11 207
14. Reflections: New York 1976–2002 214

Part Two: Women's Voices, Women's Stories
Introduction 223
Strange happenings at the
IWY Tribune: Mexico City, 1975 225
International perceptions at the
US IWY Conference: Houston, 1977 228
Working in Iran:
lost on the first day: Teheran, 1978 231
A UN water project gone
wrong in Kenya: Nairobi, 1979 237
A workshop in Liberia.
Lost again!: Monrovia, 1979..240

Gathering information at the
UN in Ethiopia: Addis Ababa, 1979 246
Cleaning up after the
Mid-Decade Conference: Copenhagen, 1980 251
International Women's Day
in Chile: Santiago, 1983 254
Women sacrificing their
daughters to get water: Peru, 1983 258
Getting information
in the village: Kenya, 1984 261
If it's not appropriate for women,
it's not appropriate: Nairobi, 1985 263
Computer training for women
in Zimbabwe: Harare, 1988..268
An Australian woman
diplomat in Nepal: Kathmandu, 1989..............................271
Pacific women using
space technology: Vanuatu, 1989...................................... 274
Discussing rights with a
village woman: Turkey, 1992...276
A 'comfort woman' tells her story: Vienna, 1993 280
A personal friend in Nepal: Washington, DC, 1994.......288
Scary stories in Beijing: Huairou to Beijing, 1995...........290
Muslim and Christian women
come together: Huairou, 1995 293
Strange ideas: Nakaseke, 1999 295
Arriving back with
something to show: Nakaseke, 2001 301
A fire at the telecentre: Nakaseke, 2002 306
Anastasia: Nakaseke, 1999–2007..309

Appendix
Letters and messages from women worldwide to the
International Women's Tribune Centre when Anne S
Walker retired as Executive Director, December 2002 ..*313*

Acknowledgements...322
Index 324

Preface

This book began as a collection of stories about events that I was part of during three decades of working with women worldwide. The thought that it might become a book did not initially enter my mind. Then, with thirty stories completed, I continued on writing stories from my early life and the journey travelled that culminated in those decades of being part of the global struggle for the recognition of women's rights.

I am gratified that others have found these stories worth publishing. My hope is that many of the women with whom I worked may also begin writing. There are so many stories to be told. Don't let our achievements and the story of how we won so much be swept under the carpet of history.

There are many people not mentioned in the following pages and for that I am sorry. Please know that I have not forgotten any of you. Some are women activists, others are close family, and lastly there are the people who have welcomed me into their lives since my return home to Australia in December 2002. I made the decision to finish this book when I left my position as Executive Director of the International Women's Tribune Centre in New York and a wonderful new life has been built since then. My own family has expanded and changed and I have added a whole new family in that time. Perhaps there is another book of family dramas yet to be written!

Finally, as time went by, I became convinced that the early chapters of this book should be removed. I put what I thought was a strong case before my wonderful editor Bev Roberts. She persuaded me that those chapters gave context to all that followed and were therefore important and should be retained. And so they have been kept. Bev's editing work has been extraordinary and I thank her for all that she has done to make this book a reality.

Anne S Walker
January 2018
Melbourne, Australia

Part One

1

Melbourne, early years

I was born in a fog on 4 June 1937. Being Melbourne, Australia, it was mid-winter in a time when winter was truly cold and often foggy. Unlike today when the winters are often mild, almost temperate.

My mother went into labour in the late afternoon as the fog was moving in and my father took her to the car, a black Studebaker – square-cornered with a running board that looked like the cars that the gangs in Chicago drove. We had two cars; the other was a canvas-topped Plymouth. We needed two for all the times that one broke down and the other had to be driven off to tow it home.

Dad headed the Studebaker for Mosgiel, a small private hospital in Surrey Hills where all of Mum's babies were born. He apparently got a bit lost in the fog and only just arrived in time for the birth. I guess with me being the number six baby there was less worry about it all. At Mosgiel, Mum was met by Matron Andersen, who had been in attendance for the birth of all of my sisters and my brother. When Robert was due in June 1942, Matron Andersen came out of retirement so that she could be at every one of the births.

Mum ran the boarding house of Box Hill Grammar School, a Methodist coeducational boarding school ten miles outside central Melbourne. Dad was the Headmaster and had been since the school, at that time a private school for boys only, had moved to Gwynton Park in Box Hill South in 1930. He had briefly been Headmaster of BHGS when it was still in Rose Street, Box Hill, in 1925/26, but just for a year and a term. He had left to take up a business appointment in the city for two years. But when the Methodist Church bought the property at Gwynton Park and took over the running of the school, they asked him to return as Headmaster once more.

Mum and Dad arrived to live at Gwynton Park in 1930 with three little girls – my older sisters Mavis, Jean and Kathleen. Ruth was born in 1933 and Evan in 1935. After me came my little sister Frances and then my little brother Robert.

Box Hill Grammar School was to be our home for the next 34 years. As already mentioned, the school was for boys only, so when Mavis started school, she was sent to the Horton Girls' School in Box Hill. But the school was closed in 1933. There was a small building at Gwynton Park called 'The Summer House'. Dad had that brought down near the boarding house and Herb, the school's handyman, renovated it. A woman teacher was hired and a small girls' class was started. In 1935, it grew to ten pupils with some a bit older and needing secondary education. After some persuasion, the School Council agreed to allow girls with the boys in the secondary part of the school. Dad wrote later: 'No boys left the school and so began co-education at Box Hill Grammar School in 1935.' He remained a fervent believer in co-education for the remainder of his teaching career.

In his book of essays on education Dad recalled what it was like when he first took over as Headmaster of the school in 1926 and said: 'Had I known the difficulties ahead of me I do not think I would have taken up the task'. And to read of how things were at the beginning, you can understand how he felt. When they moved to the new premises in 1930, they had six boarders and 25 pupils in all. There was a large, rather rundown main house and several even more rundown farm buildings. The country was in a severe economic depression. There was no money available to spend.

Dad set to work. First he hired a young builder by the name of Herb who had been thrown out of work by the Depression. The large house at Gwynton Park, formerly the residence of the Edward's Tea Company founder, was turned into a boarding house. A couple of the farm buildings were turned into classrooms. Herb served as builder, cleaner and maintenance worker for the day school and the boarding house. One of the outer buildings at the top end of the property, known as The Cottage, became a home for him and his wife and small family.

A large part of the property had been leased to a farmer by the Methodist Church, initially to help pay the rates. But the farmer fell into arrears and Dad offered to pay the rent himself. And so he did, running 18 acres of the school as a farm that provided dairy products, vegetables and more to the school for many years. As the herd of cows grew, milk was sold to a local dairy. We all learnt to milk cows, make butter, plough fields, grow vegetables, mow lawns and chop wood. The school was completely supplied with milk through the war years and was only stopped when the Commonwealth Government started the program in 1946 that supplied free milk to all schools. The vegetable gardens had to be demolished in 1953 because of the fruit fly problem.

Dad ran the boarding house as his 'own concern', paying for all foodstuffs and wages and receiving a fixed payment per week per boarder from the school Treasurer. Over the years, he and Herb (with help from building assistants who were frequently his own family and other school children that he paid during the holidays) built classrooms, dormitories, cowsheds, a dairy complete with separator for cream and skim milk, a piggery and more. Some of the Chinese boarders from Rabaul and Kavieng in Papua New Guinea did quite a lot of work for him; one of them went on to become a builder and real estate developer in Rabaul when he left school. Dad always believed that hands-on training was what we all needed if we were to have options in life!

For 15 years, part of the property was leased as a riding school to a Miss Tunbridge, and generations of children learnt how to ride and care for horses. A feature during that time was the Annual Gymkhana and people came from miles around to take part in that event.

Gradually more buildings were constructed – or carted in from other places – for more boarders and more day pupils. From Dad's essay about this time, it would appear that most of the additional classrooms and boarding accommodation came as old buildings from the more wealthy and established Methodist institutions such as Wesley College, Methodist Ladies College and Queen's College as they expanded and replaced old buildings with new ones. There was also a dormitory building that was adapted from an old building from the North Melbourne Methodist Mission. And an initial block of three brick classrooms was built for £2,300 in 1930 with the help of 'several wealthy members of the church'.

As time went by, the number of boarders grew to 50 and the number of day students to 200. Mum looked after all the boarders at the school, the children ranging in age from 4 to 16 years. Whole families came to live with us along with individual children, many from the country. All became part of our family. Mum was always busy, too busy really to have had eight children but she always said she just loved having babies. I heard a story about that from Jean who was eleven years older than me. She told me that the local baker's wife came to visit Mum following the birth of Frances, two years after my birth. They did not have any children of their own and she put it to Mum that she had so many, especially girls, she could give her this latest baby girl so she could have one baby of her own! Jean says the horror on Mum's face was memorable and she asked the baker's wife to leave. The thought of one of her babies being taken away was anathema to our Mum. She loved us all so very much.

The next few years of my life are something of a blur. I have heard stories passed down by my older sisters, but there are so few photos … 'because of the war' was the usual refrain. Being the sixth born and the fifth girl, who came after the joy of the first boy, is more likely the reason.

I gradually became part of the fabric of the school, that busy place that hummed with life and happenings. Friends in later years have asked me where I slept as a baby. I would ask Mum and she would say, 'You remember: you slept in a cot in the alcove on the far side of our bedroom until you were big enough, and then you went off to the little girls' dorm. And you couldn't wait until you went there!'

In his education essay Dad wrote: 'I had six girls and two boys in my own family. These were distributed round amongst the boarders. My wife and I lived in the school-house (the boarding house). Pressure for boarding accommodation was great. I remember trying to inveigle my School Council into erecting new dormitories, or at any rate additional dormitories. I had taken too many enrolments and fitted up the Assembly Hall to take ten beds, and had boys there as a dormitory. Three or four of the School Council came to look at it and considered it a good idea. They recommended the purchase of a few bedside rugs'. Incredible: bunks erected in the assembly hall because the School Council wouldn't build more dormitories and all they would offer was bedside rugs!

In 1938, Dad bought the house 'over the road' for Mum's mother to live in with her sister. He bought the house from his own mother who had lived there for some years. Then he built a bungalow at the back of the house and fitted it with double bunks for four girl boarders. Still not enough space however, so he put four girls into the house. Having learned that he was being paid per boarder to run the boarding house, I now understand why he kept enrolling more and more boarders and fitting them in wherever he could. I never heard a word of complaint from Grandma Ingamells yet it must have been difficult for her. No wonder her sister left to live somewhere else.

For me as a child, the dorm (and I slept in many) gave me a feeling of security and comfort. In the 'little girls' dorm', attached to the main boarding house downstairs, there were six beds stretched in a row, the most sought-after beds being those at either end. At one end the bed was under a window looking out across the playground to the kindergarten building, at the other end you were closest to the bathroom. In the days when Frances and I were both in that little girls' dorm, we would stake out our claims to our favourite beds long before the other girls arrived each year. We regarded that as one of the privileges of the school being our home.

The arrival of baby Frances had been a very big moment in my life. We were to remain close from a very early age. I have some early memories of being with her – in particular I definitely remember the moment when she learned to tie up her shoelaces before I did. I was mortified and have thought of that moment from then on, certainly every time I tie up my shoelaces! Frances and I grew up together. We shared the same dormitories, the same sports, and yes, she wore my hand-me-down school uniforms. But then, I wore Ruth's hand-me downs.

And another big moment of that time was the birth of our little brother Robert. Frances and I were over the moon at his arrival! We were so proud of him and showed him off to the other kids whenever we could. We were his sisters so in our eyes we had special privileges.

But back to our life in the dorm. Our mother took special care of the smallest boarders and our dorm was not far from Dad and Mum's bedroom. I was a voracious reader from a very early age (I'm told I could read by the age of three and was sometimes taken to the front at school assembly time to read the catechism). I do remember often sneaking into Dad's library in the night and taking books to read under my bed covers. After lights out, I would take out my trusty torch and read the books, mostly with little understanding but always pushing on until I had finished them. Sons and Lovers by D H Lawrence was a bit problematic for me. I tested some of the words out with adults, and remember being insulted when they laughed at my efforts. It frequently meant me retiring from their presence in some disarray.

My reading opened up a mysterious world of adults, and an equally mysterious world where children lived in families in a house of their own, with just their mother and father, brothers and sisters. This was a source of wonderment to me, but not one for which I yearned. Quite the contrary. I was happiest surrounded by other children and with the ability to get lost, almost invisible, or so I thought. And it pleased me not to be under the constant eye of Mum and Dad, especially Dad. He was our father but more importantly our headmaster, in charge of everything in our world. He was a force with which to reckon.

A great source of books for me was the Box Hill City Library, situated behind the Box Hill Town Hall. We would ride the bus up to the Box Hill railway gates, cross the railway line and walk down Bank Street to the Library. There I discovered Mary Grant Bruce's Billabong books and would anxiously wait for each title in that fabulous series about an Australian country family. The library was a haven and I went there as often as I could for many years.

Back at the boarding house meanwhile, in our dorm world, there would be much whispering and laughing, with things being passed between the beds and the patter of little feet as we went from one to the other telling secrets, borrowing things, checking whether someone was asleep or not. Often, there would be my mother's voice calling out 'Anne … get back into bed.' It was usually me doing the wrong thing it seems. We would discover to our dismay that she was sitting outside our door, waiting for us to fall asleep. In later years I have realised she was probably resting herself there, taking a break from the busyness of her daily life with so much that always needed to be done. It's a memory I carry with me. Maybe she's still sitting outside my door until I go to sleep. I like to think so.

Robert was growing fast and had become everyone's favourite. He was such a happy, bright little boy and fun to be around. He was usually with his little friend Lesley, the daughter of one of the matrons, Mrs Beaton, who looked after the older boys in the cottage at the top of the oval.

On one awful day, Robert and Lesley disappeared. We searched and searched the various buildings at the school where they might be hiding, in the extensive grounds, everywhere we could think of. Finally the police were called and they joined the search. In my memory (and I have been questioned about this by my older brother and sisters who have a different memory of how it ended) it was me who found them, after hearing them calling out from a large water tank in the front corner of the grounds. It was getting dark outside and we were all becoming increasingly desperate. I remember beating on the side and the two of them beating back and calling with frightened little voices.

I rushed to get help. They were inside the tank in ankle-deep water. These two little four- year-olds had climbed up the side of the tank and fallen in the small hole at the top. Thankfully, there was hardly any water in the tank otherwise they would have drowned. It's impossible to imagine losing Robert as a little boy and not having him as our brother.

Robert recently told me that the water tank where he and Lesley were found was partly buried and that's why they could climb up the side easily. He remembers jumping into the tank, not falling in, and kidding Lesley into jumping in with him: 'It's beaut in here. Come on in!' And he also remembers my face being the first to look down at them through the round hole in the top of the tank. So maybe my memory is not too bad after all.

And there's another memory from that time. A friend at school who was a day student invited me home for dinner one day and Mum thought that would be a good idea. I think she was well aware of the fact that her children rather liked being part of a large group, not singled out too much, and probably wanted us to have some individual socialising in a family home.

So I went off with Joanie Snow to have dinner at her house. We walked there from the school and as we went through her front gate, Joanie's mother appeared at the front door and called out to us: 'Hello girls. And Anne, how wonderful to have you here with us for dinner!' Or something like that. I felt as though a spotlight had been turned on me and I froze. She then came towards us, holding out her arms for a hug. What could I do? Without thinking, I turned and ran. Out the front gate, up Station Street, running and crying. Then the rain began and I got drenched.

I rushed through the front door of the boarding house, into the breakfast room, the living room-cum-dining room at the core of the boarding house, where kids went whenever they wanted anything. I wove my way through a crowd of people and huddled up to the open fire on the far side. I planned to dry myself inconspicuously and then retreat to the safety of the dorm.

The phone rang. It was one of those 'daffodil' type phones with a long body and a receiver you picked up from a rest. I heard Mum saying 'What Mrs Snow! She ran away? I'm so sorry! Oh. One moment, I think I see her in front of the fire with the others. Yes. She's here. All's well. Sorry again and thank you'.

The remarkable thing about such a sad little story is that I was not reprimanded or made to feel ridiculous, as I could very well have been. Mum fetched a big towel and came over and started to dry my hair and my arms and took me off to the dorm to find some dry warm clothes. She seemed to understand that it might have been a bit early for socialising in someone's home, with just me and Joanie, one mother and one father. Too much individual attention for me! And she was right.

Around this time, we boarders were all taken on a bus trip to Mt Donna Buang. There was snow in the Alps and we were all mad keen to experience walking and sliding through this magical stuff of which we had only read in books.

Somewhere near the top of the mountain, I began to feel very sick. It was my head and I got dizzier and weaker with every step. Dad summoned some of the senior boys and together they made a chair with their hands and carried me down that mountain, through the snow. It can't have been easy. At the base of the mountain, we all boarded the bus and went directly back home. Mum took over my care and I was bundled into bed with some hot soup and an aspirin.

I only mention this episode because it probably relates to what happened to me very soon after that excursion. I got a terrible earache, the kind that reduces you to tears and constant aching pain. Dr Chenhall, the local GP who looked after all the boarders at the school, was called. He peered into my ear and thought it might be an insect trapped in the depths of my eardrum. I was laid out on a couch in the breakfast room while he proceeded to wash out my ear. I screamed with pain and had to be held down by several people. The procedure in fact burst an abscess in my ear and I was left in considerably more pain.

The pain moved into an unbelievable headache, the kind that feels like a thousand spears are being shoved through your skull. I was rushed off to hospital in an ambulance, an old bumpy thing that I recall to this day every time we drive over the old bridge at Fairfield. I felt every bump, every movement in excruciating detail and that bridge stands out as a major source of pain.

I lay in a semi coma for the first week, with strange memories of Mum and Dad dressed in white gowns with white masks and caps, sitting on either side when they visited, no words. I couldn't move myself. It was too painful. I couldn't open my eyes.

One evening, there was a doctor's round with a group of young medical students. One of the students accidentally bumped the bed and I let out a little yelp of pain. The young student said he was sorry and the doctor in charge said something like 'Not to worry. She'll be gone by the morning'. I was horrified – I was dying! And I couldn't speak or move or even open my eyes to let anyone know I was very much alive inside!

A spinal tap carried out at the hospital confirmed that I had spinal meningitis. A year earlier and I would not have survived, but I was saved by the advent of penicillin and sulfa. I recall having to drink massive amounts of water, something I could hardly ever keep down. A young boy, who lived down Surrey Street opposite the school, had been taken away in an ambulance with what turned out to be spinal meningitis just one year before me. And he never came back. I knew about that and was very afraid.

My time in Fairfield Infectious Diseases Hospital stretched into eight weeks, during most of which I was not allowed out of bed. I got into constant trouble being caught by one of the fearsome sisters with starched stiff headgear and long dresses that creaked as they moved. I was usually kneeling beside my bed to get crayons and paper or something out of my bedside table. Or trying to look out the window into the garden.

The child in the bed next to me stopped breathing one night and I remember the noise of sheets being torn into bandages that they used to wrap him up like a mummy before they wheeled him out on a gurney. It was close to the time I was to be released and sent home and I knew he had died because I looked it up in the paper after I got home. And there was his death notice. Aged six.

One of the most terrifying thoughts I had in those eight long weeks in hospital was that everyone had forgotten about me. Surely someone at the school must have noticed I wasn't there? Hadn't my friend Nancy Wilson noticed I was no longer in the bed beside her in our little double bedroom at the top of the stairs? It's true that every once in a while, a book, or a bottle of lemonade, or some new crayons would appear with a note from Mum. But that was a rare event. My child's head told me everyone, especially Mum, was just too busy. There were too many other kids at the school, too much going on.

Then finally I was to go home. I was taken from my bed, put into a bath of what smelled like kerosene and scrubbed with a rough scrubbing brush until my skin was red and sore. Then I was dressed in clothes that didn't quite fit me as I had lost so much weight and grown a few inches. The nurse walked me out into a dreary waiting room ... and there was my Mum. I hardly recognised her. She put her arms around me and just held me tight. I couldn't believe she had bothered to come and get me. I acted cold and indifferent. How could she have just left me there and forgotten me!

Once home at the boarding house again, I began to hear about the daily trips she and others had made to Fairfield from the school, delivering books, soft drinks, special treats, drawing materials, letters and cards from the family and all my friends, special artwork and crafts done by the other kids. All left at the guard's box at the front gate because no-one was allowed in, but carefully labelled with my name and special instructions for it to be delivered to my bed. What had happened to all of these things? I certainly had not received most of them.

It seems that the sisters at the hospital thought I must be a very rich and spoilt child to get so much stuff, and in their wisdom had decided to not give most of it to me. Instead, they divided it up and handed it around to all the other children who were not receiving much of anything. It was not given to the children in my ward, though. I might have seen it being delivered to the beds around me and that would be bad.

So I was left to come out of the experience closed down inside myself, unemotional, not wanting to be hugged or touched, unbelieving of anyone's attentions towards me. It took time to get over. To this day I am so sorry that I distanced myself from my mother in that dreadful waiting room. If I'd known how worried she had been, how much she cared, how many trips she and others had made to leave all that stuff for me at the gate, then I would have been overjoyed to see Mum standing there with such a smile on her face.

The boarding house and school years went by. It was in many ways a privileged life; living as we did on a large property of 24 acres, mainly open fields with a boundary of tall trees. For us, it was a wondrous world, even though there was no family residence and in Dad's words, we Walker children 'were distributed round amongst the other boarders'. We played amazing games on that property, including Kick the Tin, Sardines, Charlie Over the Water, with around 50 children ages 5–16 years involved, and much planning and strategy required. We climbed trees, built tree houses, fished for yabbies in the dam and cooked them in a special yabby stove in the laundry.

And it was essentially a farm school, certainly during the Depression and war years 1930–1945. Dad was never happier than when working on the property. He had a draught horse called Nugget, and with an amazing contraption that was composed of about 12 small hand mower heads, chained together and pulled by Nugget, Dad would mow the school ovals, walking behind holding the reins. When Herb left early in the war years, taken away by 'Manpower', Dad had a series of groundsmen. Because many of the boarders were from the country, they also helped with the milking and care of the animals at the school. I learnt to milk cows during that time and also became quite a good horseback rider.

The war years were years of much anxiety for all of us

children as we grew up. The morning newspapers were full of army movements across Europe and South-East Asia, and with a high proportion of Australia's young people, mainly young men, fighting on the front lines, everyone knew someone who was in the army. In our case it was Uncle Gordon, Mum's younger brother. Grandma Ingamells had pasted a large map of Europe on her kitchen wall and when she heard news of Gordon's battalion, she would stick a pin marker on the map.

We heard stories of prisoner-of-war camps, the building of the Thai-Burma Railway by the Japanese and the terrible condition of the Australian and British work gangs. And there were accounts of ships loaded with both army and civilian passengers being torpedoed just north of us, the bombing of Darwin and the fact that two Japanese submarines made their way into Sydney Harbour. These last incidents caused the authorities to order all schools to be prepared for possible air attacks, and at Box Hill Grammar School trenches were dug across the basketball court for us to jump in if there was an air raid. I remember thinking the practice drills were rather fun. We would all be gathered in the Assembly Hall, the school bell would be rung and we would run down the steps across the yard to the basketball court and jump into the trenches. After a few minutes of further instructions, all of which I have forgotten, we would climb out and head for our classrooms to get on with the day.

Dad was adamantly against war and spoke frequently to us about the importance of supporting those in power who talked of peacekeeping and peace-making. He was a fervent supporter of the United Nations set up in 1945 and was President of the Eastern Suburbs Branch of the United Nations Association of Australia for many years. He was a great supporter of Dr H V Evatt and hoped that he would become Australia's Prime Minister following the war.

Dad also wrote many letters to *The Age*, Melbourne's premier daily newspaper. Most of his letters were against chemical and biological warfare and atom bombs, following the terrible events of World War I when Australian soldiers were gassed in the trenches (including his own brother Ivan) and the subsequent events of World War II when atom bombs were dropped on Hiroshima and Nagasaki. I admit that as a child, I would become embarrassed when people in the local shops asked if I was related to the strange guy who wrote all those letters to the paper. And I would invariably say that I was not. But I deeply admire his tenacity and foresight now. He was a voice crying in the wilderness as far as the public went, but he did have a school full of children to talk with about it and he frequently did. It probably provided a base for my life as an anti-war, peace activist.

We loved going to the movies on rainy Saturday afternoons. The Rialto in Box Hill ran a lot of serial flicks. Each episode ended on a thrilling, dramatic note so to miss an episode was an awful thing. I recall cowboys hanging off cliffs, people tied to railway tracks with a train heading towards them … and we prayed for rain, just to see the next episode of the movie.

But if the sun shone we generally had to walk across through the dairy farms of Box Hill South to Wattle Park. Mum and Dad and the boarding house staff needed a break one afternoon a week. Not that we didn't have fun at Wattle Park. That park is one of the treasures of the south eastern suburbs of Melbourne and still stands as one of the most wonderful, natural reserves left in Melbourne.

Our public transport in Box Hill South for almost everything was Frank Rennie's bus. It went from Box Hill Station to Burwood, past the school front gates. A ride from the school to Box Hill Station cost one penny. Once when I managed to get a free ride, I remember excitedly running in to tell Mum how clever I had been and waving the penny around in my hand. She sent me back to the bus stop outside the front gates where I had to wait until the bus returned from Burwood. I boarded the bus, walked up the stairs and handed the penny to Frank Rennie behind the wheel. Lesson learned. Didn't do that again.

The other ride we really loved was not public transport but on the back of the milk cart, drawn by a large draught horse. Milk was delivered daily to the boarding house in big silver milk cans, straight from the dairy, and the cart was shaped a bit like the chariots in Ben Hur. At least we thought so. We would sometimes ride all the way back to the dairy with Mr Coridas, the dairy owner, and then walk back to the school. Terrific thrill!

When Frances and I were about 10 and 12 years of age, we were taken on an excursion to Melbourne's Luna Park with others from the school. Luna Park has the famous Scenic Railway roller coaster, opened in 1912, the oldest continuously operating roller coaster in the world, and we all headed straight for a ride on that. But the ride we really wanted to go on was the Big Dipper, with much steeper climbs, turns and descents. We had been told, and who knows who told us, that we should sit in the front seats of the first carriage because the back carriage flipped over the top of a steep climb and would make us feel sick.

So Frances and I sat in the front seat. All went fine for the first twists and turns, and then we began the first of the really steep climbs before the first main descent. Over we went and found ourselves staring down at oblivion. Frances began screaming at the top of her voice. I totally froze, not breathing, in complete shock. It was another defining moment. One of us screams when in danger, the other freezes. I know what's the best and most effective response and it was not mine.

In early December each year, we packed up the camping gear and headed for the Mornington Peninsula where we camped for five to six weeks. Campers would consist of our family plus a few boarders who either couldn't go home yet because they were from overseas or whose parents had paid for them to come with us to camp for the first week. The camping equipment was loaded onto Uncle Gordon's fruit truck with its high wooden sides, stacked to the hilt with tents, poles, tables, carpets, stoves, lamps, and all of the stuff needed for almost two months camping amongst the ti-trees around Port Phillip Bay.

Camp Walker was usually the first camp to be set up on the bay foreshore and Dad had the choice of camping ground before the majority of campers arrived a week later. We would set up the sleeping marquees and the smaller two-people tents around the large central 'Circus Tent' where the cooking, eating and game-playing took place. I can recall camping in McCrae, Rosebud, West Rosebud and Rye, then in my late teens, Balnarring.

Those weeks at camp seemed endless and were a time for us to be together as a family. My memories of Christmas Day are all centred on camp. We would track down a good-looking ti-tree branch (if there is such a thing) and tie it to one of the Circus Tent poles and decorate it as best we could with tinsel and Christmas trinkets. Our gifts from Mum and Dad were usually books, big expensive ones, and we looked forward to that enormously.

The gifts to the family from Frances and me had been carefully selected by us during our annual train trip into the city centre of Melbourne a couple of weeks earlier, a trip we saved up for all year long. We weren't very old when we started being allowed to do that train trip. It showed enormous confidence in us as little girls, but also is probably a sign of how different things were then.

It was at camp where we Walker kids learnt much of our technical expertise, way before computers. From an early age, we were competent with Tilley and Coleman pressure lamps, portable gas stoves, erecting various kinds of tents and marquees, including the Circus Tent (which was in fact a Boer War-era post office tent), putting up camp beds, rowing a round-bottomed wooden boat out into the bay to fish, fishing, gutting fish and cooking our catch on the beach. All of these skills have stood me in good stead through my life. Maybe not the gutting and cooking of fish on the beach, that was never really fun, and is probably now banned.

We learnt how to swim in the ocean. This came into good use on many occasions, one of which was during another sun-filled day on the beach. Dad was in his usual place at the top of the sand, apparently dozing in his floppy white cricket hat but keeping an eye on all of us swimming, playing cricket on the sand, making sand fortresses, etc. Suddenly, he called out to me with an urgent bellow, not to be ignored: 'Anne! Go out and get them, NOW!' And I looked up in time to see a small inflatable raft heading out to sea with three small children on board, howling and shouting.

Dad would never let us have inflatable rafts because of the suddenness of an offshore breeze that might arrive in late afternoon. And this had happened while the parents of these children were clearly not paying attention. I ran out as far as I could on a sand bank. Thankfully the tide was nearly out. Then I dived into the sea and began to swim. The raft was moving fast and gaining speed as it went into deeper water. I called out to the children to sit down and stop waving and shouting. I was afraid they would fall over the edge. One of the children was no more than three years of age; the others more like four and five.

Finally I reached the raft and swam around to the far side to begin the long swim back, pushing the raft in front of me. We made it to shore and the kids climbed out and rushed off screaming to their parents. I collapsed on the shore exhausted. Then I looked up to see if Dad had noticed my heroics. But he was already dozing off again. He was not one to make a fuss of things like that.

Another memory concerned me and my sisters Ruth and Frances, and two young men who came down to join us at our Rosebud camp one year and wanted to go boating, in a boat with a motor. Our own boat only functioned with oars. The five of us drove down to the town to hire a boat, then off we went, heading out into Port Phillip Bay, sitting back enjoying the sunshine and letting the motor do all the work. That in itself was unusual for Ruth, Frances and me. We had never been in a boat before that we didn't have to row ourselves, often with Dad sitting in the middle of the back seat and two of us, each with an oar, heaving away.

We started to become a little uneasy as we travelled further and further out, way further out than we would ever venture when rowing. We suggested we stop and turn around but David and Alex, who unbeknown to us had never been out in a boat before, seemed confident. In fact, they turned the motor off and started to clown around, rocking the boat and singing. Frances recalls Alex standing up in the boat and singing 'Rule Britannia'! That must have been when the boat almost capsized.

And then the motor wouldn't start. No matter how hard David and Alex tried, they couldn't get that thing going again. They then took an oar each and tried to row. It turned out they hadn't done that before either. So Frances and I took over the oars. It was a long, hard haul back to the beach where the boat rental place was and we arrived totally exhausted and collapsed on the sand. The owner came up to us in the near darkness and helped us haul the boat up. Then he told us about 'an old man with a white floppy hat' who had arrived late afternoon and sat himself on the sand with a pair of binoculars and had watched as Frances and I took over the rowing. And had watched until we were almost safely back before he got up and drove away. Did we know who he was? Yes, we said. That would have been our Dad. He was the one who had taught us how to row and had supervised our rowing since we were small children and had complete confidence in our ability to make it back.

Dad never mentioned that he was anxious that day, nor that he had gone down there and watched us row home. He was probably worried that we were in the hands of two young men without any boating ability and probably didn't think the owner of the boat rental business would know he was there.

Every Wednesday afternoon at the school, we walked over the fields to the Box Hill City Baths for swimming classes. Come rain or shine, there we went, doing lifesaving and practising our swim technique. I was to be very grateful in later years, in fact during those years, for those classes.

Attached to the City Baths was the Surrey Dive, an old quarry no longer in use since digging had struck a spring deep underground and the quarry had flooded. You had to be a certain age (I think it was 14) and be able to swim a certain distance before you were allowed through the gate at the back of the baths, down the steps to the wooden platform on the side of 'the Dive'.

We older girls loved going there because it gave us some privacy. One day, several of us dived into the quarry and swam across to the other side. There we lay in the sun for an hour or so, chatting, laughing, and enjoying the moment. Then it came time to swim back to the platform and up to the City Baths and back to the school. Halfway across the widest part of the Dive, where it was rumoured to be the greatest depth, I heard a gulping little voice call out 'Anne'. I looked behind me and to my horror was just in time to see Robert sinking below the surface. He had followed me through the gate and walked around the top edge of the dive, up on the cliff, and had watched us from behind a bush.

I swam to him and grabbed him on his third sinking. He was exhausted. I put his two hands on my shoulders, his body beneath me and breast-stroked him back to the platform. There we lifted him up and began to press on his chest until all the water spilled out. Then we all sat there, scared out of our wits and full of the knowledge that if this episode became known, it would probably be the end of any of us swimming again in the Dive.

And so we told no-one. Another secret of childhood never divulged – until I did tell Mum on one of my trips home years later, when she was long retired and living across the road. I don't know why I did, maybe needed to get it off my chest. And the look of horror on her face was enough for me to know she would have been shattered at the time.

Secrets. When do we keep them and when do we finally spill them? That is the question for all children growing up. At the time when I was living across the road with three other girls, in the bungalow Dad built behind Grandma's house to extend the boarding capabilities of the school, we lived through a moment that we all agreed to keep secret and we did. We had been involved in a series of tit-for-tat pranks with the senior boys who lived in the cottage at the top of the school grounds. And had been able to hold our heads high until one certain night.

We were all fast asleep when the first alarm clock went off. We sprang out of bed and tried to find it, but couldn't. So the clock noisily rang its course and we fell back into bed and asleep. Then the next alarm clock went off and again, we couldn't find it. This went on through the night. It was about 4 am when we began to pull down the lining of the walls, where we finally found the clocks, neatly hanging on nails that had been hammered into the inside of the lining all over the interior of the bungalow.

We sat on the floor that night and discussed how we could ever match this, and knew there was no way we could. So we decided to stay dumb, to pretend that nothing had happened and we had not been kept up all night. Of course there were questions asked and we could see the ones who were anxiously waiting to hear what an awful night we'd had. But we never said a word.

Evan was one of the boys who had thought up this major prank. It was at his 60th birthday I think that I told him that the alarms had kept us up all that night. He was furious!

Apparently they had gone over everything they had done step by step, had thought the alarms had not gone off, tried to get back in to the bungalow to retrieve their clocks but we made very sure they could not do that. He couldn't believe their prank had worked but we'd never told them or anyone else about it. Maybe we were unfair. I don't know. But we knew we couldn't top it. And we now owned some very nice alarm clocks!

In my teenage years, I often went with school friends to their farms to spend the holidays. Again, I now believe these were efforts by our mother to get us socialised into family living outside the confines of the boarding house. On those holiday trips into the country, I would begin each trip by focusing on the steam train ride from Spencer Street Station to Albury, usually a day-long trip, arriving in Albury to be picked up by the family of whoever I was to stay with. I visited Katie Murrell's farm in Corryong, Doreen Lord's farm in Eskdale, and once went to Florence Kennett's farm in Mitta Mitta. I was usually very anxious before setting out, a bit fearful really at spending time within a family in a strange place. I loved the train trip though, so would focus my mind on that!

But the holidays on those farms are a memory to treasure. The horseback riding, the milking of cows, the feeding of pigs, the rounding up of sheep. And the kindness of the parents as they looked after this rather naïve and shy city girl. So many memories.

There were 'Balts' living in an outer house on the Lord's farm in Eskdale, men who spoke no English and who came from the Baltic states of Eastern Europe to find a better life in Australia. I have often thought about them. Probably some of them were trained doctors, dentists, engineers, maybe they had owned and run their own businesses. But here they were, dressed in old clothes and old gumboots, rising at dawn to milk cows and feed pigs, living in substandard housing. What has happened to all those men I wonder? I can only hope they made a better life for themselves and were able to bring out their families.

On one memorable occasion, I rode on horseback with members of Katie Murrell's family up to Mount Kosciusko from Corryong, via Thredbo I think. We were accompanying other horses laden with salt for the cattle grazing on the high country. We stayed at cattlemen's shacks along the way with names like Charlotte's Pass, Dead Horse Gap and Seaman's Hut. There were no roads and hence no traffic, just wild bush country and days wending our way across rivers, over passes and along endless dusty trails.

One night, at the Dead Horse Gap cabin, where we had travelled part of the way fording rivers in an old army truck, I was taken out into a paddock on one of the trucks in the middle of the night on a mystery mission to see something they believed I would never forget. The truck stopped and the headlights were turned off. We sat in silence for about ten minutes. Then suddenly, the headlights were switched on and there before us, spread across the paddocks as far as the eye could see, was a moving carpet of rabbits, feeding on the grass. Ear to ear, tail to tail, head to head. They all looked up startled, then scattered. I was introduced to the major ecological tragedy of the day in one swift unforgettable second: rabbits out of control! I had to repeat that story years later in a biology class at Indiana University when the professor found out he had an Australian in the class who had witnessed the worst of the rabbit invasion, pre-myxomatosis.

My first overseas trip came in 1951 when I was almost 14 years of age. There were families of children that came to the school as boarders and some stayed many years. Amongst these were the Wilsons. Mr Wilson was the Administrator of Norfolk Island for some years and in 1951 invited our school concert troupe to come and perform in halls across the island. Dad thought it a great idea and so plans were made. I begged to be able to go, even though I think I was just under the allowed age.

We flew from Melbourne to Sydney and out across the Pacific on a DC3 plane, my first ever flight. On arrival, we were welcomed like rock stars by a large group of Norfolk Island locals who all came to the airport to see who these people were coming to their island. Lots of excitement!

Norfolk Island was rather isolated at that time, still predominantly inhabited by descendants from the crew of the ship Bounty made famous by Captain Bligh and the mutiny that took place there. We were introduced to the residents of Norfolk Island, many of them still carrying the surnames of the Bounty crew, including Christian (from Fletcher Christian), Adams (from John Adams), Ellison (from Thomas Ellison) and so on. Our troupe was divided up and sent off to stay with residents in their homes. I was part of a group of six girls who stayed in a lodging house at The Cascades, a gorgeous part of Norfolk Island where you could stand on the cliffs and look down at the ocean crashing into the rocks below.

We stayed on Norfolk Island for about two weeks, with concert performances every couple of days in different church and community halls. I was part of a trio – Evan on violin, Ruth on the cello and me on the piano – and we played at each performance. In between performances we were taken on wonderful excursions, including a horse ride around the island, an outdoor feast, and places relating to the convict history of the island.

The farewell at the airport on the day we left was the most amazing thing. Crowds of islanders pushed up against the wire fence that ran alongside the runway, cheering and waving and shouting out our names. Never to be forgotten! In fact years later when I was living and working in Fiji, I was at the home of the mother of one of my kindergarten students and telling someone about my Norfolk Island visit, when there was a shout from the kitchen and the mother came running out and threw her arms around me. Turned out that she was a teenager living at the Cable House on Norfolk Island with her family when our concert troupe arrived and my sister Ruth had boarded with them. Suddenly she had put the name of Walker together with my name and was totally thrilled. And one of her strongest memories of the time we spent on the island was the farewell scene at the airport.

I've never been back to Norfolk Island but the memory of that visit remains with me. It is a special place, full of history and charm. And it was my first overseas trip.

There is much that I have left out, as one does when recounting memories from so long ago. For example, those were years of all kinds of subtle discriminations, mainly around the fact that I was a girl and clearly in my father's eyes, headed for marriage and children. No matter that I had an early interest in international affairs and news of the world, having read the newspaper from the age of three. And I had an affinity for science and technology, for architecture, for art and design, showing some talent in drawing and painting from a young age and in the planning and designing of furniture and houses.

But Dad had a dictum, remembered clearly by Frances and Robert, and it went something like this: 'If you educate the boy, you educate the man. If you educate the girl, you educate the family.' Girls should therefore be trained as wives and mothers first and foremost.

In fact I dreamed of becoming an architect, even before my brother Evan thought of becoming one. Evan wanted to be a carpenter when he was a teenager. Or a farmer. He spent a lot of time on farms belonging to the families of boarders and loved the work. But after almost a year working as a farm hand after he left school, he made the decision that it was not to be for him. Dad agreed. Evan was to become a world-renowned architect and social reformer, and a politician who helped change the face of Melbourne.

Suffice to say I was taken out of algebra and geometry classes, at a time when I recall being quite good at maths. I was transferred to domestic science. And I was almost prevented from taking part in art classes, although that was mainly Cedric Newbury's problem, not Dad's. Mr Newbury was our art teacher and he didn't want girls in his class. Not that it stopped me drawing: I studied art anyway, sat the exam for my Intermediate and passed just fine. Which is more than some of the boys in his class did. I also continued with history, geography, English literature, English expression and French classes and did okay with all of them.

But instead of maths and science there I was doing domestic science, which included sewing and cooking, the latter at Box Hill Girls Technical College. And here I should put in a word for the teacher of those classes at the Tech. She was strict, stern, expected nothing but the best from us – and immensely proud of us when we turned out a wondrous sponge cake. I have remembered her always for that (and for how to clean up in the kitchen as you go along!).

2

Teacher training college and teaching experience

On completing my Leaving Certificate, which entailed sitting finals at the Royal Exhibition Building in Melbourne, a terrifying experience in itself, I was informed that I would be going off to college to do kindergarten teacher training. Probably this was part of Dad's plan to have all of his children help him run the school. Already Mavis, who trained as a primary school teacher, had taught at the school briefly and then spent some years as a matron in the boarding house, looking after the little ones, especially during the time when Mum had to have a break from exhaustion and illness. Mavis stayed on as a matron even after her marriage and she and her husband lived at the school before building their own place in Burwood, not too far away. And Kath, who had gone to work as a comptometrist, returned to run the school office for the whole time that Dad was overseas doing further studies in education. Ruth returned to teach at the school after completing teacher training. Even Evan spent some time as a housemaster in one of the boys' dorms, as did Robert a bit later. Frances, who went off to the University of Melbourne to study science, came back to the school, now called Kingswood College, many years later, long after Dad had died, and taught there for 17 years. He would have been very proud.

I think Dad saw me as returning after teacher training and taking over the school kindergarten. And so I sat for a scholarship to the Kindergarten Training College in Kew, and found myself heading off for the first time in my life to an outside learning establishment.

I found those first days at KTC quite confronting. My life had been contained within the grounds of Box Hill Grammar School and those grounds were most surely my comfort zone. And I had never had to commute to school. For those of us living in the boarding house, our morning commute had always been a short walk up the path beside the tennis court and there we were at the classrooms. Now suddenly, I was having to get up in the early hours, catch Frank Rennie's bus to Box Hill station, catch the 8.05 am train to Glenferrie Station, then the tram up Glenferrie Road to Cotham Road and another tram to Kew Junction before the walk up Studley Park Road to KTC. And then to find myself in a group of 60 other young women, all strangers, except for Marian Clarke, the daughter of my kindergarten teacher. Otherwise I was on my own and quite literally overwhelmed for the first days and weeks.

But in the end I loved my three years at KTC. We were taken through complete courses in drawing, painting, sculpture, dance, music, woodwork, interior design, current affairs and politics. I was given the Middle East to study and report on as part of the International Affairs subject and there was hardly anything about that region of the world in our papers. How things have changed! Of course we also studied in depth child psychology, children's art, children's music and children's literature. But the college had a mantra of educating the teacher before specifically focusing on the child and for me it was a revelation. I blossomed and grew, met some lifelong friends and expanded my horizons.

Yes, I would have loved going to university and studying arts and architecture. But on the other hand, in those heady days of early childhood education training, when the focus was on creativity and the stimulating of both teacher's and child's imaginations, on creating open spaces for learning, on opening up new worlds and new adventures, the skills I learnt stood me in good stead —especially when undertaking low-cost media workshops for rural women and girls around the world.

On graduation from KTC, I was appointed Director of a large kindergarten with two separate playrooms, offices, kitchens and playrooms, one for 3–4-year-old children and the other for 4–5-year-olds. There was a second trained teacher for the 3–4-year-old group and I ran the 4–5-year-old group. The kindergarten was in a low-income part of Melbourne called Montague which was close to the docks, with Station Pier just a short train ride away. Sometimes, with the help of parents or other family members, we took the children down there to see the bustle of what was a very busy port. This was way before the age of containers and container ships of course, and the Port of Melbourne provided thousands of jobs for 'wharfies'. Many of the parents of the children worked on the wharves and the children loved watching their father or mother at work.

One memorable time, we watched a ship full of migrants arrive at Station Pier, an amazing sight, with the passengers almost entirely female and crowds of men on the pier, waving, yelling, sometimes pointing at a woman and shouting out a marriage proposal. It had been the policy of the Australian government for years to bring out male migrant workers to work on farms or provide labour for manufacturing industries. This had left thousands of men without wives and families, or in many cases, without any chance to find a wife.

There were language problems as well as other forms of discrimination that kept these men a lonely and separate part of the community. A large number of them, commonly known as 'Balts', spoke languages such as Estonian, Lithuanian, Bulgarian, all utterly foreign in this isolated corner of the world. Until I went to Europe I had no idea what 'Balt' meant, except that it was a man who spoke in a strange language and kept himself separate from everyone else.

These excursions caused much discussion amongst my group of four- and five-year-olds and I like to think our long talks helped them sort out their own lives and make them more tolerant and understanding of the children in the group who spoke limited English.

I was in no way prepared for the conditions I encountered in Montague, and the different cultures, ethnicities and languages I had within the group. It was a gritty, factory and warehouse area, and the children came from tiny workers' cottages or terrace houses. Most of the mothers and fathers were factory workers or dock-workers, while others came from generations of men and women who had been labourers. Others were newcomers, facing many problems being accepted in this tightly-knit community.

Early on, I instituted weekly home visits, when I would call on the families of the children in my group and have a cup of tea with whomever I encountered. Often this would be the grandparents, sometimes one or other of the parents who were working nights and had the afternoons off. And there were occasions when I found the child home alone. The condition of these houses was usually bad: damp walls, toilets way down the back, minimal kitchen facilities and floors covered with ancient, tattered linoleum. It was a hard life and the family members were usually happy to talk about their problems with me. It made my job as a teacher much more productive when I understood more about what the children and their parents had to cope with. Frequently, the child would have to translate for me as the only one in the family who could speak any English.

I remember a little girl in my group, aged five but with an old and worldly wise face that I found hard to understand. I had to break up the occasional game of 'Doctor' with this little one, usually at the back of the adventure playground, hidden by bushes. I would be told by others in the group that she was up to something 'scary' and would I please check to see what might be going on. Or I would find her myself. I asked the mother several times if I could set up a time to visit her at her house and discuss what might be the problem. It was definitely a very problematic game of Doctor on many counts.

Finally I decided to make a surprise visit to the home, which was close to the kindergarten in a row of old terrace houses. I knocked on the door. After quite a wait, the little girl opened the door, looking startled. She slammed the door and shouted out for her mother, who appeared at the door, hair tousled, barely dressed ... I could see my presence was not wanted. I apologised and asked if she would come to see me at the kindergarten instead.

She did, and we talked at length. It was obvious that the house was in fact a brothel, something I knew very little about. But although I was only 19 years of age, I like to think I was understanding. In fact I do recall congratulating the mother on sending her little daughter to kindergarten. She told me it had been a hard choice as the girl was very useful opening the door to the 'clients'. She convinced me that her daughter did not take part in providing any of her services and begged me to keep her at kindergarten so she would be a little prepared for school the following year. And I did, of course. Knowing her home situation put an entirely different slant on her behaviour. My only condition was that the mother would keep the daughter far away from the activities of her clients, and I suggested it might be preferable if the little girl lived with her grandparents who I knew lived not too far away. And this is what happened. I'd love to know where the little girl ended up.

Such a lot of changes were already happening to that closely-knit neighbourhood in 1957 and by 1958, many of the residents – none of whom owned their homes – had been moved far out of town by city planners and developers who could see that the location was a desirable one for wealthier city workers and their families. Factories were closing down and warehouses were moving out. I frequently had some of the parents who had been moved out as far as Broadmeadows on the very outskirts of Melbourne, come back to Montague and visit me at the kindergarten. There would be tears of anguish as they told me how difficult it was to live so far out. There were no schools, no shops, and no neighbours, at least not the ones they had known for generations. They felt dispossessed and angry, especially as they observed the renovations of their terrace houses and the new buildings going up, for new owners with more money than they had ever had. People who had no knowledge of what had gone before in that community.

When I returned from overseas travels in 1961 I went to visit Lady Northcote Kindergarten in Montague. Things had changed so much in the three years since I had left that I had difficulty finding it at all. There were new streets, factories had disappeared, buildings were gone, new high-rise apartments had gone up. I finally found my building, squashed between two new buildings, my wondrous adventure playground gone, replaced by several offices. But the building was no longer a kindergarten. My orange Marimekko curtains that hung floor to ceiling were no more and the spacious playroom had been divided up into work areas. It was a workplace for people with disabilities, and they were fascinated to hear my stories of the time this same space had been bursting with four- and five-year-olds. This was no longer a neighbourhood of young families but of urban professionals and offices. Things had changed very rapidly indeed.

Back in January 1957, I had been very surprised to be appointed as a Director immediately on graduation. As the youngest student in my year (not yet 17 when I started college) I was expecting to be an assistant somewhere, as most of my friends started that way. But in retrospect, I believe it was because I had been thrown into a situation in my final year at college, which meant I was actually in charge of the kindergarten where I was a student teacher.

The Director at this kindergarten was a woman who had

emigrated from Germany. She was frequently away because of a rather frail young son. In one of her absences, I had transferred a four-and-a-half-year-old girl from the three-year-old group into the four- to five-year-old group, at the request of her mother who could not understand why her daughter was in the younger group and wanted her to become more prepared for school the next year. The little girl was highly intelligent and it wasn't long before she became my right hand assistant, arriving early each morning to help me set up for the day. Together, we ran the group, the music sessions, the reading groups, the painting and art groups, and the outdoor activities. I won't ever forget that bright, energetic and sociable little girl who saw me through a difficult few months as a student teacher.

Then the Director arrived back, took one look at my number one assistant and called me into the kitchen. There she shouted at me, told me in no uncertain terms that this little girl had to leave the group immediately. She called in the President of the Mothers' Club who continued the haranguing. Did I not understand my position as a student teacher? I must listen to the Director and do what she told me to do.

I was totally nonplussed, but I stood my ground. I told the Director that if my small assistant were removed from the group, I would return to the college and report that I had no placement for my final year of training.

Suddenly I was presented with a different face from the Director. Couldn't I understand her position? This little girl was Jewish! (I had not noticed and anyway, it would have made no difference to me.) She (the Director) could not be expected to be in the same room as such a disgusting child. I was informed that she had to cross the street whenever she saw a Jewish person walking towards her. If I had been a member of the Hitler Youth as she had, she said, I would then understand where she was coming from. I was horrified. And I was angry. My voice uncharacteristically rose. I made it clear that if the child went, I went too. Which placed the Director in a tough spot as I was running the place. She was stunned. Then she turned on her heel and marched out. I didn't see her again until the final days at the kindergarten, leaving me to be totally in charge for that final term.

Back at the college, my student adviser had somehow found out about all this and called me in at the conclusion of that final year. I didn't know why I was being called in and was somewhat fearful. Had I not passed after all? Would I have to repeat that year? I was worried because my friend Natalie had already been told that she would not graduate because she had not completed some assignments. We were all very shocked by that as she was an amazing teacher who had excelled in everything through three years of college. We felt the decision of the college made no sense at all. Was I also not going to graduate?

My fears of being held back a year were unfounded. My adviser told me that the college had discovered what had been happening, and wanted to thank me for the way I'd handled it. She went on to say how much they wished I had reported it earlier so that they could have helped me more.

In addition, I was informed that the Director of that kindergarten had now lost her teacher's registration and would not be in charge of a kindergarten in Australia again. I became tearful and enormously relieved, not just because I had not failed the course but also because the Director would not be running a kindergarten ever again.

1938: Girl boarders at Box Hill Grammar School.

Back row, l. to r.: Heather MacDonald, Margaret Boardman, Isobel Rochford, Helen Johns, Margaret Maddison; front row: Betty Melville, June Alexander, Ailsa Webb, Mavis Walker holding Anne, Elwyn Cox, Jean Walker, Kathleen Walker and Ruth Walker seated in front

1942: Box Hill Grammar School students.

C.F. Walker (Dad) middle centre, E.A Walker (Mum) sitting in front of him, Jean to the left of Mum, Kath to the right, then Mavis, Anna Wilson, and Ruth. Front row: Evan third from left, Frances in front of Mum, Anne to the right of Frances

1943: The Walker Family.
Back row, l. to r.: Jean, Kath, Mavis, Ruth. Front row: Frances on Dad's knee, Evan, Robert on Mum's knee, Anne

1958: Box Hill Methodist Women's Cricket team.
Frances Walker front left, Anne S Walker front right

1961: Box Hill Methodist Women's Cricket Team.
Frances and Anne opening bats

1962: Camp Walker, Balnarring Beach. Anne and Ruth Lechte with their parents.

L. to r.: Roy Walker, Anne, Ethel Walker, Ruth Lechte, Doris Lechte and Don Lechte

3

Sailing away in search of the world

Things changed dramatically for me in December 1957. Between Boxing Day and New Year's Day, I had gone to a Methodist Youth Fellowship summer camp at Ocean Grove for a week with all my Box Hill MYF friends and with young people from all over the Melbourne area. For years, I had resisted these camps, feeling that I had no appetite for a week in a dormitory crowded with other young people – I had grown up in dormitories! And I had reached a point in my life where I was now enjoying having my own space.

But at Ocean Grove I met Ruth Lechte, one of the leaders at that camp, and I was bowled over by her enthusiasm for life, her gift for making things happen, her sheer exuberance. I wanted to spend more time with her. So when I left to travel to Albury to attend another camp, I promised as soon as I got back that we would meet up again. And that we did.

However, Ruth was planning to leave for England in May of 1958, having won a scholarship to a youth training course at one of the Selly Oak Colleges in Birmingham. She had brought such a whirlwind change into my life and suddenly, she was to be gone. Strange how a person can appear in your life and change things forever. In retrospect, this is what happened to me.

By December of that year, I was on a ship bound for England myself. It was a year earlier than I had planned with my KTC friends but I wanted to join Ruth in London. Plus my sister Jean had written to say I could join her at Kingsley Hall, a community centre in the East End of London. At the last minute, Judy Toy, a friend from the Box Hill MYF, asked if she could join me on the voyage. Judy had had a long relationship with Evan but it was now over. She wanted to find something new in her life and we both agreed it would be wonderful to have company on the five-week ship journey across to the other side of the world

England

We docked in Southampton one early morning in late January 1959 as the dawn broke. Here was England, the place still called home by Dad and most of his generation. His mother had sailed from here with her family as a 16-year-old girl from Cornwall, and they made a new life in faraway Australia. But Dad's grandfather on his father's side had sailed out as a child with his family, in 1841. Our roots in Australia were deep. Yet still the pull of England was there.

Jean was on the dock waving to us, an enormous thrill! She had sailed to England a year before and was working at Kingsley Hall, a community centre in the East End of London in a suburb called Bromley-by-Bow. She had come down to Southampton by train to meet us and escort us back to London. We unloaded our gear and headed for the railway station. I remember being a bit taken aback by the extreme cold, the bitter wind, and the fog. Judy and I were deeply tanned, our hair bleached from the sun after five weeks' sailing from Australia, and we were not prepared for this.

We reached the fabled Waterloo Station in London and took a taxi to Kingsley Hall. I had heard so much of this place, set up by two quite wealthy women, Muriel and Doris Lester, who had wanted to work with and on behalf of the poor who lived in Bromley-by-Bow. There were many such community centres in different parts of the East End, sometimes set up by private groups, more often by county councils. People were struggling at the time and needed support. This community place was loved by the people who lived around Kingsley Hall, and there was a healthy youth club with young people who poured in the door every evening to play billiards, table tennis, cards and more.

Judy and I lived at Kingsley Hall initially, but she soon moved to join some shipboard friends who had found a flat in the West End. I decided to stay with Jean for a few months, taking on the youth club and various other activities.

I slept in a cell on the roof. It was cold up there and the air was filthy. The winter of 1958–59 was one of the last of the great smogs in London, mainly due to charcoal fires still being widely used, and coal smoke and ash pouring into the sky. The first night that I ventured out for a walk I got hopelessly lost and became quite frightened. I could not see a foot in front of me and had a scarf wrapped around my nose and mouth because of the black smog and the atrocious smell. My head was full of Jack the Ripper, of course. That walk was to be my last for a while, at least on my own. I got very lost and took ages to find my way back to Kingsley Hall.

Ruth Lechte was teaching in a girls' school in the West End, having completed her youth work course in Birmingham. I was delighted to be in contact again and we saw each other frequently, usually at the opera at Covent Garden or the ballet at Sadler's Wells, with an occasional play in the West End. I was lapping up the culture of this great city. We were there for the first of the many seasons that Joan Sutherland sang at Covent Garden. What an extraordinary thrill to hear her sing with that incomparable voice in that wonderful place, albeit from a position high in the 'gods', in the standing only cheapest seats. Often we would wait outside the stage door afterwards just to catch a glimpse of Joan. She would always stop and chat in her easy, friendly way to her compatriots standing outside in the cold at the stage door. It always made us laugh with delight to hear her real Aussie accent just minutes after she had been singing in perfect Italian or French.

I began relief teaching in those first months, riding a bike to various schools in the East End to teach primary classes. I taught six- and seven-year-olds in Poplar, Bethnal Green and Stepney, struggling a bit with the accents and with many cultural situations from time to time. It was in these schools I encountered children who had been 'sewed up for the winter', dressed in head to toe woollen underwear that covered their whole body, arms and legs, with only an opening for going to the toilet. They were dressed in these and sewn in for the entire winter. I had encountered this in my first teaching assignment in Melbourne some years before. Parents wrote notes asking that their children be excluded from medical examinations by the county nurse because of that.

During Easter of that first year, I decided to go hitchhiking to the Lake District by myself. Ruth was not available to come with me and I figured that with all my Australian hitchhiking experience I would be fine. So I took a train to the outskirts of London and set off.

I don't have a diary from that time unfortunately, and most of my memories of the trip have faded with the years. But I do recall the kindness of strangers, particularly truck drivers, who picked me up and took me long distances to wherever they were headed, and some even invited me into their homes to have a meal with their family. I also remember the ones who got excited to find I was Australian and would immediately ask me if I knew some relative who had migrated there and with whom they had lost touch.

I was struck by the contrast between the green rolling hills of England, the tiny villages with their stone walled thatched cottages, and the rugged, dry, endless vistas of Australia with highways into nowhere. For English families, the disappearance of their family members to this other reality on the far side of the world was probably akin to death. So they were anxious to hear news of this distant place, anything that could draw them a picture of what it was like.

I loved the Lake District. Each night I stayed in a youth hostel, doing my share of the chores before leaving in the morning, and wandering beside the most beautiful lakes and through delightful small villages. At the end of the week, I set out on the highways and byways to head back to London, feeling refreshed and happy to have experienced a little of rural England for the first time. And thirsty for more. So it was that I planned a more extensive hitchhiking trip around the UK, with Ruth and her friend from Australia, Barbara Harris.

We set off, in the summer of 1959, staying in youth hostels throughout England, Scotland, Wales and Ireland. The first part of the trip would be without Ruth who was going to a week-long event on the island of Iona, off the west coast of Scotland.

It was extremely hot weather that summer, unusually so, but we felt we should take at least one plastic raincoat each in case of rain. This was, after all, the UK, known for its rain, wind and cold through the summers. The plastic raincoats were never brought out – it didn't rain for two months, at least not where we were. During August and September of 1959, the sun shone brightly.

We went through Cambridge to Norwich, then through King's Lynn and onwards to Hull. We slept in youth hostels all along the way, waking early and hitting the road with nothing but a pack on our backs. Moving steadily north, we went on to York and up to Newcastle, heading for the Scottish border and Hadrian's Wall. Along the way, we stopped to wander through magnificent cathedrals and old castles, some of which doubled as hostels and we slept in their ancient, crumbling dormitories.

In Scotland, we spent time in Glasgow then headed across country to Edinburgh, in time for the Military Tattoo in Edinburgh Castle, one of the few more touristy things we had added to our otherwise rather loosely organised meanderings. As we continued north, we stayed in one youth hostel where, when we produced our youth hostel passport showing we were Australians, we were charged an extra shilling 'for the Australian room'. which turned out to be the shower! And we sure did make use of that room after a day on the road.

We hitchhiked our way steadily north to Tongue on the far north coast of Scotland, then to Thurso where we were to meet Ruth coming by boat from Iona and stay a night in a hostel there. The next morning, we hitched a ride on a fishing boat headed to the Orkney Islands and set sail in quite rough seas that made it difficult to hold onto the deck rails without being swept overboard. In the Orkneys, we got off in the port of Stromness to have a look around and stay the night. No youth hostels there so we slept on the floor of a church hall. Next morning, we travelled by another fishing boat to the Shetland Islands, passing Fair Isle on the way. The Shetlands were much more rugged and isolated, very windswept. From memory, we stopped in Scalloway, and it was there we saw the hulks of old warships at the bottom of the shallow waters of the harbor, remnants of World War II.

We had reached the furthest parts of the UK and it was time to turn around and head back south. Which we did, making good time first by fishing boat back to Thurso and then down to Glasgow and on through Lockerbie and Carlisle, heading towards Wales.

Exactly where we crossed on the ferry over to Northern Ireland I can't be sure. But I believe we crossed the Irish Sea from Stranraer, directly to Belfast. From there we hitchhiked our way up to the North Coast to see the Giant's Causeway. Standing on those colossal pillars of stone is not something I would ever forget.

From the Giant's Causeway we hitched our way from youth hostel to youth hostel through Londonderry and down to Sligo and on to Galway. Somewhere in Connemara, Ruth and I found ourselves very far from any youth hostel with night coming on, and it was a very desolate place. We had slept one night already under a hedge and did not want to do that again. Even though the weather was dry, it got cold at night and we had not found the experience too pleasant. So we began knocking on doors, asking of we could possibly sleep the night on their floor, or in an outside shed. Ruth did not like the leaping dogs that would occasionally answer our door knock and on one occasion, I went alone to knock and was totally bowled over by an enormous dog. A nice woman came to my rescue and took us both in. We ate well that night, and slept beside an open peat fire in the living room, in our sleeping bags.

It took months to remove the smell of peat from our clothes and backpacks. In fact, some clothes we had to toss out. But it was a memorable night in a little stone cottage in Connemara, with some very nice people who were totally fascinated to have a couple of Australians sleeping over.

From Connemara we continued south through County Clare and into Limerick and on to Kerry. Throughout our time in these parts of Ireland, we bought water from people selling it from donkeys. The lack of rain was an ever-present thing. We had always thought of this place as green and verdant with lots of rain. But that summer, there was none of that, and they had no reservoirs to cope with such a situation.

In Kerry, we headed for a youth hostel near the Gap of Dunloe where we had heard we could ride horses through the Gap. Very good way to see the gorgeous scenery we were told. So, after a good night's sleep at the hostel, we were introduced to the horses and set off.

After the Gap of Dunloe, we hitched our way to Cork and Killarney Castle in order to kiss the Blarney Stone. I don't think we totally understood that you had to lean backwards over the edge of a tower and kiss the stone upside down, but we both did it because we were there. Crazy really. But we have kissed the Blarney Stone and are now apparently capable of as much blarney as we wish to speak. Onwards through Waterford we went and finally to Dublin. We went from the youth hostel straight to Dublin Castle to see The Book of Kells and spent most of the day there, marvelling at the exquisite painting of this extraordinary book.

From Dublin, we crossed by ferry into Wales, to Fishguard port I think, and down to St David's Cathedral on the west coast. From youth hostel to youth hostel, we made our way through Swansea and on to Cardiff, crossing over the Bristol Channel to Bristol.

Then to Cornwall, where I remember visiting King Arthur's Castle in Tintagel. It was fun to be actually climbing around a place where Arthur had lived, fought and ruled the round table of knights. Or did he? I don't know; but it was a great visit. As was our walk across the causeway to St Michael's Mount near Mousehole.

On we wandered, hitching rides with strangers who quickly became friends. By the end of that gloriously sunny summer, we were ready to return to London. I think we took a train for the last part, arriving one late afternoon and making our way to Bromley-by-Bow and Kingsley Hall.

Ruth had resigned from her school at the end of the previous school year and now joined me at Kingsley Hall. She had loved teaching at a girls' school in London and had stayed at a women's hostel. But she was intrigued by the activities at Kingsley Hall and was pleased to join me there when Jean left to do a diploma course in religious education in Birmingham.

Kingsley Hall is where Mahatma Gandhi chose to live when he came to the UK for talks with the British government on India's independence. He chose it because it was in a poor part of London and he wanted to meet the people who lived there.

Gandhi slept in a small cell on the roof of Kingsley Hall and when Ruth came to join me, she took over that very cell.

She and I ran the activities at Kingsley Hall from September 1959 until June of 1960. In the process, I became quite competent at table tennis and billiards, even entering competitions in table tennis with other youth club members from Kingsley Hall and playing against other community centres in the East End.

In the Easter break of 1960, I went with Carol, a Kingsley Hall friend, to Europe by ferry and hitchhiked around the Netherlands for about a week. We had a great time. I remember climbing the steep, narrow stairs of a church tower in the middle of the Netherlands and being able to see the whole of the country from there. I also remember spending a day in the Keukenhof Gardens and being totally dazzled by the flowers and landscaping of that incredible place.

We also discovered the magnificent art galleries of the Netherlands, including the Anne Frank House and the Van Gogh Museum. One very special day trip took us some distance outside of Amsterdam, to a place called Otterlo. In the midst of a forest was the Kroller-Muller Museum, including an art and sculpture garden. I was blown away by Vincent Van Gogh's paintings and remember standing alongside and looking across the painting to see the depth and richness of the paint. (That's what you don't get in prints!) There were also paintings by Mondrian, Seurat, Braque, Gauguin, and Picasso, all this in a private collection.

Hitchhiking around Europe

As the time approached for Ruth and me to leave Kingsley Hall, June 1960, we began to plan a trip to Europe. We wanted to attend the Rome Olympics, having been to the Melbourne Olympics in 1956. In fact, I think we were probably part of a generation of Australians who figured we would attend the Olympics every four years from now on, once having experienced such an amazing event.

I know somewhere there is a thick journal in which I wrote down every town, museum, every art gallery, every cathedral, every place of interest as we hitch-hiked our way across Europe that summer of 1960. But I can't find it and probably that's just as well.

Ruth, her friend Barbara and I headed north from London in late July 1960, catching a ferry from Newcastle to Oslo, Norway. It was a stormy passage across the North Sea. We landed in Oslo a bit the worse for wear and went straight to the Oslo youth hostel to recover. The next day, we wandered around that beautiful small city with its harbour and central park, visiting the museum to see the works of Edvard Munch and others and generally relaxing after the North Sea crossing. And then it was off across the Jotunheimen Mountains towards Stockholm amidst spectacular scenery and soaring mountain peaks. It was incredibly beautiful but hard going and we varied that journey with some stretches riding the train. We stayed one night in a youth hostel that had a roof of thick grass that several goats were enjoying!

In Stockholm, the youth hostel was a three-masted schooner anchored harbourside and we slept in cabins down below. The old town of Stockholm is exceptionally beautiful and we wandered those streets for hours, soaking up the atmosphere and sipping coffee in the sunshine. Then off south on the train towards Malmo for the crossing to Denmark. It's now an incredible bridge and tunnel that spans that crossing, but for us, in 1960, the train drove onto a ferry and we rode on top with magnificent views across the Oresund Strait.

A brief stay in Copenhagen, a city of canals and much beauty, then by train south towards Germany. I remember falling asleep briefly during that train ride, and waking up to see a railway official walk past my carriage wearing a high-fronted cap reminiscent of those worn by Nazi soldiers. We were now in Germany and I got a fright: I grew up as a child with a great fear of that uniform, even in faraway Australia. We became accustomed to it as we travelled through Germany and Austria. I guess we thought that was one of those symbols that would have been done away with following the atrocities of the Second World War.

We had bought tickets for the Oberammagau Passion Play before we left London, so on arrival we looked for the youth hostel that was providing our official accommodation. To our surprise, we found we were in temporary hostel conditions, a tent in a paddock outside of town! But the time spent in that medieval village was wonderful, surrounded by townspeople who all took part in the play. Which meant all the men had very long hair and long beards, a unique sight in 1960.

After Oberammagau we travelled south, through the picturesque mountains and valleys of Austria, mostly hitchhiking, occasionally jumping on a train. We were heading for Rome and the 1960 Olympics. Down through Italy we travelled, all the way to Florence. What a fabulous city that is, so full of antiquity in buildings, art, sculpture, fabrics, craft of all kinds. We loved our brief time there. But we had tickets to events at the Olympic Games so pressed on, hitchhiking our way down through Arezza, Perugia, Terni and on to Rome.

In Rome we headed for the youth hostel, expecting that we would at last have a comfortable bed under cover to sleep and prepare ourselves for the Games. On arrival we were informed that they had vastly overbooked the hostel and we would have to sleep on the open rooftop. Up the stairs we trudged and sure enough, we would be sleeping in the open with just the night sky full of stars above us.

But we were in Rome and the next day, we set off to the Opening Ceremony of the Olympic Games. The Opening was dramatic as all the competing nations marched, led by Greece, but very soon after came the Australians with a squad of 189, only 29 of whom were women.

I have terrific memories of those Games. It was the Olympics of Herb Elliott who won the Gold in the Men's 1500 metres; of Murray Rose who won a swimming Gold in the Men's 400 Freestyle, Jon Konrads, Gold in the Men's 1500 Freestyle and of course, Dawn Fraser, Gold in the Women's 100 metre Freestyle. In fact Australian athletes won 8 Gold, 8 Silver and 6 Bronze, a total of 22 medals which put them 8th on the Olympic ladder. At that time, a great effort.

One of the most memorable athletes was Wilma Rudolph of the US, a former polio patient, who won three Gold medals in sprint events on the track. And Abebe Bikila of Ethiopia who won the marathon bare-footed to become the first black African Olympic champion.

The Closing Ceremony was somewhat terrifying when the crowd started lighting newspapers and other bits and pieces lying around and waving them in the air. We were wearing skirts in those days and it became very dangerous with flames licking at our legs. So we left early.

From Rome, we headed north once more, hitchhiking up the coast highway to Pisa where we wandered around the sloping verandahs of the Tower of Pisa marvelling at the fact that we were allowed to do that. Then on to Genoa and north to Milan. We wanted to see the Michelangelo mural of the Last Supper housed in a very small building, a masterpiece somewhat damaged by the German occupation of the building during World War II. Apparently they had used the building as a stable for their horses.

Then to Turin and back to the southern coast, heading for Nice and Cannes in France. From Cannes we hitched our way to Avignon and its famous Pont d'Avignon, and Nimes and Montpelier, making our way steadily towards Spain. Moving south, we wended our way to Barcelona. We wanted to see the Basilica de la Sagrada Familia, one of the most famous landmarks in Barcelona. We spent the best part of a day wandering around that extraordinary place. It's one building

I wouldn't mind going back to see one day.

After Barcelona, Madrid – such a bustling, exciting city. We were overwhelmed by the numbers of people in the streets and happy to find the youth hostel and retire for the first evening and night. But a wonderful few days were spent there, before we boarded a train to head back into France.

On the border with France. Ruth and I settled in for a read and a sleep, aware that we were the only tourists on board the train, at least in the third class carriage, and neither of us able to speak Spanish. We did however speak to each other, and the others in the cabin became wildly excited when they found we were speaking English and came from Australia. We were somewhat nonplussed, not understanding why they would be so excited. A little girl crept over to my side and started to stroke my fair hair. Others came closer and spoke to us more and more excitedly and we were totally useless, not understanding a word.

Finally, one of them ran down the corridors to a first class carriage way up the front of the train where they apparently knew someone who could translate. She appeared at the door of the carriage, a young woman who was a nanny for an English family, and finally all became clear. Or as clear as was possible with a translator who spoke very limited English.

It turned out that our fellow travellers were a family taking one last trip to visit relatives before they all migrated to Australia. The questions came thick and fast. Did everyone there look like us? Were there some people with dark hair and complexion? What was the weather like? Did it snow? Would they be able to find jobs? Did they have to speak English? Was there nobody there who could speak Spanish? And on and on.

After a couple of hours, Ruth and I were exhausted and asked the young translator to let them know that we had been very happy to answer as many questions as we could, and we wished them every happiness in their new country, but now we needed some sleep. The translator was exhausted too and was happy to return to her carriage. For us it had been a real lesson in the trauma and uncertainties faced by immigrants coming to Australia and leaving all that was familiar and comfortable behind them. Most of all, facing a life where they could not speak the language. That's real courage. I sincerely hope those we met that day on the train to San Sebastian prospered in their new country.

From San Sebastian, we hitched our way across the border into France, then through Bordeaux, Poitiers, Tours, Orléans and finally Paris. At that time, not many people in France spoke English and my schoolgirl French was not too successful. We sort of stumbled our way north, using public toilets and scavenging for food as best we could. The youth hostels were not clean and had quite disgusting toilets and bathrooms. This meant that we just slept in the dormitories and travelled on as fast as we could. By 'scavenging' I mean we would buy something very cheap in a café and stock up on bread, sugar, packets of salt and pepper and butter and whatever else came with the meal. By public toilets I mean holes in the ground, usually in the village square, within small brick structures, where if you didn't jump fast enough, an automatic flush would almost swill you down the hole. Toilet visits required considerable athletic ability.

In late September 1960 we caught the train to the ferry and crossed the English Channel back to England. It was good to be back again even though the two months on the road had been extraordinary.

I found a job with the Royal Hospital Chelsea, in the office, while Ruth found a job at Parliament House. We were making plans to drive back to Australia from London, something several Australians were doing at the time. We wanted to see something of the countries east of Europe, the Middle East, South Asia and South-East Asia. So we started writing to various companies and possible sponsors for a Land Rover, camping equipment, funds for petrol etc. And to our amazement, we were getting good responses. Two of the young men from our youth club at Kingsley Hall got very enthused at the thought of the journey and asked if they could come too. We were delighted at the thought of having two strong young men with us, mainly for security reasons.

Everything was coming together nicely and the trip was taking shape. Then came the message from the doctor of Ruth's father. He genuinely felt that our planned trip could very well bring on a heart attack for her father, who suffered from angina. It was the end of those plans. We wrote letters of thanks to all our sponsors and turned our attention to another plan of action. We would migrate to Canada where my brother Evan was and make our way home across North America. Off we went to Canada House to start the Landed Immigrant process.

Canada and the USA

Winter in London in 1960–61 was freezing, and somehow the icy rain and biting cold as we set off each morning from our temporary North Finchley home to the tube station really got to Ruth and me. Huddled in our heavy coats, scarves wrapped around the neck, wool hats and wool gloves, our thoughts turned more and more to home where our families were enjoying beach weather and endless sunshine.

So it was good when we heard from Canada House that Landed Immigrant status was granted with our Canada sponsor now in place (Evan Walker), and we would be sailing from Southampton on the Cunard liner RMS *Saxonia* to Halifax, Canada in January 1961. We would be crossing the Atlantic for £100 each; we were happy with the arrangement and began to prepare ourselves for the trip.

Of course it was mid-winter and we should have prepared ourselves for that. But when the first of the storms hit, we were not at all prepared. One day we were walking around the deck enjoying the brisk air, playing table tennis and other indoor pastimes. The next day we were banned from going outside at all and watched in amazement from behind locked doors as waves smashed over the top of the ship; the seawater turning to ice before it hit the decks. That was before we had to retire to our bunks with seasickness. And we were very sick.

The ice storm that our ship had run into was so severe that entry into the harbour at Halifax was impossible. The port was totally iced over. So an icebreaker ship was sent out to travel in front, breaking the ice as it went, in order for our ship to be able to creep into port.

Finally we were at the pier. We disembarked with many other Landed Immigrants and were ushered into an enormous reception hall on the pier. Waiting for us were immigration and customs officials, social services staff, and clergy, who with church volunteers handed us bags containing some essentials such as tooth brushes, soap, hand towels, gloves, hats. We were very touched by this and in recent times here in Australia, I have wished my own country had been as welcoming and supportive of new arrivals. Canadians went all out to make us feel at home and we were very grateful for that.

Then we boarded the waiting train for Toronto via Montréal, and off we went. Once outside of the shipping and piers area, we were astounded to find ourselves in a total winter wonderland. Houses were covered with snow to their rooftops; cars parked beside roads were mere bumps in the snowscape. But we were snug and warm on the fabled Canadian Pacific Railways, trains that we had been told by Canadian friends in the UK were the best in the world.

And so they were for the first day or so. Then disaster struck. The ice storm was so severe in the Province of Quebec that it had brought power poles crashing over the rails and our train could go no further. Not that we knew that at the time; we came to a grinding halt and that was that. Hours went by.

One of us tried to walk along the train but couldn't open the doors at each end of the carriage. We didn't know what was happening and were starting to get cold and hungry. A young man in our carriage volunteered to climb down the stairs and walk up towards the engine and see what was happening. We all donated our coats and scarves and rugged him up to his teeth and out he went. Then we got worried as time passed and he didn't reappear. A search party of fellow passengers was being assembled when he finally banged on our door and we dragged him up the steps.

When he could get his lips moving again, he struggled to tell us what he'd found. There was no engine on the front of the train and no dining car either. They were gone. Apparently some repairs had been done to the track that would allow just the engine and one or two carriages (including the dining car) past but not the rest of the train. We were stranded in the middle of nowhere with nothing to eat.

At the last station before all this happened, we had all jumped off and rushed into the restaurant in the station and tried to buy food. Ruth and I were the only ones who managed to purchase anything at all – a bag of chips (crisps) and a small bar of chocolate. When the train was stopped in the middle of nowhere some hours later, this food was what sustained the entire carriage for an entire 24 hours.

Finally, with the carriage now extremely cold and all of us on board very hungry and thirsty, we heard a train horn in the distance and the sound seemed to be coming our way. We all stood up and cheered. Then the great thump as the engine was attached, the triumphant shriek of the train horn and we were moving at last! Afterwards we found out that teams of men had been working to clear the railway tracks ahead of us, mainly from electric poles that had iced up in the storm and split down the middle before crashing across the rails, taking the wires and everything else with them.

It was a major ice storm for Canada and most especially for the Montréal area. As our train lumbered across the bridge into Montréal, I was able to get some English news on the little portable radio I had bought in Germany. Travellers were being warned to stay off the bridges leading into the city because of icy stalactites hanging from the rafters above. I recall hearing these words as stalactites crashed onto the roof of our train and ice skidded down the frosted windows. Quite alarming!

At last we arrived in Montréal Railway Station. Ruth and I disembarked, found our luggage and proceeded to the main waiting area. It was packed to the rafters: apparently the ice storm had destroyed the power systems across the region and farmers and other country folk had no power for light or heat. Thousands had come into Montréal proper to camp out in railway stations and other major public buildings until the power could be switched back on.

We were told that our train would not be continuing to Toronto and that we would have to wait for a connecting train. So we waited. And we waited. Thankfully we found food and coffee and began to feel a bit revived from our journey through the storm. After some hours, we found that there would be a mail train making the journey from Montréal to Toronto and we bought our tickets quickly before it was sold out.

It was a mail train and not meant for passengers so seating was rudimentary and uncomfortable but we were at last on our way to Toronto. We arrived in the middle of the night and all was pitch dark. The railway station was empty and there was no-one to meet us. But we had expected that would be the case as our train was so overdue. We decided to settle ourselves down on a couple of benches in the waiting area, and very soon we were fast asleep.

As dawn broke, I woke to the footsteps of someone moving across the waiting hall. It was a young man, with somewhat dishevelled hair and the beginnings of a beard, and clearly he had been sleeping and was not yet fully awake. But he seemed to be on a mission, heading towards the information desk, even though there was no-one yet on duty. Then to my utter surprise I realised it was Evan so I jumped up and chased after him. It was such an amazing relief to find him waiting for us there. It had been a very worrying few days with no news of where we were or what had happened to our train in the ice storm.

Evan and a friend, George Hume, a fellow student at U of Toronto, had given up trying to get information over the phone and had gone down to the railway station to sleep until something turned up. And their plan had worked.

Toronto is such a special city, in many ways very like Melbourne though it is located on a lake rather than on a river. Lake Ontario, in the summer, is a wonderful playground for Toronto residents. But it was winter still and very cold, so we had to get out and buy ourselves more suitable clothing to cope with the ice and snow. Then we needed a job.

I was the first to find one: at the University of Toronto Library, where a vast collection of books was being transferred from the old Dewey Decimal System of organisation to the Library of Congress System, and they needed unskilled labour. Ruth found a job as a motor scooter courier, zooming around Toronto with documents and parcels from office building to office building. A job she enjoyed for a few weeks but she soon became tired and a bit bored. I was making more money at the U of T Library, so Ruth joined me there. By now I knew the ropes and could fill her in on the job we were to do. We needed to make money not just for our share of the rent at the share house we were living in, but also towards a major expedition we were planning in the summer. These were plans that had been afoot since before we left London.

USA: 'The Grand Tour'

Ruth and I were on our way home to Australia after being away three years (for Ruth) and two years (for me). We were now planning to continue our journey home by driving around the USA and catching a ship in Vancouver to cross the Pacific for the last leg. We planned to undertake what we were now calling 'the Grand Tour' with Evan and his college friend George Hume. Ruth and I agreed to raise the money needed for trip incidentals if Evan could raise the money to buy a new car. And he did, working day and night as a draughtsman with an architect's firm to raise those funds and buy a new car, though his choice was questionable. A Vauxhall for goodness sake, an English car that had never been seen in the USA before, at least not by any service station or mechanic that we met over that long, extraordinary summer! It was fortunate that Evan had invited George to come with us as he knew about cars – at least more than any of us did.

This is an excerpt from a long letter that Evan wrote home about the plans we made for the Grand Tour:

Initial plans are to visit the university towns of Hanover, Andover, Boston, Cambridge, Wellesley and New Haven (Yale) – and then New York. The next part of the plan is to visit Princeton, Philadelphia and Baltimore, also spending time in Washington to visit the White House, the Capitol Building, and several of the well-known memorials in the US capital.

The next leg of the journey will see us pass through Virginia, North and South Carolina, Georgia, Florida, Alabama, Mississippi and Louisiana with New Orleans to be our next 'rest spot'.

The plan is to then take in Houston, Texas, and then San Antonio, Del Rio and El Paso, following the famous Rio Grande for several hundred miles, and following along the border between the US and Mexico. Leaving Rio we are to make our way through the arid, mountainous wastes of New Mexico and Arizona to Tucson, Phoenix and Tempe, and then tour the Grand Canyon and Hoover Dam. We plan to have a quick look at Las Vegas and then enter sunny California, heading for San Bernadino and Los Angeles.

Next we plan to head north along the coast to San Francisco. From there we head inland to Denver, Colorado, plus a detour to visit the new Air Force Academy at Colorado Springs. Then north again through Cheyenne in Wyoming to Nebraska and the Black Hills of South Dakota, taking in the Mount Rushmore National Monument where the likenesses of Washington, Jefferson, Lincoln and Roosevelt are carved into the face of a mountain. Yellowstone National Park will see us enjoying our fourth rest stop for a few days. Then on through Montana to Alberta, Canada, for a short stay in Taber [with a fellow student from Toronto].

Then through Calgary into the famous Canadian Rockies, visiting Banff, Lake Louise, Revelstoke, Kamloops and arriving in Vancouver, all being well, on 24 August. It is in Vancouver that our party is to diminish by half, as Anne and Ruth will leave us to embark on the SS *Oronsay* for home on 8th September 1961.

Incredibly, the planned tour outlined in this long letter was pretty much how it all happened. On 1 July 1961, we finally departed on our great adventure, heading first for Montréal, such a completely different city in the summer, with no ice or snow to be seen!

A day in Fiji

The trip on the good ship *Oronsay* was in great contrast to the disastrous trip across the Atlantic in January of that same year. The weather was great, the accommodation more than fine and the food and entertainment world class. We had two ports of call on the way home. The first stop was in Honolulu where we spent a day exploring the town. The second stop was to be in Fiji, with a day to explore Suva. Ruth had written ahead to her mother's cousin Dr Esther Williams in the hope that we could see her while we were in port. We had not heard back from her. Dr Williams had spent years in Fiji, initially as a teacher but later, after returning to Australia for medical training, as a doctor. She was known nationwide, particularly for her care of Fiji-Indian women, and spoke fluent Hindi.

We dressed in holiday gear for our day in Suva, expecting to spend time in the market buying crafts and maybe duty-free electronics for our families back home. We also had a plan for some time on a beach nearby. That was the plan anyway.

But our day was to be nothing of the sort. On our arrival at the pier, there was Dr Williams waving her hands and shouting out to us. Without much ado, she loaded us into her little Morris Minor and we went rocketing off from the wharf through the town and up to Government House! We drove past the gates with Royal Fiji Military Force guards on either side in their bright red shirts and white sulus, saluting us as we passed by, and then up the long drive to the very grand front entrance to this magnificent old colonial building set in expansive grounds. Lady Elnor Maddocks, the wife of Fiji's Governor, Sir Kenneth Maddocks, greeted us at the top of the steps and led us inside.

There we were seated amongst the gilt of times past and served tea and sandwiches by uniformed servants. Lady Maddocks, after welcoming us officially to Fiji, began to discuss with us the purpose of the visit. Apparently, a group of women had been meeting in Suva for some time with a view to starting a YWCA in Fiji. There was growing concern in the community about the numbers of young women coming into town from villages, often with no job training and little preparation for city life. And with the recommendation of Dr Williams, who knew both Ruth and I had teacher training and social work experience, plus Ruth's youth work diploma gained while she was in England, Lady Maddocks had convinced this group that we would be the perfect people to come to Fiji and get the YWCA going.

To say we were taken aback would be putting it mildly. We were firmly set on returning to Australia after years away, and our only experience with the YWCA was being turned away by the Vancouver YWCA when we were looking for somewhere to stay, just four weeks earlier. So we gave a very tentative response, saying that we first had to return to Australia and once there, would give the matter further consideration.

Then it was time to return to the Oronsay and sail away as the sun set over Suva Harbour, with Dr Williams waving us off from the wharf. It had been quite a day of surprises and we had much to think about.

A couple of days later we arrived in Sydney, rising from our bunks at dawn to watch the sunrise as we sailed through the Heads into Sydney Harbour. We joined many other passengers, mostly Australians who had also been away for years, for an emotional entry into that magnificent harbour. We were not to know that it would be the only time we ever sailed through those Heads again as air travel would take over all of our future travels overseas. This was the end of a circumnavigation of the globe for Ruth and me, a journey by ships taken in three parts over three years.

From Sydney we boarded the train and travelled down to Melbourne. We were home again. It's always strange to come home after a long time away and this was certainly the case for me. But I knew I needed to find a job and to map out what my future would be now I was back in Australia.

The first need was almost immediately answered when Dad asked me to work in the school office. I was not enthusiastic at first, but then agreed to his request, thinking I would be looking for a kindergarten teaching position for 1962 and may as well be earning a little money meanwhile. So I started work at the school.

The office was no longer based in the boarding house but was in an extension that had been built on the assembly hall, a weatherboard building across from the Cloisters building. Each morning I presented myself there and set to work. It was a remarkably busy office with all the regular administrative needs complicated by constant visits from school children needing some kind of assistance. I enjoyed my few months there and learnt a lot about the smooth running of the school. And the not so smooth: these were Dad's final years at the school and he was fighting a losing battle with the School Council.

But the group of women in Suva kept up the pressure for Ruth and me to return to Fiji and help set up a YWCA there. We discussed the possibility endlessly. There were many pros to the idea and also many cons. Finally, however, we agreed to give it a try. We thought we would go for one year just to get something off the ground.

Meanwhile, Ruth was to fly to New Zealand and visit several YWCAs there to discuss the setting up of initial activities. I was to fly alone to Fiji to set up a multiracial kindergarten as the first YWCA activity. It was a daunting thought to go alone and I was hesitant. However, in February 1962, I flew from Essendon Airport to Sydney, and then across the Pacific to Fiji. I remember looking out of the small window of the plane at the crowd of family and friends, including Ruth, who were lining the top of the old terminal at Essendon and waving me goodbye. And I wondered what on earth I was doing.

4

Fiji: a decade that changed everything

When I first arrived in Suva in February 1962 I stayed with Dr Esther Williams in her little flat in Gordon Street. She lived on the top floor of a four-storey building called Gordon Flats. On the ground floor lived Miss Hollis and Miss Jennings, known as Holly and Jenny. These extraordinary women had been Anglican missionaries in China and had amazing stories to tell. I spent quite a lot of time with them, hearing about their work in China. Holly had spent years in a Japanese prisoner-of-war camp. She was imprisoned along with the children from the school where she had been a teacher and continued teaching inside the prison camp to keep their minds occupied and off the thought of food. She and the children had tried to escape the Japanese soldiers with a long trek over the mountains but were eventually caught and imprisoned. I wondered if the film starring Ingrid Bergman about such a trek was based on Holly's story. After the war, both women headed south to Fiji and settled there, teaching at the Chinese School in Suva.

Dr Williams had a medical practice that spanned the city of Suva and its environs and I would often go out with her on her rounds. I saw some shocking living conditions, most especially the toilets – or more correctly, the lack of same – and more than once witnessed Dr Williams so nauseated she would throw up on the way back to the car. She was totally dedicated to her job as one of the only women doctors to look after Fiji Indian women, and treated them in their homes. It was no surprise then that so many Fiji Indian babies were called Esther, many of them Esther Williams.

But my task was to get a kindergarten off the ground as a first activity for the fledgling YWCA. I visited several possible locations and decided on St John's/Red Cross Hall in Rodwell Road, opposite the Phoenix Theatre. I had lots to do back at Dr Williams' apartment and I worked hard on an application form for the parents to fill out, making copies on an old Gestetner mimeograph machine. I put out a call for Fiji mats, tables, chairs, wood blocks, crayons, paints etc. to the wonderful women of the Pan Pacific South-East Asia Women's Association (PPSEAWA) in Suva who had led the effort to get a YWCA started in Fiji. Lady Maddocks at Government House donated most of the mats. And we actually opened within two weeks of my arrival in Suva.

First, however, I needed to take down the necessary contact details and other information for each child and I organised to see parents or carers before opening. I expected a dozen or so might turn up, but when I arrived at St John's/Red Cross Hall I found a long line of people waiting for me. There must have been at least 40 children in the line, of many ethnic groups including Fijian, Indian, Tongan, European and Chinese.

I had decided I would interview each adult and child briefly and get to know the children a little. Up stepped a handsome Fijian woman with her little girl beside her. I went through the first part of the form then got to the part where I asked for the occupation of the father. The woman said 'RokoTuiViti' and I said something like 'would that be a carpenter, or maybe a person who works on the wharves or something like that?' To which she replied, 'No. It means he's the Paramount Chief of Fiji'. I was mortified and apparently showed my embarrassment because she patted me on the arm and said that I shouldn't worry.

Some months after that, a New Zealand mother asked if her child's best friend at kindergarten, who happened to be the daughter of the woman who had been so understanding on that first day, could come home for a sleepover. The arrangement was made and shortly after, off went little Adi Kaunilotuma Cakobau. The next morning, the NZ mother came in to the kindergarten and pulled me aside: 'Who on earth is Kaunilotuma?' I asked why she needed to know. Apparently, whenever the house girl and the little visiting girl were in the same room together, the house girl sank to her knees and reversed out of the room. I said I hadn't thought it necessary to let the mother know that Kaunilotuma was the daughter of the Paramount Chief of Fiji. In the kindergarten she was just one of the group. But of course, the young woman who helped at home recognised the distinctive eyes of a Cakobau and was totally overwhelmed at having her in the home.

That first kindergarten group was made up of children from all areas of life in Fiji, including colonial servants, Fijian chiefs, house girls, tradespeople, shopkeepers, public officials, teachers, nurses and bus drivers. It was multi-racial, multi-ethnic, and represented all the faiths and beliefs of Fiji at that time. And because of this, we immediately became a source of much interest. The Education Department sent groups of teachers and officials to observe the phenomenon. I was told in no uncertain terms that it could never work. At that time, the schools of Fiji were all segregated by race and religion; there was no integration at all. I was to find out more about that as time went by.

A month after my arrival and a couple of weeks following the opening of the first YWCA kindergarten, Ruth flew in from New Zealand. She had gone there from Melbourne to meet and talk with YWCA leaders and to find out some basics about this world organisation of which we knew very little. Dr Williams and I had been scouting out possible places for Ruth and me to live and we had found an old house on the corner of Thurston St and Gordon Street that seemed to fit the bill. It was actually half a house with the elderly woman who owned the building living on the other side. There was a large garden at the back and plenty of room inside.

Ruth and I moved in and set about organising. We had no funds to speak of, no office and no staff other than the two of us. Gradually we pulled together a group of young women and started the discussions. Meetings were held at our place. We made it clear that we had not come with any pre-arranged ideas as to what was needed and were reliant on the community to guide us.

We knew only the basic need as it had been expressed to us before we had come to Fiji. The Pan Pacific South-East Asia Women's Association Suva branch said there was a major problem with young women coming in to Suva from villages and rural areas without skills and in some cases with little education. The concern the PPSEAWA had was that they were 'falling into the wrong hands' and out of this concern Ruth and I had been invited to start a YWCA.

The first plan that came out of the early talks with young women from the community was the decision to invite them and others to come up with activities that they thought were needed, and then for us to find a leader or leaders and a place for those activities. If the activities did not prove to be successful after a few trial weeks, then we would celebrate the effort with a 'Failure Party' at our house, to which everyone was invited. We promised that we would assist in every way possible with logistics, equipment and moral support. We made it clear from the beginning that if it involved cooking, sewing or any other domestic skill of that nature, we were totally dependent on them to find the necessary leadership as we were hopeless in those areas. If an activity was a success, we would expand and publicise it so that more young women could take part.

Those parties were an enormous success, and we had lots of them in those early months. In fact, during that first year, the owner who lived on the other side became increasingly anxious about our activities and began to complain about the noise. And it was not just the parties that she didn't like. It was also the fact that all of the activities were being run out of our house. Day and evening, that old wooden house was rocking with laughter and movement as more and more young women began to take part. It was clear that we needed a place separate from our home to run the activities, and fast.

So we began discussions with the Suva City Council. Was there any available space amongst their properties where the fledgling YWCA could conduct its growing list of activities? Much to our delight, they offered to rent us the first floor at the Suva Town Hall, a great location on Victoria Parade in the centre of town.

However, this meant we had to raise funds to be able to pay the rent. We also needed funds to pay our salaries and to bring on local staff to work with us. It was during this time, when we were discussing the financial plight of this new organisation, that Ruth and I made the decision to peg our salaries to those of local Fiji teachers. This was done for many reasons, the main one being that we wanted to be on a par with local professionals. But we also were very aware that we had to raise all the money ourselves and we wanted to spend our time on the growing number of activities, not trying to raise too much money for our own salaries. Membership fees were basically out of the question and the shilling per day that the kindergarten parents paid barely covered kindergarten equipment and supplies.

This decision to pay ourselves local salaries was to plague YWCA staff in the years after Ruth and I left because these salaries were so low. We combined our two salaries to make ends meet, and the YWCA Board agreed to pay the rent for our house and the cost of running a car. These two additions to our salaries made it possible for us to continue. Of course, we had to raise the funds that the Board was allocating towards the rent and car as well. But we thought we would only be in this position for a year or two. That was the initial agreement.

How could we raise money? The need was urgent. And so the first YWCA old clothes stalls started in Suva Market. We collected from everywhere and anywhere, with the bulk of the clothes coming from the homes of the families of public servants, most of them from the UK, New Zealand and Australia, but also from shopkeepers, teachers, nurses and others who wanted to see the YWCA succeed. And Ruth and I donated many clothes of our own. We were shopping locally now for the lightest and coolest clothes and much that we had brought with us was inappropriate.

In addition to the weekly old clothes stall, we also started planning for an annual bazaar. For this, we rented the main hall downstairs in the Suva Town Hall and began working on it many months in advance. There were stalls for fruit and vegetables, crafts of all kinds, cakes and scones, plants, used clothes including school uniforms and much more. Some of the most popular stalls were those where morning tea was served, and those where you dipped apples into a pot of toffee, or where you could throw a ring at a post for prizes. We had great crowds. And I remember the first year that we raised over F£1000, we were as excited as if we had raised a million pounds. F£1000 was worth a lot more in the 1960s.

Once we had a little money raised, we looked around for our first local staff member. We already knew Amelia Rokotuivuna as she had taken part in some of the discussions in our house at the very beginning. She was working at the Fiji Broadcasting Commission as an assistant technician. Amelia had been educated at Adi Cakobau School (ACS) that was initially set up as a 'sister' school to Queen Victoria School, a college for the sons of Fijian Chiefs. I'm not sure whether ACS originally only accepted the daughters of Fijian Chiefs but by the time we were in Fiji, it had evolved into a school for high achievers.

The YWCA program just kept growing and we were somewhat overwhelmed in those beginning days by the numbers of people arriving and wanting to take part. Very early it became clear that this was to become an organisation for both young men and women. Not in every activity for sure. Some of the first activities were training courses for young women in secretarial skills – typing, organising and budgeting. Other training courses were in reading and writing, and domestic skills such as sewing and cooking. More and more local women came forward to be leaders of these groups. And we started multi-racial sports teams, including hockey, cricket and basketball. All of our activities were multi-racial, which was in many cases a first for Fiji. And we also started a Youth Club that was for both young men and women, and organised a Friday Night Dance Club that became an instant hit.

Ruth, Amelia and I fell into a routine each day for running this expanding organisation. Amelia had joined Ruth and me at our house and we would all set off together in the mornings, Ruth and Amelia to the Town Hall, me to the St John's/Red Cross Hall in Rodwell Road. The YWCA kindergarten now catered for 60 children aged between three and six years of age, and I needed more equipment and supplies. We had started with only mats on the floor and very basic supplies of chalk, crayons, paper and some educational toys. But this was not sufficient. I now had an assistant to help with setting up each morning and supervising various activities. And we were feeding the children with milk and fruit each morning so I needed help in the preparation of that. We already had a waiting list.

We needed more furniture and equipment, so I set about designing and drawing up specifications for low tables, painting easels, large and small building blocks, family-corner furniture, etc. All equipment was designed to fit on a trolley that we pulled out from under the stage each morning, unpacked, and then repacked for rolling back under the stage at the completion of each session. The hall was used every afternoon and evening for other activities.

Then I contracted a local carpenter to build them. He did an amazing job with very little money, sourcing local timber and using great ingenuity to achieve a very professional final product. I was delighted. With this equipment we were able to expand our activities and set up a very functional and exciting educational space.

We were by then having regular visits from groups of teachers sent from the Education Department to observe this 'experiment in multi-racial education', an experiment they were certain could not work because of the different languages.

But it became difficult for the St John's/Red Cross people to continue to accommodate us as their own activities were expanding. They needed their hall, so I was out looking for another place once again. I found the Mormon Hall in Desveoux Road, a large, modern facility with a functioning kitchen and some surrounding grounds that we could utilise for outdoor activities. And they also had long trolleys that rolled out from under the stage. So we moved there in, February 1963.

With the kindergarten progressing well, I was able to join Ruth and Amelia at the Town Hall for YWCA activities in the afternoons and evenings. Almost from the beginning I was in charge of youth activities both at the Town Hall Y headquarters and outside in nearby villages and rural settlements. With sports training sessions, posters to make, bulletins to type up on stencils and copy on the mimeograph machine and events to organise, life became extremely busy. Our days went from 8am each morning to 8 pm each evening, and midnight on Fridays when we ran the Friday Night Dance Club. The upstairs area at the Town Hall was bursting at the seams. As more and more training sessions were organised we took on whatever staff we could afford. In addition to staff, young women volunteers from New Zealand and British youth volunteer programs came to work with us.

A major problem emerged early on with our growing list of sports activities. For instance, basketball in those early days, specifically the Suva Women's Basketball Association, was restricted to European players, or players who had some European heritage. We were totally opposed to this kind of racial profiling and attempted to enter a YWCA team of mainly Fijian players. The YWCA team, under Amelia's leadership, had quickly become very good. Amelia was an amazing sportswoman and in addition to the captaincy of the team, had also taken on the role of coach.

The YWCA application was turned down. So we decided to set up another basketball competition, open to all. With Ruth and Amelia leading the effort, eight teams were quickly signed up and the competition was on its way. More and more teams joined each season, some from high schools, some from former students, others made up of young women working or training for jobs in Suva.

It was not long before the new Suva Multiracial Women's Basketball Association became the largest and most successful in town. Finally, the original Suva Women's Basketball Association, now down to only four teams, knocked on our door and asked for a meeting, at which they graciously invited all the teams from the multi-racial association to join their association. And so the two associations became one.

In the case of the YWCA hockey team, we again had Amelia, one of Fiji's premier hockey players, in charge. She developed a YWCA team that became famous for its athleticism and winning ways. The Y took a leading role in setting up the Suva Women's Hockey Association and assisted with the organising of that competition.

One major sport that was not available to Fijian young men or women in those early days was tennis. The Suva Tennis Club did not admit Fijians at all, saying they were not interested in the sport. We had, however, found otherwise: there was great interest in tennis. So we began coaching sessions on the public courts in Albert Park and quickly formed a steady group of young players eager to learn. I had received tennis coaching myself when much younger so undertook the coaching. I immediately found not only much interest but also much talent. And it wasn't too long before we entered several names for membership to the club. After a certain amount of confusion and lengthy discussion within the club, they were finally accepted.

At the end of the year Ruth and I needed to find another place to live. I remember taking a map of Suva and marking all the main Y program areas, with the Town Hall headquarters in Victoria Parade and the kindergarten at the Mormon Hall in Desvoeux Rd central to our needs. Then there were the sports activities at Albert Park to be taken into account. I drew a line between the three main areas and came up with the top of McGregor Road, where Desveoux Road intersected. And I began to knock on doors in that area. One woman, after telling me they were not leaving their home, pointed across the road and said 'But they are!' It was a NZ Air Force family moving out after a term serving at the Laucala Bay Air Force Base. I hurried across the road. The people were indeed busy packing and were somewhat startled by my appearance at the back door.

They gave me the name of the landlady, and I walked further up McGregor Road to the house where she lived. After much discussion she agreed to our taking over the lease, with some strict provisions that included looking after the garden and not making too much noise. Ruth was a great gardener so that was no problem. The other part of the agreement did cause some problems over the years though.

So began our years at McGregor Road, not too far from the first house we had lived in just down the road in Gordon Street. The house was an old wooden house divided into two, just as the first house had been. Sadly, both houses are gone now. They were historic reminders of earlier days in Fiji, complete with hurricane shutters, windows that folded open to the air (and mosquitos and cockroaches) way before air conditioning. The main feature of the house was its incredible view across Suva Harbour to the mountains beyond. Over the years we spent there, I painted that view at various times of the day, in oils and in watercolours. I still have one of those paintings. The others were sold at various Fiji Arts Clubs exhibitions and I wish now that I had kept them.

I was able to walk to work, just a few steps to the kindergarten where I would arrive early to set up and prepare for my group of 40 children. I had one or two five-year-olds who would come early to help. Michele Taylor was one of these. She and I would pull out the long trolleys and unload all the tables and chairs, the mats, the easels, the paint pots, the blocks and family corner furniture and set them up. Then we would mix the paints, prepare the clay for modelling, and hang up the posters, the paintings, the pictures around the walls, and all the rest that made up our space. It was an instant kindergarten, one that was unpacked each morning and packed up each afternoon.

Once the morning group was over, I would walk down to the Y headquarters, into my office there and begin the afternoon programs. By now, the YWCA was also offering lunch on the terrace above Victoria Parade and this was very popular. People would gather to talk and eat, and young people would then stay on for the afternoon activities. The YWCA was rapidly becoming 'the place to be'.

On many afternoons, Amelia and I would drive off to YWCA groups that met in people's homes or villages surrounding Suva. These groups ranged from training sessions to craft, sports, and leadership sessions. We were not only training young women for sports teams and for jobs, but also for leadership positions in community and social groups. As more and more young women's groups developed, we took on additional staff. Seniloli Tora joined us and took over the running of craft groups.

Early on in the YWCA beginnings, we organised camps for young women, particularly those who were on committees and helping with groups and classes. One of the earliest camps was at Nadarivatu, situated in the mountains inland from Tavua. It was of particular interest to me because I had heard about the Methodist Rest House there, set up for missionaries and their families when they needed a holiday.

In between camps and excursions, the work of the YWCA steadily grew. We continued expanding the number of young women's groups in areas all around Suva, with interest growing outside the urban area. Groups for young Indian girls were introduced on demand, some at the office in the old Town Hall but most out in the areas where many of the girls lived. These were called Blue Triangle Clubs and for a while we were overwhelmed with the numbers who wanted to join. Again, the program was set mainly by the girls themselves and usually each club started with a lot of games, music and much laughter. Then they would settle into discussions about their rights, many of them struggling with the things they were not allowed to do. This would develop into information and cultural sharing, with many girls then asking for some training in basic skills such as typing, and in some cases English language.

Many of these young women were married off at an early age to men they had never met. There was not much we could do about that except provide a supportive ear and encourage them to seek ways of keeping up their studies and learning new skills. Many did do that and in later years would come to the YWCA and thank us for the encouragement.

Interest in the YWCA kindergarten also grew steadily. We now had a growing waiting list and a group that numbered 60 four- to six-year-olds. I had a fulltime assistant working with me each morning and always some 'senior' five-year-old students who worked alongside me setting up each morning and leading small groups as needed. But it was obvious that we needed more trained teachers and more groups. So we began talks with the government about the possibility of scholarship support to send a young woman to Australia for training. I was also in contact with the Kindergarten Training College in Melbourne and, with full cooperation from Heather Lyon, then Principal of KTC, we were able to get scholarship support from the Fiji government.

We advertised in the *Fiji Times* and interviewed applicants to be sent to Melbourne for training. Adi Davila Uluilakeba was finally chosen on the basis of her scholastic results at Adi Cakobau School and her enthusiasm for a career in early childhood education. She flew to Melbourne for the start of the college year in 1963 and spent the next three years training. When she returned in 1966, we opened another YWCA kindergarten group, this time in the Fiji Arts Club building, across the road from the first group, now situated in an old house leased to us by the Education Department in Desveoux Road.

Meanwhile, we continued to run the kindergarten in the Mormon Hall for three more years, setting up each morning and packing away at the end of each session. It was back-breaking work in many ways and I was feeling the strain with a bad back from a fall in my teens. In fact, I had to spend some weeks at Colonial War Memorial Hospital at one stage while an orthopaedic specialist tried various treatments to relieve the pain.

One of the very bright moments in that period was the arrival in 1963 of a large wooden shipping crate from Australia, containing music percussion instruments for the kindergarten. A young friend from the Box Hill Methodist Church days, Elizabeth Lade, by then a student at Methodist Ladies College in Melbourne, had raised funds as part of her social service activities at the school, and had used the funds for musical instruments for the YWCA kindergarten in Fiji. It was an extraordinary gift and proved a great hit with the children.

We used the instruments almost daily in our music groups, inside and outside in the playground. For the children it was an opportunity to make music themselves in a way they had never tried before. And the whole group formed an orchestra that performed at kindergarten pageants and concerts to the delight of the parents. Several children became very expert at conducting.

Later in 1965, Ruth was invited to participate in a World YWCA International Training Institute in Geneva. I think Elizabeth Palmer, the General Secretary of the World YWCA, had become very curious about the work being undertaken by two Australians in Fiji, neither of whom had ever been members of the YWCA before and certainly neither of whom had any YWCA leadership training. It seemed a good idea for Ruth to go off for the three months, and a volunteer from the UK was sent to assist us while Ruth was away

Little were we to know that this would be a seminal time in the political history of Fiji. While Ruth was away, the British Government sent an emissary to Fiji to test the waters in this British colony, and see whether there were any independence rumblings. There had been considerable unrest in the colony, mainly around the Colonial Sugar Refinery and the 99-year leases on sugar cane plantations that were coming to an end. This whole period of negotiations had been tense as Fiji Indian families, most of whom had leased and worked their own sugar cane fields for generations, were facing expulsion from this land. The land belonged to local Fijian mataqalis (tribes), and they were demanding them back. Almost all land in Fiji belongs to mataqalis, a right won back in the 1930s when the Native Land Trust Board was formed with Ratu Sukuna as the first director.

As these important negotiations were going on, discussions were under way in both the UK and Fiji on the future of Fiji, although as far as the community knew, these were happening behind closed doors. The colonial system was long entrenched, with power in the hands of British civil servants under a British Governor and special rights held by Fijian Chiefs, all part of the Council of Chiefs. The non-chiefly members of the population, along with the Fiji Indian population, were very much on the outside of decision-making at all top levels. This was a real bone of contention with the Fiji-Indian population, particularly as they were by now not only the backbone of the sugar industry, but also the backbone of most of the retail trade, industry and professional life of the colony.

Ruth and I were not very knowledgeable about the recent history of Fiji before we arrived in 1962. In particular, it would have been good to have known more about the extent of the strikes and disturbances that took place in 1959/60, led by union leaders Apisai Tora (Fijian) and James Anthony (Fiji-Indian). These had caused considerable angst in the British Colonial Office and were being mainly characterised as race riots and anti-British disturbances. The troubles had clearly confused the colonial government because they were led by a Fijian and a Fiji-Indian and could not easily be characterised as Fijians rebelling against Fiji-Indians.

In fact, the strikes and marches were more against low wages and work conditions, a fact admitted much later in the writings of Sir Kenneth Maddocks, the British Governor of the time, and others. But the British Colonial Office was reacting because of the violence and loss of colonies in India and Africa. This was probably the reason for the heavy-handed treatment by the Fiji police and military forces in dealing with the demonstrations; and this violence, considered uncalled-for by most of the population, was still fresh in the memories of many in Fiji when we arrived.

In 1965, Eirene White, Parliamentary Under Secretary at the Colonial Office in what was now a Labour government in Britain, arrived for a familiarisation tour of Fiji. Her task was to report back on issues that might be raised at a forthcoming constitution conference in Britain. Many years later, Brij V Lal,

Fiji-Indian historian educated at University of South Pacific, now an emeritus professor at Australia National University in Canberra, wrote:

She heard a wide range of opinion: from Muslims about separate representation, from Fijians about their special interests — including political leadership of the country — from the ever-mercurial Apisai Tora about deporting Indo-Fijians as Ceylon and Burma had done, from the Council of Chiefs reiterating the terms of the Wakaya Letter, from Indian leaders about common roll and the need to promote political integration, from journalist Alipate Sikivou expressing the Fijian nationalist line that the Indians could always go back to India, the Chinese to China and the Rotumans and other islanders to their respective islands but the Fijians, the indigenous people, had Fiji as their only home. Sikivou was not alone in holding such extreme views. Many others were of the view that, as Ratu Penaia Ganilau and Ratu George Cakobau had said in 1961, at independence, Fiji should be returned to the Fijians. (*A Time Bomb Lies Buried: Fiji's Road to Independence, 1960–1970.*)

We knew little of all this at the YWCA and were oblivious to so much of the political discussion swirling around Government House where there had been a standoff between the new Governor Sir Derek Janeway and A D Patel, the Fiji-Indian lawyer and leader of the time. Then we received an invitation from the government to attend the one public meeting planned for Ms White where women's non-government organisations (NGOs) could meet with her. The YWCA was allotted 12 seats to participate in that meeting.

I discussed this with the staff and other Y members and it was agreed that we should place a poster on the main announcement board situated halfway up the stairs to our headquarters, inviting whoever wanted to be at the meeting to write their name in the spaces below. There was no pre-selection. The invitation was open to anyone from the Y.

Twelve of us turned up for the meeting in a hall above a bar in downtown Suva. Those of us representing the YWCA had not met beforehand to establish any specific position. We just wanted to hear what Eirene White had to say and then speak if any of us felt the urge to do so. We sat along the back row in one long line. I think the expectation was that the meeting would be somewhat boring and we would probably want to slip out early.

Eirene White gave a very brief introductory talk, stating basically that she just wanted to hear from the people about their thoughts on the future of Fiji. Then she opened the floor to comments. We heard from Fiji Girl Guides Association, TISI Sangam, Sri Sewa Sabha, Soqosoqo Vakamarama, Pan Pacific & South-East Asia Women's Association, Fiji Catholic Women's League, the Fiji Muslim Women's League, Fiji Red Cross Association and more. Our back row began to get fidgety. Without exception it seemed that each of these organisations wanted things to remain as they were. One after the other, they gave pledges of allegiance to the Queen and stated their wish that Fiji would always be a Crown Colony. One representative of an NGO even went so far as to state that her organisation wanted Fiji to have the same status as the Isle of Man!

A note was passed along the back row to me that said simply: 'This is awful. Can we speak as individuals?' And I sent one back that said: 'Of course. That's what we're here for!' And one by one, these women of the YWCA stood up and walked to the front to speak their mind. They included Suliana Siwatibau, Amelia Rokotuivuna, Taufa Vakatale, Charlotte Cheddie, Anaseini Qionibaravi, Esiteri Vakalala, and Dr Anarieta Vakalala. One by one they stated that they wanted an independent Fiji, one where everyone could vote for the candidate of their choice and not necessarily from their ethnic group, and one where every child could get an education in whatever school they chose.

The response from Eirene White was electric. She had been

sitting back almost looking as though she was dozing off and now suddenly she was sitting straight up, eyes alight, an enormous smile on her face. But that was not the reaction in the rest of the room; there were mutters of disapproval and no applause.

Afterwards, we found ourselves in a huddle in the entrance area, talking together in hushed tones. Eirene White walked through the doors, spotted us and walked into the middle of our group. She looked like she wanted to hug the lot of us, and told us that what these women from the Y had said had made her entire visit to Fiji worthwhile. She had been so distressed at previous meetings that she thought she would be returning to London with very little that was positive to report, but now she was excited and hopeful.

The next day, the Fijian language daily newspaper *Nai Lalakai* came out with reports from the meeting, with headlines that the women of the YWCA were treasonous and clearly part of a conspiracy to destroy Fiji and cause a revolution. They called for Taufa to lose her job as Principal of Adi Cakobau School, and for the others who were teachers, nurses, public servants and so on to lose their jobs.

We all gathered at our house in McGregor Road to discuss how to handle the situation and ways in which we could support each other through this time. Some of the women were afraid to walk down the streets of Suva. One or two young women moved in with us until the tension died down.

The Fiji secret service began appearing in the YWCA offices, searching for evidence that we had met beforehand and prepared these statements. They searched our records and our program brochures, looking for clues. And the phone calls started coming. In the end I hand-printed a notice that stretched across the front of the reception desk to be read by the young women who answered the phone. It read: 'The YWCA does not tell people what to say. Neither does it tell people what not to say'. It stayed there for weeks.

I have told this story for many reasons, the main one being that as good as Brij V Lal's detailed historical writing is on the events of that time, and most especially the events surrounding Eirene White's visit to Fiji, none of this appears in his writings or other writings. And I believe it is important that the courage of these young women of Fiji should be remembered. What they said that day to Eirene White mattered greatly, and played a definite role in the search for an independent and democratically elected multi-racial Fiji.

Around this time, we were having lunch on the terrace at the YWCA when we heard the sound of chanting and singing and some kind of clashing noises below us. We all stood and leaned over the balcony to see a crowd of what appeared to be villagers storming down Victoria Parade, dressed in Fijian traditional attire, including sulus, long leafed skirts and carrying spears and cane knives. Several had banners and signs that said things like: 'Indians go home' and 'Give us back our country'.

To say we were taken aback would be an understatement. As far as we were concerned there had been no indication of any troubles. In fact, some of us thought the whole thing quite amusing and there was laughter and waving as the march went by. The marchers were clearly against any talk of a common roll for Fiji. And they had gathered together leaders from rural areas and warned them they would lose their ancestral lands to foreigners and their country to Fiji-Indians if that happened. At the time, we thought this was fanciful but in later years, many of these fears would come back to haunt Fiji. In fact, it has now come to be known as 'the land of coups'. But that was unthinkable in 1965.

From 8 to 18 December 1966, the Second South Pacific Games took place in Noumea, New Caledonia. This time, I was to be more personally involved than in the First South Pacific Games, held in Suva in 1965, as I was chosen to be a member of the Fiji table tennis team. This meant dawn practice sessions for weeks before we left for Noumea, under the careful eye of our captain and coach K.C. Ramrakha. My experience playing table tennis competitively in the East End of London served me well during that time.

We flew off to Noumea with high hopes of doing as well if not better than Fiji had done in Suva at the 1963 Games. There, Fiji had come on top of the medals ladder, winning 84 medals. Second in the medal tally had been Papua New Guinea with 32 and New Caledonia and French Polynesia were third and fourth with 27 and 10 respectively.

However, the French had clearly left Suva very disappointed in 1963 and had determined that this would not happen again. On arrival in Noumea, we found that a sporting transformation had taken place in that very French city. The French Government had spent an estimated AU$14 million on developing world-class sporting stadiums, swimming pool, velodrome, indoor sporting hall and various training facilities. In addition, they had sent athletes from New Caledonia and French Polynesia to mainland France to get experience and coaching and French athletes had been imported three years earlier to be sure they fulfilled residency requirements and could compete.

This made for a very unbalanced situation at these Games. No other Pacific country had anything like this kind of money to spend on coaches and facilities. From the beginning, there was a feeling of deep unfairness and injustice amongst the athletes from all the non-French speaking countries. Added to this was the varying standard of accommodation and food provided for each team. The French countries were housed in upmarket accommodation with three course meals served by French chefs. The non-French-speaking teams were housed in school dormitories and the food was definitely not good and certainly not plentiful. I can speak from personal experience regarding that!

The results from the Games were predictable. New

Caledonia had a massive medal haul of 99, with Fiji a distant second with 59. French Polynesia came in with 30 and Papua New Guinea with 29. Fiji's women were the major contributors to Fiji's tally, with Ana Ramacake the star of the athletics team, winning a gold medal in the 100 metres. The Fiji table tennis team took out the silver medal. I was in the doubles team and we came through without losing a match.

Back in Fiji after the Games, we made the decision to move the kindergarten out of the Mormon Hall. This was mainly because we had found that the Mormon Church was broadcasting worldwide that we were part of their mission, a totally erroneous claim. Word got back to us from friends who had attended the 1964 New York World's Fair that they had seen a photo of the group with me as teacher, on a giant feature wall in the main Mormon Exhibition Building at the Fair. Our kindergarten was clearly being used as an advertisement for their mission work in the Pacific.

Another major reason for moving was to allow us to set up an educational space that would be more permanent and would not need to be packed away each day. Although we moved from a modern hall to an old wooden former residential building, we now could develop a space of our own, one that we filled with the results of each day's work. Children's handiwork covered the walls and windowsills – murals, sculptures, collage as well as large easel paintings, science experiments and cardboard models.

Davila had now returned from training in Melbourne and we set up a second group in the Fiji Arts Club building directly opposite the old house in Desveoux Road. We had a bit more leeway in that building and were able to keep much of the daily setup in place there – unless the Arts Club was to hold a function or an art display, when all the equipment had to be packed away.

By now, the children from our two multi-racial groups were being accepted at all of the primary schools in Suva, including the Suva Primary School, previously only open to those with some European heritage. That battle was fought and won around 1964/5 when I found that the Headmistress of that school was turning down applications from non-European children – children without some European heritage. After several very upset parents had come to me, I took the matter up with the Education Department. A meeting was held with senior members of the department, at which I was told that it was definitely not racial discrimination, but rather just a language problem.

I then accompanied one of the parents and their child to an interview with the Headmistress, and saw the confrontational way in which she undertook the interview, so that the child became confused and tongue-tied. It was a pattern of intimidation with a clear message: non-European children were not welcome at Suva Primary School.

And so at the end of the kindergarten year, after asking parents which children would be applying to Suva Primary School, I started daily role-playing of interviews and played the Headmistress, using her abrupt and confrontational manner. This would initially be a shock that sometimes produced tears, at which point we would stop the game. As the days went by, the children would get into the spirit of it all and start to enjoy it. Gradually they became more confident and more Fijian and Fiji-Indian children began to pass the interview.

Finally came the day when the Headmistress called me and said in a resigned voice: 'Okay then. Just send me a list of all the children who are applying from your kindergarten groups and that will be that!'

This was another important part of our strategy at the YWCA to work towards the development of an equal playing field for all of the young people of Fiji, whether it was in education, sports or choice of vocation, with no discrimination on the basis of racial or ethnic background.

With the success of the scholarship for Davila, we had

decided to apply for more scholarships from the government, this time in the area of youth work, as we needed trained youth workers for the greatly expanding youth activities at the YWCA. Initially we were able to get two scholarships. We advertised widely and chose Nina Buresova and Raijeli Panapasa, both of whom flew to Melbourne for Youth Work Training in 1964 and 1965. Nina and Raijeli were highly acclaimed in their studies and did exceptionally well.

However, both of them met and later married Australians and, except for one year in the case of Nina, both went on to live in Australia. This had an unfortunate effect on our overseas scholarship plans and we were not able to obtain more from the government. It became clear that from now on, we would need to set up training courses in Fiji.

A very important woman during these mid-1960s years was Marjorie Stewart, who had come to Fiji at the request of the South Pacific Commission to set up a training course for women in Suva. Working with the Fiji government, she had founded the SPC Community Education Training Centre in Nausori as a centre of excellence for women from all over the Pacific. In the year-long training at CETC, these young women were trained as community leaders in appropriate technology, including how to make smokeless stoves, water-sealed toilets, charcoal and water-cooling cupboards and a host of other village essentials. They also learned the essentials of diet and nutrition, new ways of cooking, the art of public speaking and a host of other areas needed in community development.

But Marjorie also brought with her a knowledge of building and leading a YWCA, having done this in Jamaica in her earlier years. She was an enormous support for Ruth and me, encouraging, challenging and always there when needed.

In later years, I met up with Lucille Mair, Jamaican Ambassador to the United Nations. She was interested in my background with the Fiji YWCA and asked to have lunch with me one day at the UN. No doubt she was also curious about the fact that two Anglo-Australians had been able to achieve something important in a country like Fiji, given that Australia was noted at that time for its racist government immigration policies known collectively as the White Australia Policy.

Part way through lunch, I mentioned Marjorie Stewart and Lucille exclaimed loudly: 'Of course! All is clear: Marjorie Stewart is the reason I am who I am. I have everything to thank her for. She took me in to the fledgling YWCA in Kingston and it changed my life!' Apparently Marjorie being in Suva at the same time as Ruth and I was all she needed to know about the growth and success of the Fiji YWCA.

In 1968, three major events took place in the Pacific that changed forever how these isolated small countries scattered across a vast ocean saw the world. One was the introduction of US Peace Corps volunteers. The second was the opening of the University of the South Pacific. And the third was the beginning of French nuclear tests in Mururoa, French Polynesia.

The Peace Corps volunteers were spread across the region and worked alongside local staff in community organisations, government projects and schools. They brought with them new ideas, new skills and a different outlook on life. At the Fiji YWCA, we were fortunate to have a few talented Peace Corps craftswomen who worked with us in training workshops as part of our small business skills program for young women. Many volunteers also helped with youth work activities that we were involved with as part of the newly established Fiji National Youth Council. Ruth and I were two of the founding members of the Youth Council and held various positions as President, Secretary and/or Treasurer over the years. And through the Council we established a Fiji Youth Training Program that brought youth leaders from all over Fiji. Peace Corps volunteers assisted us with this training.

The second important event was the opening of the University of the South Pacific. This meant that Pacific Islanders could now be educated in the region and not have to go overseas to get professional qualifications. It was a masterstroke towards real Pacific independence in terms of staff at colleges and schools, and the training of professional leadership in all community, government and other public groups. With the opening of regional USP branches throughout the Pacific, we also saw the beginnings of a regional transformation from former colonial dependency to truly local independence.

I was honoured to be at the official opening of USP in the enormous hangar at the former Laucala Bay Air Force Base, now transformed into the university campus. I sat amongst the crowd in that vast space and heard the speeches of the Queen of England (and the Commonwealth), the King of Tonga and of the newly appointed Pro-Chancellor Fetaui Mataafa of Samoa. It was a momentous occasion not to be forgotten. And I strongly approved of an air force base being turned into a centre of learning!

The third major event of 1968 was the commencement of nuclear tests at Mururoa Atoll in French Polynesia, an event that changed forever the entire Pacific region. We were suddenly faced with the reality of a major world power, without any discussion with or regard for the inhabitants of the region, sending nuclear pollution into the sea and air in a succession of horrendous explosions that on occasion could be seen in the sky from Vanua Levu.

Initially, we in Fiji thought we could call upon our friends in the world to help with this devastating situation. We called on the UK, the USA, Australia and New Zealand, all seemingly to no avail. Then, with the arrival in the region of Greenpeace ships to patrol the test area and attempt to stop the tests, it was discovered that the US and the UK were all reaping valuable information from the tests, with their research ships patrolling around the edges of the test area.

I truly believe it was this realisation that changed everything in Fiji. Suddenly, this important Pacific region knew they were on their own and could not count on help from outside for support in this new reality. I believe a certain innocence and trust was lost at this time, and the foundations were laid for much of the political tumult that was to happen in Fiji and the Pacific region in the coming years.

The YWCA became a major leader in the protests around this time. Amelia, Ruth and I and others in the YWCA, with USP students from all across the Pacific region, organised mass rallies, protest marches, spot actions outside the French Consul's offices in Suva and at the regional South Pacific Commission when regional meetings were being held. It was the beginning of a very active and vocal public affairs initiative at the YWCA that changed everything. We were suddenly flung into a much greater awareness of global affairs and the way in which these affairs affected our region.

The YWCA had already become a leading community affairs advocate and now we were expanding these activities into a broader range of public affairs that stretched across the country and the entire Pacific region. Within all of this, basic rights were being discussed in relation to education, job training, community and government leadership positions. And the Fiji YWCA was at the centre of much of the discussion. Fiji was still a British colony, but talk of independence was everywhere. A new form of government was being discussed. Major changes were on the way.

5

USA: a chance to work with global women activists

In 1969 another World YWCA International Training Institute was to be held, this time undertaken by the YWCA of the USA. I was invited to participate and, if I accepted, would fly to New York a few months ahead of the actual Institute to assist with planning and implementing the program.

I was intrigued by the focus for this ITI on the use and adaptation of the arts in programming, aimed at YWCA program directors from all over the world. Following an initial briefing and arts immersion experience in New York, the group was to be divided into teams that would fan out across the country to undertake community projects at local YWCAs, learning from these local groups and sharing their newly gained skills.

I decided it was time I had some further training in the arts and communication for programming as I was increasingly becoming more involved with the youth and women and development groups of the YWCA. I was also now the main developer and producer of pamphlets, flyers, banners, notices, program outlines and more, and wanted to expand my knowledge and expertise in all of this. So I accepted the invitation to participate in the ITI and prepared to leave for New York.

I flew from Fiji in October 1968, through Hawaii and Los Angeles to New York. I was to stay in the YWCA on the corner of 8th Avenue and W 53rd Street, a large multi-storeyed building not far from Times Square and Broadway.

Planning for the upcoming ITI began to occupy more and more of my time. With the ITI Director, Jimmie Woodward, and others on the leadership team, we were contacting artists and YWCA staff who would be working with us as leaders as well as making final decisions on participants from every world region. Forty-six participants, representing staff and volunteers from YWCAs in 31 countries, were to be selected and notified. The ITI was planned to open up a world where art in all its forms and renditions would be used in YWCA programming. Early on in my stay, the decision was taken that instead of me representing Fiji at the Institute, I would be one of the leaders, which opened up the opportunity for another representative from Fiji to be chosen. I was delighted of course, and especially so when Anaseini Qionibaravi was chosen.

The YWCA in New York also made it possible for me to sign up to some evening courses while I was in New York City during those months leading up to the February 26 1969 start of the ITI. I began oil painting classes at the Museum of Modern Art plus some animation and cartoon drawing classes downtown at the School of Visual Arts. Both classes proved wonderful experiences and I was able to extend my painting and drawing abilities greatly.

In December I travelled to Toronto, Canada, for Christmas to join my mother, who was visiting Evan and his Canadian wife Judith and their new baby Christopher. Returning to New York after Christmas, I continued the preparations for the International Training Institute. The first day finally arrived and I, along with other staff and volunteers from the YWCA at 600 Lexington Ave, met the 46 participants. We had an opening luncheon for all of us to begin to get to know each other and to start forming a world community for the next three months. Then the next day we set off in a bus to Planting Fields in Oyster Bay, Long Island.

We had chosen this wonderful estate on a beautiful sunny day in the Fall of 1968, thinking that the grounds would be perfect for walks and workshops. We never imagined that we would be met with a blizzard. On arrival, we found the place buried in snow, much to the initial delight of the participants, especially those from Africa, the Pacific, the Caribbean and Latin America, most of whom had never seen snow before. But the delight was short-lived and we quickly had to cope with the business of finding appropriate clothing for such intense cold.

A number of the staff, myself included, were housed some distance from the main building in a gatehouse cottage and had to make our way each day up the snow-filled, icy drive by car. I was often the driver for this daily trek and more than once we found our car fetching up in a snowdrift by the road. We had to find someone to come and attach chains to the tyres. My experience driving on the gravel roads of Fiji helped to a certain extent but not totally!

Our activities were confined to the main house for the two weeks we spent there, which made for a very intensive and powerful experience for the whole group. We had various artistic leaders come in to lead us in dance, music, art and crafts, most of whom had to stay overnight because of the weather. And we had our in-house team of artists who stayed throughout the two weeks.

It was two weeks of incredible intensity and drama, of music and dance, of art and film, and we all came out at the end as different people in many ways, more attuned to ourselves and to the world around us. On the final days we held team meetings and discussed preparations for the field assignments that would take place in local YWCAs throughout the USA. These assignments were to take the form of projects, 'laboratory experiences that would be chances to try out new media, new skills while working with staff in local associations' as team leader Jean Plaxton explained it. Each assignment would consist of three or four ITI participants who would be flying off to their assigned YWCAs around the US for a month, in which time they would be undertaking a community project using arts as a tool.

As I was now one of the ITI leaders, I would be flying to several of the projects to see how the teams were progressing and if they needed any support. I was looking forward to that. And there would be four Regional YWCA Conventions taking place during the time our teams were on assignment. The ITI leadership team would be attending each of these to work with the various teams in that region on a creative arts presentation of some kind. It was all very ambitious with lots of unknowns.

But first, the whole group made its way back to New York. One of the group described this as 'an astronaut's re-entry into the world's atmosphere' and it was a bit like that. We were coming out of the cocoon of the mansion at Planting Fields, buried in snow from a mighty winter blizzard, into the bright lights of Manhattan.

The first week back in New York was geared towards building a sense of urban environment and human community. By bus and on foot we explored uptown areas, housing settlements, community projects and special arts programs. We wandered through downtown areas and saw how spaces had been changed through redesigning to include small parks, how ugly walls had been transformed by paint. We were introduced by community leaders to the problems of racial groupings, of hungry people. We met with New York City officials and discovered what essential role the arts played in the life of that city. We heard plans for 'Summer in the City' that would take place throughout the city. And we experienced New York's art galleries, studios, museums and theatres.

We travelled out to New Jersey to visit the Jersey City Job Corps Centre and saw how crucial vocational training was for school dropouts. At the Museum for Contemporary Arts we learned about international craft merchandising, basics of good craft design, and possible resources for future reference. And we went to the United Nations to meet with an officer of the UN Social Development Section of the Department of Economic and Social Affairs.

One of the other highlights of that first full week in New York City was a visit to Radio City Music Hall. This followed a dinner party at the home of Mary Rockefeller in Park Avenue. Mary was the President of the YWCA Mutual Relations Committee and she, along with Elizabeth Luce Moore, had been integrally involved in the planning for the ITI. Mary had arranged for us to see the backstage workings of the mammoth Music Hall stage, and we saw some of the preparations underway for the next show.

The very full weeks in New York came to an end and the teams prepared to leave for their field assignments. Groups of four made their tearful farewells and left for the station or the airport. They went off to Pittsburgh, to San Francisco, to St Paul-Minneapolis, to Atlanta and many other YWCAs across the country. We would all meet up again at the regional conferences. Meanwhile, we would maintain contact as best we could and make sure each team had everything they needed.

At the two-week mark, I was sent to Cleveland, Ohio to check out a situation at the YWCA there. We had been receiving very unhappy calls from our team of four who were undertaking a quite difficult community project. But it wasn't the project that was causing difficulties. It was clearly some other problems that needed sorting out.

I arrived to find that the African and Caribbean ITI team members had been housed in dark, damp rooms in the basement of the Y. The Canadian and US team members had been placed in much nicer rooms upstairs. I talked at length with the General Secretary and asked for a change to be made. But it became clear she could not see any problem with the arrangement. So we went looking for alternative accommodation in town and found an apartment with four bedrooms quite close by. After discussing it on the phone with the leadership team back in New York, all of whom agreed the situation was not good, our team of four moved out of the Y and into the suite. It was the best solution to a very tense situation that was jeopardising the project. And it was very much a sign of the times. I believe there was a change made in the leadership of that YWCA shortly after the project finished.

Then in April and May, the four regional conferences took place. I flew from New York to Asilomar, California for the Western Regional Conference, 12–16 April, where we were responsible for the opening celebration, art media workshops and some parts of the closing ceremony. There were four ITI teams who joined us there from their various field assignments and I flew in with some of the ITI leaders. We were thrown immediately into preparations for the opening. It was our first large-scale presentation and took hours of rehearsals and stage set-up. I was in charge of the music machine and the visual and light effects, which included slides, strobe lights and more. We put on a quite spectacular event to rousing applause.

Team members and ITI leaders also took part in the consciousness-raising sessions, workshops, excursions and much more. After four full days, we said goodbye to our team members working in that region and flew on to the next regional conference in Memphis, Tennessee, 20–23 April, for the Southern Regional Conference.

As we flew into Memphis, Kathy, who was African American, confided to me that she did not want to be in the South and most certainly not in Memphis, where Martin Luther King had been assassinated just one year before. I was aware of the racial tensions still very much present. Kathy Grant, our African-American dance instructor, asked that we share a room at the hotel and that I stay very close at all times. I could feel her nervousness and of course agreed.

We went straight into rehearsals with the four ITI teams that were undertaking projects in this region and put on another opening celebration of arts and dance, with light and visual effects and everyone invited to take part. But Kathy became almost ill with anxiety and I went with her to discuss her situation with ITI leaders. We all agreed she should fly back to New York after the opening, an event that she was directing and producing. And that's what she did on the morning after.

At the end of the four days of workshops and sessions, I flew with the rest of the leadership team to Philadelphia for the Eastern Regional Conference, 25–27 April. Kathy re-joined us there. We again began rehearsals immediately with the ITI teams working in that region and put on another major multi-media opening celebration, this time involving 40–50 conference delegates in the presentation along with our ITI team members.

And then we flew on to Chicago for the final conference, the Central Region Conference, 2–4 May. With the ITI teams working in that region, we produced a completely new lot of banners, posters and murals to use in yet another opening celebration. However, those of us doing the lights, the slides, the music and the scene setting encountered a real problem in Chicago, where everything was union run and we non-union members were not supposed to touch any sound or light equipment. By now, Lynda McNeur, Kathy and I had developed a way of coordination that required us to touch and work with a lot of equipment and this was going to be very difficult. However, after watching us rehearse with the teams of dancers, singers, artists, the union men agreed to just stand around and 'supervise' while we got on with it.

After a five-day visit to Washington, we returned to New York for a night and then headed to Waltham, Massachusetts for a final two weeks of evaluation and the business of relating all of our learnings from the past months to our own home YWCAs. The final two weeks began with a multimedia symphony concert at the Boston Town Hall, a magnificent concert that featured Arthur Fiedler and the Filmore East light show and was quite spectacular.

We were divided into regional groupings in Waltham – European, North American, African, Asian and Island –so that we could plan more specifically for our individual needs back home. We had studio times also, where we continued with the silk-screening, the banner-making, the music and dance, the light-boxes, films, slides, charts and printing layouts.

And then we were back at the National YWCA in New York and it all came to an end. When the ITI participants packed their bags and flew away it was a sad day for us all. We had become a large family of close friends and probably would not see each other again.

I had been asked to stay on for another month to write the final report for the ITI and I moved into a room at the YWCA and settled down to do just that. During these intense few weeks, I was pulling together all the ITI information and trying to produce something that illustrated the creativity of those three months.

I also went to several other YWCAs in New York State to talk to groups about the YWCA in Fiji, and one young woman from Rochester became very enthused about it all and later flew out to Fiji to spend some months working with us as a volunteer.

I was feeling the need to get out of New York City during that time. One of the reasons was the sense of being trapped under a leaden sky: I felt claustrophobic and at times it was hard to breathe. I wondered how anyone could live in that place. I remember one Saturday in desperation catching a train up the Hudson River in my quest to find a little bit of blue sky. I went as far as the Palisades Park and wandered amongst the trees there. And yet, I still could not find a blue sky. It was before the Clean Air Act of 1970, an act that made an enormous difference to New York City as I was to discover when I returned in 1976. I could not believe the difference in the quality of the air – I could actually see the blue sky!

In June 1969, it was time for me to return to Fiji. I had made plans to go home via Europe so that I could visit funding agencies in London and Germany and the World YWCA in Geneva to discuss the building plans for the Fiji YWCA. The Suva City Council had given us a 99-year lease on a wonderful property on Suva Harbour and we now had to raise the funds to design and build our own headquarters.

In London I visited the people at the UK Department of International Development and discussed the YWCA project with them. It was not a great time in the UK as funds were being withdrawn from former colonies worldwide, most notably the British Council in Fiji, which had always been a great supporter of our work with young people. But I gave them the Fiji YWCA building book that described the project and the funds needed.

From London, I flew to Bonn, Germany and met with Bread for the World, an ecumenical funding agency that supported the work of YWCAs, mainly in Africa. The man I met with started the conversation by saying that Bread for the World did not fund buildings. And he was surprised when I said I had not actually come to ask for funds, but to thank Bread for the World for past help with our activities. He was so taken aback he suddenly became interested in what we were trying to do.

From Bonn to I went to Geneva for a few days with the World YWCA, then on to Rome for my flight connection to Australia. In Melbourne I had a few days with my family, and connected briefly with old friends before flying back to Fiji.

Returning to Fiji

My return to Fiji was wonderful and it was great to be back with Ruth and all my friends. I settled back into the daily routine quickly, no longer teaching at the YWCA kindergarten but still involved in the running of its activities, now four groups in four different locations. My main work, however, was as National Program Director, in charge of youth work activities, women and development groups, women's rights and community programs. This also involved public relations, publicity, development of all program materials, posters, leaflets and other visual materials.

We also now had a kindergarten group in Lautoka where a new YWCA office and programs for young people and women had been set up with Amelia in charge. Davila was running the Fiji Arts Club YWCA kindergarten in Suva and three other fully-trained expatriate teachers were in charge of other groups in Suva. The demand had become so great we had no option but to expand the program as best we could. We were now raising funds to build our own two-group kindergarten building on the Desveoux Road site. The government had given us a long-term lease for that property and planning was already under way.

For the Fiji YWCA building quite separate from the kindergartens, we had contracted the architectural firm of Jackson and Walker in Melbourne, and they had begun the work of designing a new, purpose-built place. This would allow us to not only undertake the growing program of activities but also to be as self-sustaining as possible.

Work began on the harbourside site, and concrete piles were dug into the reclaimed land on which we were to build our headquarters. A work building was constructed on site, and one day, I took the youth club down there loaded with pots of paint, to paint all sides of the work building with quotes, words, diagrams and balloons that expressed the excitement and pleasure of this important moment in the life of the Fiji YWCA.

Into all this came Elmyria Hull, sent by the YWCA of the USA at our request to assist in the setting up of job skills training courses at the Fiji YWCA. Elmyria, an African-American, had been the director of a very large job skills training school for young people in Brooklyn, New York, as part of the US Government sponsored Job Corps. We were thrilled to have her and her 10-year-old son Clinton with us and they settled into a flat quite close to our house in McGregor Road. She was with us for a year, and during that time the job skills training expanded dramatically and the need for more space became even clearer.

Somewhere in the midst of all this, I flew to Kiribati to help run a low-cost media workshop for young people at the request of Jean-Michel Bazinet, South Pacific Commission Youth Director. Kiribati, one part of the former Gilbert and Ellice Islands, is a collection of tiny atolls connected by causeways. Our little plane flew via Tuvalu, which was formerly the Ellice part of the Gilbert and Ellice Islands. The plane landed at Funafuti airport in Tuvalu but had to buzz the airstrip first to scare off the cows and goats feeding on the grass strip. The villagers live around the airstrip which takes up almost all the middle area of Funafuti.

Then we flew on to Kiribati, landing near the capital Tarawa. We stayed in the most beautiful little cabins right on the lagoon and went swimming first thing each morning. A highlight of our stay was when Jean-Michel and I were taken sailing one day in an outrigger across the main lagoon. The Kiribati outriggers are known as the 'greyhounds of the Pacific', long and sleek, beautifully carved and finished, unlike the Fijian outriggers that are hewn from logs and more sturdy. The skill of the Kiribati sailors is legendary and Jean-Michel and I were quite breathless at the speed at which we crossed the largest of the lagoons. Not to mention the speed of the turnaround at the other side, during which both of us were tipped over the edge, to the delight of the helmsman!

The workshop took place in a large bure with open sides in the village of Bikenibeu at the southern end of the string of atolls that made up Tarawa. We were driven across causeways to reach the meeting place each morning. There was absolutely no power so it was all hand-printing, simple line drawings, cut and paste in preparation for offset printing. Out of it came a full-colour manual on Youth Ideas for the South Pacific, a manual that was used across the region for many years.

In 1970 came Independence for Fiji, and the YWCA was deeply involved in much of the preparations and planning for this We took part in countless celebrations, ranging from garden parties at Government House, sports carnivals, marches and parades, ballroom dancing, and of course the main ceremony at Albert Park where the British flag was lowered and replaced by the new Fiji flag. Elmyria and Clinton became very involved in all of the independence celebrations and were very much affected by being a part of such a momentous event.

Both Ruth and I were very honoured to be presented with the Independence Medal of Fiji. But the coming of independence meant many changes for us. New regulations came into play concerning the status of expatriates in the country, mostly relating to length of residency and work. We agreed with the new laws, believing strongly that Fiji needed to pave a new way for itself and its citizens. However, one of the new requirements was that once a local Fiji citizen was trained to take an expatriate's position, the expatriate had to leave Fiji. Given that the training program of the YWCA was an essential part of everything we did, and that we were constantly training local Fiji personnel to take over our various roles in the organisation, we knew we would have to make a difficult decision.

We had come to Fiji from Australia during the time of the infamous White Australia Policy, and that policy was still the law in 1970. We both firmly believed in a multicultural society, one where people of all races, ethnicities and faiths would have equal rights and opportunities. And Fiji was now very much our home. We had made lifelong friends there and our lives were intricately involved with this community. And so we decided to become Fiji citizens. It was a momentous decision and one we did not take lightly. I was not to know how dramatically my life, and Australia for that matter, would change in the next couple of years, and felt we had made the right decision.

In May 1971, I received the news that Dad had cancer and did not have many months to live. This was terrible news and I knew that I needed to fly home to visit him. There was a slight problem in that he refused to believe he was ill, as he didn't believe much in illness. So I conjured up a story of a YWCA meeting that I needed to attend in Melbourne. Then there was the problem of money to pay for the airfares. Ruth and I together had no savings. So I approached Susan Parkinson, a Suva friend and member of the YWCA Board, also a renowned government nutritionist. She loaned me the airfare and I flew home immediately.

At home in our house across the road from Box Hill Grammar School, I settled in for a two-week stay. Each morning I travelled into the city where I did indeed have discussions with the staff of the National YWCA of Australia about ways in which we could work together on various activities. Then in the afternoon I would return to sit with Dad and discuss whatever he wanted to talk about. It was a special time and one I won't ever forget. He handed me several books that I was to read while at home so we could discuss them together. These included *Essays of a Humanist* by Julian Huxley, *In Praise of Idleness* by Bertrand Russell, *On Aggression* by Konrad Lorenz, *The Territorial Imperative* by Robert Ardrey and *In Fear of China* by Gregory Clarke.

My nights were filled with speed-reading as I caught up with the thoughts and intellectual musings of my father. He was a man who refused to acknowledge that he was dying and preferred to continue educating others and discussing the deep philosophies of life. And he wanted to know what I was doing with my life. If I wasn't going to get married and have children, what then was I going to do?

It was very good for me at an important moment in my life. I think it was then that I decided to move into another career and add to my teacher training education by going back to college and studying development communications, specifically for women involved in development activities in the so-called Third World. It would be a year and a-half before I was able to do that, but the beginning of a plan was formulating.

Dad died in October of 1971. I was not home when it happened but flew home from Fiji to be with the family at his memorial service at Box Hill Grammar School (by now called Kingswood College).

But I needed to return to Fiji where there were many things brewing, including the completion of the new YWCA kindergarten building in Desveoux Road in addition to the building of the new Fiji YWCA building on the harbour front. For the kindergarten, we had decided on a local builder who was an expert with a new kind of cement brick that 'breathed'. It was perfect for our needs. The old house had been demolished and the new building was almost complete. It was a two-group building with independent playgrounds for each group, a shared kitchen in between and verandahs around the outside.

The opening of the new YWCA kindergarten building was a wonderful moment and drew a large crowd. We finally had the spaces we needed for our groups to have the best possible early childhood education experience. The design allowed for cool breezes to blow through each main room and the playgrounds were equipped with state-of-the-art equipment.

We were also preparing for the First South Pacific Arts Festival, 6–20 May 1972. A thousand participants from 20 countries were coming to Suva. The highlights would include traditional dance, the creation of a village of traditional houses, and the sailing of traditional canoes. The University of the South Pacific would be the site for a village of houses of Tonga, Kiribati, Tuvaluan, Solomon Island, New Caledonia, Niue and Fijian. Suva would be transformed.

Everyone arrived and the Festival got underway. One of the greatest things about that whole time was the fact that you could be walking along a street in downtown Suva when suddenly an Australian Aboriginal group would begin a corroboree dance in a patch of sand they had put down on the footpath. Crowds would gather in amazement as the dancers portrayed kangaroos, emus, wombats, snakes in intricate and stomping motions. Or a group of Samoan singers would gather and begin singing in a nearby park. Albert Park itself was ablaze with colour as groups danced and sang. And the dramas enacted on stage in the evenings were unforgettable. I think the arts in the Pacific grew up in those two weeks as we all became aware of the incredible talent among us.

I was looking around for possibilities to return to college and retrain myself for a new career. After 11 years in Fiji, I knew it was time to leave, at least for a while. I needed to undertake training in the areas within which I was now increasingly more involved. These included information, communication, technical assistance and training for young people and women working in human rights, development, justice and peace activities. At that time, I thought I would complete this training and return to Fiji to train others in these new skills.

I knew I would need to apply for a scholarship so I turned to the Pacific Conference of Churches, headquartered in Suva, and discussed the matter with colleagues and friends there. They in turn advised me to contact the National Council of Churches of the USA in New York, who, in consultation with the PCC, made some suggestions as to where I could get the training I needed and what financial assistance they could provide.

After much consideration, the course offered at Indiana University in Bloomington seemed the most appropriate, with its focus on development communications and an international student body from Africa, Asia and the Middle East. And so arrangements were made for me to leave Fiji and go to Indiana University.

In our final year, the first Fiji National Youth Council youth training workshop was organised, bringing young adults from across Fiji to Suva for an intensive week of lectures, discussion groups and practical assignments. Working alongside the newly established Fiji YMCA, we trained a strong cadre of youth workers, many of whom went on to work for community youth organisations including the YWCA and YMCA, and some who went on to positions with the newly installed government.

It was a matter of some pride for Ruth, Amelia and me that we had been pioneers in the formation of several local and national groups that pulled together many of the community organisations working within the country at this time. Prime amongst these were the Fiji National Youth Council and the Fiji National Women's Council. These were important meeting grounds for groups that had not always worked together well. I like to think that they were the foundation for many of the far-reaching groups that have formed in the decades after, including the Suva Women's Crisis Centre, the Fiji Women's Rights Movement, FemLink Pacific, and the Nuclear-Free Pacific Movement.

But first, we had some more fund-raising to do for the two new YWCA buildings and we threw ourselves into that. We made a giant wooden thermometer and hung it on the front of the YWCA offices on the first floor of the Suva Town Hall. As each $500 was raised, we would slide a red block of wood down a slot on the front, gradually filling up the thermometer. An extraordinary month of activities for the month of August 1972 had been planned, with daily radio broadcasts publicising each event and the whole community involved. We had sports competitions, fairs, bazaars, stalls, dances, film shows, art shows, you name it. It was exhausting yet exhilarating to see the little red wooden blocks slide down the thermometer. Incredibly, we were able to raise $10,000 by the end of that month, an amazing amount for those times, and enough for us to really get the building off the ground at last.

And then it was time for me to leave Fiji. It had taken me a year to remove myself from all the committees I was on (I counted 40 of which I was a member and on several of those I was either the secretary or the president) to pack up my belongings, to decide what I would be taking to the USA, and to say my farewells to my family of friends and colleagues.

6

Postgraduate studies and a new career

The flight from Fiji to New York was broken with stops in Honolulu and Los Angeles. There was a problem in Honolulu when I was asked for my chest x-ray. I had not realised this would be needed and it was packed in my luggage on board the plane. So I was taken away to a small room under armed guard while they unloaded the case from the plane's hold. Then the x-ray was inspected right there in full view of all the other passengers waiting in transit. Apparently my chest passed inspection and I was allowed to re-board the plane.

In New York, I had meetings with John Backer, director of the Leadership Development Committee of the National Council of Churches of the USA. John greeted me warmly and could see I was somewhat nervous about heading off to Indiana University. He was able to put me at ease and gave me his personal phone number so that I could call him if needed. I also met with officials from Church Women United as they were the group that had raised the funds for my scholarship. I am forever in their debt and hope that my work with women worldwide has given them some pride in what they made possible. And I met with the women at the National Board of the YWCA of the USA who had agreed to assist me with a grant of $500 a year for two years towards my day-to-day expenses. It was good to be back at the National Board headquarters and to recall the months I had spent there in 1968–1969 with the International Training Institute.

Then I flew to Indianapolis and transferred to the little plane down to Bloomington. To my surprise, the airport in Bloomington was a grass one and the airport terminal a small shed. I felt at home immediately – it felt like I was back in the Pacific. Dr Denny Pett of the department in which I would be studying was at the airport to meet me and drive me to Eigenmann Hall, the high-rise dormitory building that was to be my home for the coming year.

And so I found myself in a Big Ten university in the Mid-East of the USA. My department was modest and housed in temporary buildings. It was called the Instructional Systems Technology Department of the School of Education, and the student body was multicultural, coming from every world region. I threw myself into the classes and into study: this was an enormous opportunity that had been presented to me and I was going to make the most of it.

But all was not well. I still suffered from a bad back, and it became progressively worse. I started having difficulty getting to classes. I couldn't climb the steps of the student bus. I had to stand at the back of classes leaning up against a filing cabinet or whatever was available because I couldn't sit down.

Finally, I was sent to the Student Medical Centre. There, they tried cortisone injections and tying weights to my legs as I lay on a board for days. Nothing worked. I was in terrible pain and couldn't walk. I was informed that for further treatment, I would need to pay substantial sums of money because my student fees would not cover it. So I found John Backer's phone number in New York and called him from the IU Student Medical Centre.

His voice came on the line and I began to explain about my back. I didn't get very far before the tears came. I remember him saying over and over in his calm voice that I was not to worry and he would handle everything. I was just to hand the phone over to someone in the Medical Centre. Which I did, and all was arranged.

Off I went to see Dr Haddawi, an Iraqi-American orthopaedic surgeon in Bloomington, and was admitted to Bloomington Hospital for further tests including x-rays. It was with a myelogram that the doctor pinpointed the problem, dating it back to a roller skating accident when I was 15. He operated and removed 20 pieces of calcified disc that were wrapped around the sciatic nerve in the L4-5 disc space of my spinal column.

I spent a week in hospital and then was transferred to the house of an Australian couple, Graham and Marian, who were living in Bloomington while Graham studied for his doctorate in Mathematics. They were wonderful to me and I will be eternally grateful for their care. Recuperated, I returned to Eigenmann Hall and was able to continue on with my studies.

I was called to the head of the School of Education for a meeting between several professors, one of whom was an Australian. They took down details of my three years at KTC and said they would be contacting the college to get more details. From the details they received, it turned out that I had four times more credits in education philosophy, education history, teacher training, art, literature, music etc. than required for a B Sc in Education. But I needed more credits in science and maths, so had to add those before they would recognise my first degree from KTC. I had already passed everything else needed for an M Sc.

So back to undergraduate classes I went, to a world of 18-year-olds, computer tests (unheard of in my earlier time at college) and very large classes in lecture rooms with stacked seating. But I did it and passed with As, which were required. And I graduated with an M Sc degree.

By then, I was also working as a graduate assistant in the storeroom dispensing photographic and media equipment to students, and in the media workshop, developing film and slides, producing slides for various faculties on the campus, doing freehand posters and signage and more. I was also teaching freehand lettering classes to other students. In this way, I was able to raise the money that I needed for textbooks, clothes and transport. My scholarship paid for fees and accommodation only. But this was coming to an end.

Around this time, my department head suggested that I apply for Specialist and Doctoral Studies. He assured me of a place for Ed S degree studies but I would need to sit a graduate assessment test to continue for an Ed D degree. I was told that if I agreed to continue, there would be graduate assistant positions that I could apply for that would pay my way through.

I decided to continue on at IU. When would such an opportunity ever present itself again? I was 36 years of age by now, with years of experience under my belt. I felt that I would reach 39 with or without a doctorate and it seemed to me that I should try for that. So I signed up for summer school right then and there to continue my studies. I had much to learn and felt I would never have such an opportunity again.

The team I had been working with in the IST media workroom had now been offered much better-paid positions in the Math Department. It was 1974 and the USA was supposed to be going metric (which never happened, even with the US pioneering the dollar more than a century earlier). This meant the redesigning of math materials across the board, and they needed a team to develop blueprints of textbooks that would expedite this. So we set ourselves up in our own unit behind the Math Department and started work.

In the summer of 1973, Vicki Semler had turned up at IU and joined several of the classes I was taking. She had spent years in Santiago, Chile working with the US diplomatic corps but resigned and set off to hitchhike through Europe with friends. As she tells her story, she woke up one day in Europe and suddenly realised she had to go back to college and retrain for a new career. So she hopped on a plane and flew home to Indiana and registered at IU. We became friends very soon after she arrived and she persuaded me to take my own apartment in the same complex further out of town where she was living. And this I did. After some months, I gave up my apartment and we decided to share an apartment and that is the arrangement that saw me through to the end of my studies at IU.

In June 1974, after I had completed my M Sc in Education, I was approached by several organisations with a view to taking up positions with them. The first to write to me was the National Board of the YWCA of the USA, with an invitation to become their Mutual Relations Consultant, based at the New York office. When they found that I was planning to continue with a PhD, they suggested I transfer to Columbia University in New York and work with the YWCA National Office part-time, using them as a field work placement. This offer included the possibility of a full-time position once I had completed my studies, and I was very tempted. The National Board had also assisted me with my daily living expenses at IU and I felt a certain obligation to them.

Other positions offered included one with the University of the South Pacific in their new Distance Education department, a particularly tempting prospect as I knew that having a director holding a PhD in Education (Instructional Systems Technology) – if I managed to achieve that! – would give added credibility and status to what was very much a fledgling discipline at USP. Then there was the offer from the South Pacific Commission in Noumea to apply to be SPC Youth Work Officer, and many letters from John Mavor of the Pacific Conference of Churches asking me to apply for the post of PCC Communications Director. Finally, the World YWCA in Geneva had written to sound me out as to whether I was interested in being their new Communications Director.

But I had already made up my mind to continue at IU, now

made possible by the position I held with the IU Mathematics Education Audio Visual Unit. My job meant I was no longer dependent on scholarship funds, nor did I need to be Graduate Assistant in the IST Department. This latter job and the organisations mentioned had seen me safely through to an M Sc (Education) and their support had set me up to be able to stand on my own two feet and that felt good.

I made the decision to make my doctoral dissertation one that would look at the area of communication and change in developing countries. Along with other issues around communication technology and change, I had disagreed vocally and strenuously with several professors at IU over the impact of television teaching in American Samoa, stating that the removal of trained teachers from the classrooms and villages and their replacement by TV monitors had been disastrous.

In the course of taking television and radio classes, I had developed a project that entailed the use of Sony Betamax video cameras and the training of local people to use them in gathering information on the lives of the people for sharing in a kind of revolving library. I knew there were better ways of utilising these emerging information technologies in development activities that would not mean the removal of trained teachers. And I had been challenged to prove my theory that development progressed by individuals being actively involved in the activities, both in the planning and the implementing.

I studied hard to complete all of my coursework in the 1974–75 academic year, and then proceeded to plan for my doctoral research. The first paragraph of my finished dissertation in 1976 stated:

The area of communication and change in developing countries, and in particular, the role of mass media in the process of social change, has attracted numbers of writers and researchers in recent years. From the related fields of sociology, education, anthropology, economics and politics, scholars have discussed the implications of the increasing use of mass media in the less industrialised countries of the world. Within the countries themselves, authorities have expressed concern at the implementation of projects that involve the use of advanced systems of communications technology, without a thorough study being undertaken beforehand of the long-term effects of such projects on the social and cultural life of the people.

I have to smile as I read this now: it was written in 1975, before computers, faxes, the Internet, the World Wide Web, smart phones. I was not to know that the world would be so radically changed in the next few decades and, in fact, that much of the developing world would leap over such things as landline phones, tape cassette recorders, faxes, overhead projectors and go straight to the Internet and smart phones.

The study I undertook in 1975 was to explore the use of mass media and concurrently the extent of involvement and interest in community and political affairs by the residents of three geographical settings in Fiji. I planned to undertake my research in rural, newly urban and urban areas of Fiji. Essentially, the question posed in the study would be: Does mass media usage have any relationship to community involvement and political participation?

From my years working and living in Fiji, I knew that those who lived in villages were deeply involved in community activities. But were they aware of what was happening politically? Did they care? Did they use mass media (mainly radio) to keep themselves informed? Or just entertained?

I also knew that once people moved into town where there was much more in the way of movies, telephones, radio coverage and entertainment in general, community and political involvement went down. Why was that? I wanted to compare responses to my questionnaire in rural areas with responses from those living in semi-urban/slum areas on the periphery of towns, and with those living in cities and towns of Fiji. Why were villagers so much more involved in the life of the community than the people who moved into town? And were women more involved than men? My gut feeling told me that they were, and with my growing interest in women and development and the part played by gender, this was of particular interest.

Having decided to undertake my research in Fiji, a country I felt I knew better than any other at that time, I prepared to fly to Fiji in September 1975. There had been much preliminary work with my research committee at IU, in particular Dr Dennis Pett and Dr Robert Arnove. The NCC Leadership Development Committee, because of the efforts of John Backer, provided financial assistance for travel and accommodation in Fiji. I have so much for which to thank that man.

But first there were major conferences to attend. The United Nations International Women's Year (IWY) Conference in Mexico City was to be held from 19 June to 2 July, the first UN world conference ever to be held that focused on the rights of women. A non-governmental meeting was being planned to run parallel to the UN world conference, in the same way as the NGO Tribune had been held parallel to the UN World Population Conference in Bucharest, 1974. Named the IWY Tribune, it was to be held across town from the main conference, in the Centro Medico.

I had already heard from Ruth Lechte and Amelia Rokotuivuna in Fiji that the World YWCA was recruiting women to attend the IWY Tribune, and the Fiji YWCA had been asked to suggest suitable participants from the Pacific Islands. This request came soon after the first Nuclear Free and Independent Pacific Conference that was held in Suva in April 1975. Building upon the contacts forged by Fiji YWCA members at this event with critically-minded civil society actors from a number of Pacific locations, a list of 'radical women', who were sure to pursue a provocative agenda in Mexico City, was presented to IWY Tribune organisers. These included independence and indigenous rights activists such as Déwé Gorodé from New Caledonia, Tea Hirshon from Tahiti, Hilda-Halkyard Harawira from Aotearoa New Zealand and Grace Mera Molisa from the New Hebrides/Vanuatu. They shared the strong anti-nuclear stance of the Fiji YWCA members, and were emerging as important and radical political figures in their own countries. Amelia and Ruth, with Vanessa Griffen and Claire Slatter, represented the Fiji YWCA.

Of course I wanted very much to join these women from the Pacific, having worked closely with most of them from 1962 to 1972. So I began to make plans to try and get myself down to Mexico City from Bloomington, Indiana.

I soon discovered that Mildred Persinger, the World YWCA representative at the UN, was the Coordinator of the NGO Committee organising the IWY Tribune, and I contacted her. Mildred was an old friend from my work with the Fiji YWCA and she knew of my participation in the Nuclear Free Pacific group of activists as well as the work of the Fiji YWCA in supporting the status of women in the Pacific generally. She was able to find some funds that would cover airfare and accommodation for me. In fact, with the funds provided, both Vicki Semler and I were able to go, though it meant staying at a very small and somewhat distant pensione. But we didn't mind, we were going to the IWY Tribune in Mexico City!

1963: Fiji YWCA, Suva. On the verandah of the YWCA headquarters.
L. to r.: Amelia Rokotuivuna, Seniloli Tora, Ruth Lechte, Cema and Litia

1964: Fiji YWCA Kindergarten at the (rented) Mormon Hall.
Anne playing piano. Children using musical instruments collected and sent by Elizabeth Lade and students from MLC, Melbourne

1966: Fiji YWCA Softball Team.
Back row, second from left: Anne S Walker. Front row on left: Ruth Lechte

1966: South Pacific Games, Noumea. Women's Table Tennis Team.
L. to r.: Akisi Naivaluvou, host guide, Amy Buksh, host guide, Jiko Cavu, Anne S Walker

Above

1966: Fiji YWCA headquarters in the old Suva Town Hall.

Ruth Lechte far right. Anne S Walker third from right

Left

1966: Davila Uluilakeba, Fiji YWCA first local kindergarten teacher trained at Kindergarten Training College in Melbourne, at her Graduation with Roy and Ethel Walker

Left

1967: Fiji. Director of Fiji YWCA Kindergarten, Davila Uluilakeba, at work

Below

1967: Fiji YWCA, Suva.

Friday night youth club dance upstairs in the YWCA headquarters in the old Suva Town Hall. Maraia and Anne halfway up the stairs, acting as bouncers

Above

1968: Fiji YWCA.

Group of youth club members at barbecue. Anne S Walker on the left. Ruth Lechte on the right

Left

1969: Fiji YWCA. Youth Club outing.

David Lancaster in back row left. Front row: Ruth Lechte second from left, Ecelini, Amelia Rokotuivuna, Anne S Walker

1969: USA, Planting Fields, Long Island at YWCA International Training Institute. Anne S Walker learning how to work a movie camera and direct a film

1969: USA, Planting Fields, Long Island. YWCA International Training Institute.
Drawing graphics to accompany presentations by leaders and students

1970: Fiji YWCA. Annual General Meeting, Lautoka.
L. to r.: Amelia Rokotuivuna and Anne S Walker on guitars, YWCA members holding placards indicating members of the community

1971: Fiji YWCA.

Mary Rockefeller from the USA YWCA Mutual Relations Committee visits and requests to see a YWCA rural women's village group. It rains. Anne S Walker accompanies Mary along the muddy trail to the village

1970: Fiji YWCA.

Seniloli Tora, Anne S Walker and Mary Rockefeller meet with the YWCA rural village women's group

Above

1972: Fiji YWCA farewell feast for Anne S Walker when she departed for further studies in the USA.

L. to r.: Raceva and Ethel Walker seated by the mats laden with food. They had met as teenagers when Mum was in Fiji in 1921

Left

1974: Indiana University, Bloomington, IN, USA.

Anne S Walker and her sister Frances Millar standing outside the FIJI fraternity building on the campus, deep in snow

1975: Mexico City. IWY Tribune.
Amelia Rokotuivuna on the panel about to speak on nuclear testing in the Pacific and the dire effects on the region. (Just before the Mexican government stunt that sought to portray women from every continent fighting at the microphone.)

1975: Mexico City. IWY Tribune.
Ruth Lechte on a break between workshops

1975: Mexico City. IWY Tribune.
Vicki Semler and Ruth Lechte

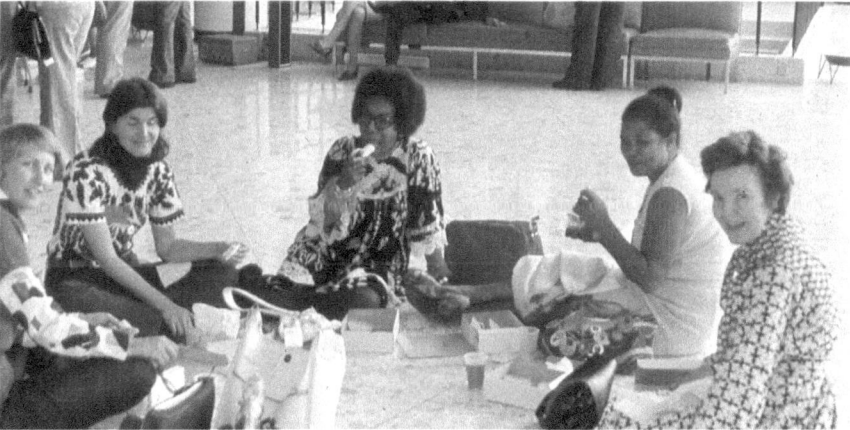

1975: Mexico City. IWY Tribune.
Anne S Walker, Vicki Semler, Dewe Gorodey (New Caledonia), Kila Amini (Papua New Guinea), Mildred Persinger

1975: Mexico City. IWY Tribune.
Vanessa Griffen and Claire Slatter from Fiji YWCA at Pacific anti-nuclear tests meeting

1975: Mexico City. IWY Tribune.
Vanessa Griffin of Fiji YWCA speaking at Pacific anti-nuclear tests meeting

7

Mexico 1975: International Women's Year Conference and Tribune

Vicki and I, with our friend Suzanne from Indiana University, flew to Mexico City in June 1975 for the IWY Tribune. Now known as the largest consciousness-raising session ever held by women worldwide, the Tribune brought together 6,000 women from every country. There was a planned program of plenaries and sessions in various auditoriums, some seating more than a thousand. And then there were the workshops. As women found each other and discovered how much we all had in common and how much we worked almost alone in our own countries, they asked for space and time to meet, to plan and strategise. The organising committee came up with a way of taking these requests each day and planning spaces for workshops for the following day. So evolved the system of organising that was to characterise the following three non-governmental meetings held parallel to the three UN women's world conferences in 1980, 1985 and 1990.

Amelia Rokotuivuna was one of the few delegates from the Pacific region given the opportunity to participate on a formal IWY Tribune panel. She spoke on nuclear disarmament issues alongside Sean MacBride, winner of the 1974 Nobel Peace Prize, and Noel Brown, a Jamaican-born representative. While each of the male speakers outlined the dangers of nuclear weapons and the nuclear industry in general terms, Amelia emphasised the impact of nuclearisation in the Pacific Islands, and highlighted local women's perspectives on the continuing influence of colonial powers in the region. In addition to this formal appearance, Pacific delegates also released two joint statements calling for an end to nuclear testing in the region, and self-rule for the region's colonial territories.

For Vicki and me, it was a liberating and refreshing time. We met up with the Pacific contingent and took part in their efforts to bring French nuclear tests in the Pacific to the attention of the world. We also participated in workshops and meetings around critical issues facing women from the Global South (the Third World of Developing Countries), e.g. food, agriculture, water, education, training, health, poverty and armed conflict. We met amazing women, some who had never been outside their village or rural town before and who were discovering the power of sharing their concerns and coping skills. Most importantly, they were discovering a world of women just like themselves, working alone and in need of support.

Across town, delegates from 133 Member States of the United Nations were meeting at the official International Women's Year World Conference. This conference set a precedent in that 116 of the delegates were in fact women. Much has already been written about this meeting, the first of four UN world conferences on women, three of them following the declaration of a Decade for Women, made five months after the conference in Mexico City.

Out of the official conference came the World Plan of Action, recognised widely as launching a new era in global efforts to promote the advancement of women by opening a worldwide dialogue on gender equality. The General Assembly identified three key objectives that would become the basis for the work of the United Nations on behalf of women:

- full gender equality and the elimination of gender discrimination
- the integration and full participation of women in development
- an increased contribution by women in the strengthening of world peace.

Importantly, the Conference called upon governments to formulate national strategies and identify targets and priorities in their effort to promote the equal participation of women. By the end of the United Nations Decade for Women, 127 Member States had responded by establishing some form of national machinery, institutions dealing with the promotion of policy, research and programs aimed at women's advancement and participation in development.

Within the United Nations system, in addition to the already existing Branch (later Division) for the Advancement of Women, the Mexico City Conference led to the establishment of the International Research and Training Institute for the Advancement of Women (INSTRAW) and the United Nations Development Fund for Women (UNIFEM) to provide the institutional framework for research, training and operational activities in the area of women and development.

But there was very little interaction between the official conference and the IWY Tribune and this caused a lot of frustration amongst the 6,000 women at the non governmental meeting. US feminist Betty Friedan mobilised many of the NGO participants, Vicki and me included, and we marched across town towards the end of both meetings, presenting ourselves outside the doors of the official conference and demanding to have our say. It did have some effect: the Pacific contingent got to meet with the Australian delegates and to discuss their concerns, especially around the testing and use of nuclear weapons in their region. Other women also got to meet briefly with their delegates.

At the end of the conference we returned to Indiana

University with a whole new world of possibilities in front of us. But first we had to complete our projects and then I had to prepare to leave for Fiji to undertake the planned survey for my doctoral dissertation. We hurried to complete the two slide-tape presentations we had begun in Mexico: one was 'Issues and Images of Latin American Women', for use by the Latin American Studies Department at IU, and the other highlighted the major issues and concerns of the IWY Tribune. We sent a copy of the Tribune set to Mildred Persinger in New York, to thank her for her assistance in making it possible for us to participate in Mexico City.

In September 1975, I went back to Fiji, staying at the new Fiji YWCA building. It was amazing to be actually living in the place we had planned for so long. I wanted to stay as incognito as possible and not to jeopardise the impartiality of my research. I therefore stayed very much to myself initially, with help from Amelia, now the General Secretary of the Fiji YWCA. She allowed me the use of the Gestetner machine and a typewriter to prepare the questionnaires. Initially in English, these were translated into Fijian so that the final ones were in both languages. These were then field-tested with a randomly selected number of households in Suva, resulting in many changes and adaptations.

To have attempted to randomly select people from all the urban, newly-urban and rural areas in Fiji would have called for financial and human resources far beyond what I had. In addition, the anonymity of the survey would have been destroyed by the resulting publicity. The best strategy seemed to be to select areas that would represent urban, newly-urban and rural areas, and to randomly select people from within those areas.

Accordingly, Suva was chosen to represent an urban area and divided into three sub-sections. Interviews were carried out in each sub-section, with every third house in every second street in that sub-section being selected. In this way, interviews were conducted in a cross section of commercial, residential and housing estate areas of Suva.

To represent newly-urban areas, scattered houses and settlements on the periphery of Suva were chosen. In areas where the majority of Indian residents lived, a Hindi-speaking interviewer conducted the interviews. In areas where Fijians were living, Fijian-speaking interviewers were used. As far as was possible, respondents were selected from every third house in each settlement.

Representative rural areas were more difficult to select. It was felt important that the rural areas chosen should not have easy access to an urban centre. Additionally, Indian as well as Fijian rural residents needed to be represented in the sample, and this meant that sugar-growing areas should be included. Respondents were chosen from every second house in a village or rural settlement. Three interviewers were involved in the interviewing of residents in rural areas, one on Viti Levu, and two on Vanua Levu.

The difficulties faced in reaching some of these villages were made easier with help from the Minister of Information, Ratu David Toganivalu, who provided all manner of support, including the 'put-put' canoes for travel on rivers, and guides to accompany interviewers through mountainous and forested regions. Each interviewer was supplied with an official ID, signed by the Minister.

When all the questionnaires had been filled out and collected, I did a spot check on every tenth questionnaire to make sure the interviews had been correctly done. Finally the forms were all loaded into boxes and sent back to Indiana University. And I flew back to Bloomington to begin the task of writing my dissertation from the mounds of survey results.

In a letter home dated November 1975 I wrote:

> I've had a busy and extremely interesting time these past couple of weeks. Bloomington has a very well put-together International Women's Year Month which is still going on

even though the 'Month' stopped on October 17th. We've had Gloria Steinem speak on campus, also Carol Brown, United Church of Christ minister, Carter Heyward, female Episcopal (Anglican) priest, though still unlawfully so as far as canonical law goes, Judy Chicago, feminist artist/writer, and Rosemary Reuther, radical Catholic theologian. I've been lucky enough to meet most of them, took part in a Home Mass with Rev. Carter Heyward, an 'illegal' occasion, as the Indianapolis bishop would not give consent for such an event.

Later in the same letter, I mentioned that I had finished working with the Math ED department and was now working full time on my dissertation. I also needed to complete French studies in order to switch from an ED.D, to a PhD. This meant some intensive work on French verbs and the sitting of yet another examination, but I managed to pull through with that.

All that was left to do was to complete my doctoral dissertation, then defend it before a doctoral committee, and my sojourn at IU would be over. My final defence took place May 14th 1976. On the advice of my contacts at the University of the South Pacific, I had applied for a job at the East-West Communication Institute at the University of Hawaii, a job that focused on research into New Media in Old Societies in the Pacific, very much within the area of my dissertation. The project was funded for three years and I was very hopeful of being appointed.

Both Vicki and I were feeling somewhat burned out by this time, and when we read in a journal that there was to be a conference on women and development at Wellesley College, just west of Boston, we decided we would apply for registration and get ourselves there. Our applications were accepted and we packed our bags and set off in Vicki's car to drive from Bloomington to Wellesley.

Wellesley College Women and Development Conference, June 1976

To say that this conference was life-changing would be an understatement. Each day was jam-packed with presentations from women academics who had undertaken research on the role of women in development in Africa, Asia and the Pacific, Latin America and the Caribbean, and Europe. We were hard-pressed to choose which presentation we would attend and found ourselves running from one to the other, trying to get as much as we possibly could from each. That was in the first two days. The organisers, however, had attempted to cram too much into each day and had left no time for questions, and this suddenly and dramatically became a major issue.

We had noticed the arrival of a large group of international women researchers on the second day. The conference was suddenly bigger and the participants came from every world region. The final count was 117 women from 32 countries – mainly from Africa and Asia with some from Latin America. They filled the front seats of all the presentations that applied to their individual regions, unable to ask questions because of time limitations and becoming increasingly agitated because of this. The group had come from another conference at Wingspread in Wisconsin, and the funding that made it possible for them to come to the Wellesley conference was confirmed at the last minute.

The result was an increasingly untenable situation. Academics and researchers from each world region were being asked to sit and listen and not ask questions of mainly US and UK researchers who had been funded to undertake research in those same regions. In most cases, these women were unaware of the research undertaken and had not been invited to work with the overseas researchers.

Things began to explode. There were increasingly animated and vocal demands that their questions and comments regarding the research being presented should be heard. All this quickly climaxed in a closed meeting in the Wellesley grounds that was restricted to the researchers from every global region who had been included at the last minute and hence had no way of taking any meaningful part.

So the final three days looked very different to the first two days. The entire program was abandoned and a new one introduced, including these researchers from every global region and allowing for questions and comments from the floor. To Vicki and me, it was a forceful example of where the world needed to go in the area of women and development. A totally new approach had to be forged that worked within each world region with women and development practitioners, activists, researchers, planners, writers, public officials, from the ground up. It was the beginning of a dramatic change in approach by funders and universities, and led to more resources being made available at that level, and not almost exclusively to women researchers in the US and the UK as had been the case until then.

We made valuable contacts among some of the best and brightest women and found our own interests and possible future career prospects growing by the minute. We were changing direction and becoming very excited at what might lie ahead. So we drove back to Indiana revived and stimulated beyond our expectations.

I still had a lot of writing, sorting and tidying up to complete and Vicki had hardly made a start on her doctoral dissertation. I had also committed myself to participate in the National YWCA Conference at Notre Dame University in Southbend, Indiana, representing the Fiji YWCA. I was to be in charge of a telephone link-up between the conference and the Kenya YWCA as part of their World Fellowship publicity. I was kept busy even before leaving Bloomington with phone calls from New York about the conference call, also from Indiana Bell Telephone Company, who seemed to think that the Kenya end of the link-up would be coordinated by rural villagers who would not be able to handle it.

Following the YWCA Conference in Southbend, I was called daily by Mildred Persinger who was responsible for getting me to the National Conference in Southbend. She now wanted me to go to New York and help handle the avalanche of requests for assistance coming from the 6,000 IWY Tribune participants. The NGO Committee had not made any plans for follow-up and were struggling to cope with these requests.

I had never planned to work in any large city on finishing at IU. My thoughts were totally focused on getting a job in the Pacific. So I was not keen on heading east to New York City. But in the end I agreed, and set off in July 1976 to see what the situation was.

8

International Women's Tribune Centre, New York

*Coping with the responses from
the IWY Tribune, Mexico City*

New York, July 1976. Fresh off the plane from Indiana, I walked in to the 8th floor of the Carnegie Building at 345 East 46th Street, New York. The lights were off; papers were strewn around the floor spilling from desks and chairs. I turned on the lights. 'No, no!' said a voice from the darkness. 'Turn them off! We don't want the management to know we're still here!' It was the voice of Mildred Persinger, the reason I was in New York.

It was a year since the International Women's Year World Conference and the parallel non-governmental IWY Tribune in Mexico City, and the committee should by now have packed up and gone home. But Mildred and Rosalind Harris, President of the Conference of NGOs in Consultative Status with the UN, were still trying to cope with the response to that landmark gathering.

Mildred had been calling me on the phone at Indiana University, asking me to come to New York for a couple of weeks to discuss possibilities for how to deal with this massive response. It was clear that the women who had been there, organisers and participants, were looking for some kind of follow-up.

We talked long and hard about possible strategies for action. A meeting of the NGO IWY Tribune Committee was called to join the discussions. Should we try to set something up? If so, what form should it take? Could we support work already underway in the regions? Were there linkages we could make?

I felt we should start at regional level and develop ways to support regional networks, rather than set up a global focal point. This came from my years in Fiji where we worked nationally and regionally wherever possible and very rarely turned to an international group for support. The exception, of course, was the World YWCA, which gave us constant moral support and offered leadership training opportunities as needed.

Within days the decision was made for me to travel to Puerto Rico to make contact with women leaders meeting at an international social work conference there. In particular, I was to find Peggy Antrobus, Head of the Women's Bureau in Jamaica, and talk with her about the possibility of a trial project in the Caribbean.

When I found Peggy she was surrounded by women eager for her time. I introduced myself and produced the draft survey. Did she think this was a good idea? Could we work with her in putting together a Regional Resource Kit for Women in the Caribbean? Peggy looked thoughtful. Then carefully said 'I really believe we Caribbean women could do a regional kit ourselves. We don't need someone from New York to do it for us'. It made sense to me and I returned to New York.

Six months later, Peggy wrote: 'I have rethought your idea of a Caribbean regional resource kit for women and wonder if you could come to a Caribbean sub-regional meeting in Jamaica in preparation for the World Conference on Women in Copenhagen in 1980. We could talk again about the kit, and begin collecting information from around the region.'

By now I was working full-time on the fledgling Tribune Centre project. Vicki Semler had joined me in early 1977 and then a third part-time staff person, Martita Midence, a fellow student of Vicki's and mine at Indiana University who now had a Masters degree in Library Science. Martita had begun immediately to build a resource centre on women and development information. Mildred was working with the project as a full-time volunteer. Already we had produced two issues of a 24-page newsletter on women's projects, issues and concerns worldwide and, now with Martita's assistance, put together a resource and database of project information, publications, names and addresses from IWY Tribune participants. Initially called the IWY Tribune Project Newsletter, it was to become *The Tribune*, a quarterly newsletter in three languages, and its constituency was to grow to 26,000 individuals and groups worldwide.

In June 1977, Vicki and I participated in the New York State meeting at Albany. We voted, along with thousands of other women, for various resolutions that New York women wanted in the final National Plan of Action. We did not however expect to be at the planned USA International Women's Year Conference meeting in November in Houston, Texas, as we were not elected delegates.

But Mildred Persinger, who was World YWCA Representative to the United Nations and the Coordinator of the IWY Tribune in Mexico City, had other ideas. The World YWCA had made it possible for a group of women representing YWCAs in Africa, Asia, Latin America, the Caribbean and Europe to attend the meeting in Houston. She wanted Vicki and me to assist with several workshops for them and to accompany them to the conference in Houston. We jumped at the chance to be part of this historic event.

From 18 to 21 November 1977, over 20,000 people gathered in Houston, Texas, to celebrate International Women's Year and identify goals for women of the USA for the next decade. This was the first and only national women's conference to be sponsored by the federal government. The primary job of the conference was to formulate and pass a National Plan of

Action, based on recommendations from the state meetings. The final Plan had 26 planks, ranging from better enforcement of existing laws to broad demands for a national health security system, full employment, peace and disarmament.

On 29 September a torch was lit at Seneca Falls, New York, site of the first women's rights convention held on 19 July 1848. A relay of runners carried the torch 2,600 miles to Houston, arriving the day before the conference began. Poet Maya Angelou wrote a new Declaration of Sentiments to parallel the one passed by the 1848 convention. The Declaration accompanied the torch on its journey where it was signed by thousands.

On 18 November 1977, the torch was presented to three former USA First Ladies at the official opening of the conference: Rosalynn Carter, Betty Ford and Lady Bird Johnson. They signed the new Declaration and then circulated it among the delegates to sign. It was a great time for the USA, and for the women from around the world. And Vicki and I felt privileged to be there. We returned to the IWTC office in New York with renewed enthusiasm for what we were doing.

But there was a problem with funding and we were running out of money to pay salaries. A grant from the Canadian International Development Agency (CIDA) had been sufficient to get the ball rolling but we needed more funds while further project proposals were being considered by European development agencies. So Vicki and I accepted consultancies, one for me to work in Barbados at the Women and Development Unit of the University of the West Indies to support the development of this new gender unit with workshops, publications, plans, and most importantly, the development and publication of a Caribbean Resource Kit for Women. I would be working with Peggy Antrobus and her staff. The other consultancy was with a group in Ghana and Vicki travelled there to work with Fanny Dontoh Russell and others on a low-cost media workshop to develop women and development materials in local languages for village communities. We were away for a month, with Mildred, Rosalind and Martita holding the fort back in New York.

Working with women in the regions

So began the IWTC process of running low-cost media workshops for women in the regions and developing low-cost, visual materials and women's regional resource kits in collaboration with regional women's groups. During the next five years the IWTC (we had decided on the name of International Women's Tribune Centre in 1978 when we were incorporated) developed strong linkages with women activists in every world region. In the process of gathering information for the kits, we shared information on resources, training and technical assistance, gathered bibliographies of women's work, and put women in touch with the resources available in their regions.

We took note of how Peggy used the first Caribbean Regional Resource Kit as a way of reaching out to women throughout the Caribbean in the beginning days of the Women and Development Unit (WAND) at the University of the West Indies in Barbados. Using the same process we had gone through together, she and her staff put together a second Caribbean Regional Resource Kit in 1981, this time with the WAND Communications Officer (Lesley Barrow), who spent the final months of production with IWTC in New York.

Peggy was uniquely aware of the need for developing strategies that would support the empowerment of women as leaders in the region. In setting up WAND in Barbados, she worked to organise at a regional level a structure of information, technical assistance, training and activism. As an activist, economist and writer, she forged a partnership between the women of the Caribbean and the governments of the region, never losing sight of the goal of putting women in decision-making positions at local, national and regional level.

Parallel to our manual and newsletter production activities, we continued our commitment to skill training through a series of workshops in Africa, Asia, the Pacific, Latin America and the Caribbean. In those early years, we were rarely all together in the New York office. From the very beginning, we offered low-cost media skills workshops for women so that they could begin to collect, develop and disseminate their own information in the language of their choice. It also meant that they could take the information that we sent them, and adapt and translate that so that it would reach a larger, local readership.

Although we were becoming more and more proficient with fundraising skills (and sharing all we were learning with other women's groups as we went along), our financial resources were constantly stretched and we were often on the verge of going under. The need to develop project proposals was a constant concern and I would frequently find myself writing a proposal for an upcoming project on a plane, flying between workshops or fundraising visits in Europe.

In early 1978, Elizabeth Reid, who had been the Special Adviser on Women's Affairs in Gough Whitlam's Labor Government in Australia from 1973 to 1975, visited IWTC. When the Labor Government was removed from office in Australia, Elizabeth had gone to Teheran at the request of Princess Ashraf, the sister of the Shah of Iran. Elizabeth was on the Australian delegation at the IWY World Conference in Mexico City in 1975 and had met Ashraf there. In Teheran, Elizabeth set up the Asia and Pacific Centre for Women and Development (APCWD) and she had seen the Caribbean Resource Kit for Women. She wanted a regional resource kit for women similar to that for women in the Asia and Pacific region and asked me to come to Teheran to work with her staff to develop the kit. Elizabeth shared our vision of making information and resources available to all women and women's organisations and had the same sense of urgency we felt in sharing as much as possible with as many as possible in the pursuit of equality, development and peace.

I flew to Teheran via Australia to first visit my mother and family in Melbourne, and Papua New Guinea to take part in an appropriate technology workshop with Ruth Lechte who was working with the World YWCA. I ran a low-cost media workshop for the group and we developed fine line drawings that were appropriate for PNG, along designs and layouts for newsletters, manuals, posters and leaflets on appropriate technology for women.

From Port Moresby, I flew to Manila and stayed a night at the Manila YWCA. There I was surprised to see copies of the book I had developed from the youth work training workshop years before in Kiribati. Called *Youth Ideas for the South Pacific*, it was full of my graphics and had apparently become very popular in the Philippines. The need for appropriate regional materials was evident and this little book had apparently found a wider audience than just with the young people of the South Pacific.

The staff at the YWCA arranged for me to go by bus up into the mountainous area out of Manila to visit some women's groups who were developing water projects to make water more available to the women and their families there. In the evening, I took part in a village celebration with fireworks and much singing. It was a memorable day and night. Then back to Manila for the flight to Teheran.

The descent by plane into Teheran was memorable. We had been flying over wide-open spaces of desert, interspersed with dramatic mountains and sweeping landscapes when I noticed an immense black cloud up ahead. I asked the flight attendant what it was and she replied 'Teheran'. Such was my first introduction to the city in May 1978. A beautiful city designed in the 1950's for a population of 1 million and now with a population of almost 5 million. It had become terribly polluted with cars and industrial pollution with the sky shrouded in blackness.

I was met at the airport and driven to the offices of the Asia and Pacific Women's Resource Centre and introduced to the staff by Elizabeth Reid. I was to stay with a young Australian volunteer in a house some distance from the offices and to travel back and forth by bus each day.

I stayed six weeks in Teheran, working alongside the staff at APCWD to put together a women's resource manual for the whole region. It was painstaking work but we were spurred ahead by the increasing threat of revolution in Iran, with daily demonstrations in the streets, outbreaks of violence, and many other reasons to fear for what was to happen in that country. I will be forever grateful for the care taken of me by the women and men of APCWD and most especially by Elizabeth Reid herself during that time.

By July 1978, the manual was virtually complete. It contained lists of women's organisations in every country in the region; a bibliography of regional women's publications; names and addresses of regional groups that could provide technical assistance and training; the basics of project-writing and lists of donor agencies; and a description of all that APCWD had to offer, with their full contact information. I flew back to New York with the almost-final manuscript. All that was needed to do was the layout and graphics, which took some time given we were still working in pre-computer times and everything was done by hand. But we did complete the manual and it was soon ready for distribution across the vast Asia and Pacific region.

We were able to put those resource kits into the hands of almost every women and development group in that region with the help of the UN pouch system (packages sent within the UN mailing system and delivered to UN Development Program offices). And when the staff of APCWD had to hurriedly leave Teheran during the Islamic revolution of 1979, the information contained in the manual was key to the reestablishment of APCWD in Bangkok. A second edition was produced after the organisation was later moved to Kuala Lumpur, Malaysia, as part of the Women and Development Unit of the Asia Pacific Development Centre.

Early on in the production of our newsletter and manuals on women and development issues, we began to get remarks from many readers that IWTC never credited the artists who were drawing the graphics. One went so far as to say 'It's typical of people who produce publications. They never give credit to artists!' So I began to put my initials on each graphic, and ASW began to appear at the bottom of each. In later years, we were able to add other artists to our small staff, in particular Grace Jung who worked with us for many years, and Laurel Douglas. Their graphics would join mine and travel the world over.

In February 1979, with additional staff and major projects underway, IWTC was suddenly informed by the Carnegie Institution that they were selling their building and moving to Washington DC. We were given very little time to find new office space. We searched all across Manhattan for the right place for our growing international women's hub. Proximity to the United Nations had become increasingly important for our work, especially with women coming from developing countries who needed a place to meet and be supported in their UN and International NGO meetings and discussions.

Finally, we found a loft space in the Albano Building at 305 East 46th Street, a building opposite where Vicki Semler and I were now living. It was totally unfurnished and needed a lot of work to be made habitable. We bought unfinished wooden doors as desktops, each of the staff sanding, oiling and waxing their own desks, formed with filing cabinets and/or shelving at each end. We also had to clear out all the old metal desks and chairs that we had inherited for use while in the old Carnegie Building. In NYC, if you want to get rid of something, just leave it out on the sidewalk overnight!

With Martita Midence running the Resource Centre, Joanne

Sandler (who came originally as an intern but returned as a permanent staff member) developing programs and deeply immersed in setting up bookkeeping and mailing list systems, and Vicky Mejia developing our Spanish-language program, we were a hardworking, dedicated team. We also needed office space for our two major volunteers, Mildred Persinger and Rosalind Harris. Mildred and Ros were important and crucial links between us and the United Nations international non-governmental organisations community. They had been part of the UN NGO community for decades and made up the core of our IWTC Board of Directors as President and Treasurer.

It was good to have our own space at last, with a much larger area for all our growing needs, including a central table for meetings and gatherings of all kinds. Into this space came Vanessa Davis, a young African American searching for a job and willing to take on anything. Vanessa was to remain with us for the next 20 years, becoming our receptionist, then accountant, and finally indispensable to all activities of the Tribune Centre. Also into this space came a growing number of women from around the world, some searching for information resources, others needing help with making contact with UN officials and delegates, and all needing support for their activities in their home countries.

In 1979, we were asked by Mary Tadesse, the Director of African Training and Research Centre for Women (ATRCW) in Addis Ababa, to develop a resource manual for women and development in the Africa region. Mary had seen the regional resource manuals for the Caribbean and Asia and the Pacific regions and wanted something similar for African women. I flew to Addis Ababa following the UN Regional Conference in Lusaka in 1979.

I went to that conference as part of my first trip to Africa. It was a long trip from New York to Liberia, Zambia and then to Kenya and Ethiopia. It began in Monrovia, where ran a low-cost media workshop as part of a larger Women and Media conference run by Elizabeth Okwenje of the African Council of Churches (Kenya) and Thelma Awori of UNDP (New York).

From Monrovia I flew to Lusaka for the UN Regional Conference on Women, mainly to be part of discussions with women from all countries in Africa as they prepared for the next UN world conference on women to be held in Copenhagen in 1980. While in Lusaka, I spent time with the Zambia YWCA who were running women and appropriate technology and support services for refugee women in camps outside of Lusaka. I went one day with the director of the YWCA to visit one of these refugee camps and was taken aback by the sheer size and lack of even the basic amenities. I witnessed an enormously long line of women lined up with buckets and pans waiting for a food handout by a UN agency, and talked with some of the women in one of the YWCA groups. It was heartbreaking to see how tough life was for them, with little hope of them returning to their war-torn home countries. It gave me much to think about in terms of the information and resources needed, and how we could work more closely with the YWCA and other women's groups in Lusaka in accessing these.

From Zambia, I flew to Ethiopia via Nairobi where I met with Mary Tadesse and several members of her staff at the African Training and Research Centre for Women. We discussed what they wanted in each section of the manual, including a section on ATRCW publications that had been produced on women and development issues in Africa, and an order form so that groups could place orders for these publications.

Following our initial discussions, I was directed to a building at the back of the centre where all the publications produced by the centre were stored. On opening the door, I was stunned to find myself faced with stacks of books, piled to the ceiling of this barn-like building. I found a ladder and began climbing up each stack to take a copy from the top of each. These I packaged and sent back to New York via the

UN mail system. On my return from Africa, we collected the books and laid them out on the floor of IWTC and invited various UN and NGO staff and officials to come and see them. They were stunned by the variety and number of publications that had been produced by researchers and writers in Africa, commissioned by ATCRW in Addis Ababa.

When we developed the African resource kit on women and development, following my visit, we included a whole section on these publications, with an order form for women so they could order copies from ATRCW in Addis. Within weeks of the resource kit being distributed to women's groups across Africa, those enormous stacks of publications had been depleted! And when IWTC was asked to produce another resource kit for the French-speaking regions of Africa, we were requested to limit the number of copies that could be ordered on the form.

At IWTC we were greatly encouraged by this, regarding it as a real sign that women and community groups throughout Africa wanted to know about the resources available in their region and were hungry for this information. The IWTC vision of information, communication, technical assistance and training for women's rights in development was expanding in ever new and global ways.

Most importantly, the more we became involved in regional and global UN meetings concerned with the UN Decade for Women, the clearer it became to us that it was essential for women to have access to information that linked what was happening at global level with what was happening at regional, national and local level. We were more and more convinced that if our work was undertaken with inclusive participation, a free flow of information, and highly visual and simple language information materials, IWTC could play an important role in the development of a global women's rights movement working towards equality, development and peace.

In early 1980, IWTC joined forces with APCWD (now in Bangkok) and the Women and Development Unit (WAND,

Barbados) to hold a Feminist Forum at Stony Point in New York. Two feminist consultants, Charlotte Bunch and Shirley Castley, were to lead us through three intensive days of study, discussion and reflection. Together with women from all regions of the world, we mapped out a feminist strategy of inclusiveness that could deepen the growing worldwide women's rights movement. Out of this forum came a booklet entitled *Developing Strategies for the Future: A Feminist Perspective* which was widely disseminated amongst women's groups around the world.

Some months after the Feminist Forum, IWTC organised INCONET, an Information, Communication and Networking forum to which women came from every world region to join us in building global networking strategies. For this major event, we hired Jacqui Starkey, consultant with expertise in a wide range of networking and arts/crafts skills. Vicki and I had met Jacqui at the IWY Tribune in Mexico City in 1975 and had remained good friends. Her support in those early days of IWTC was crucial to the ways in which we were able to develop networking and outreach dimensions to our burgeoning program.

In fact, it was in no small way that these very focused feminist forums helped all of us at IWTC grow and expand our vision of a truly inclusive and broad-based feminist rights approach to our work with women worldwide. And it was enormously important in building the groundwork for the next major UN World Conference on Women and NGO Forum to be held in Copenhagen. This time, IWTC was to be integrally involved in the planning and implementation of the event.

Copenhagen, 1980: UN Mid-Decade World Conference on Women and NGO Forum

In July 1980, the UN Mid-Decade Conference on Women and the parallel NGO Forum were held in Copenhagen. Three subthemes of Health, Education and Employment were added to the overall themes of Equality, Development and Peace. IWTC was given the task by the NGO Forum Committee of sharing information on plans and preparations for the NGO Forum with women worldwide, and we set about developing and producing newsletters, manuals, posters and leaflets to distribute to our growing mailing list of women's organisations in every world region. By now, the use of graphics had become an essential part of all of our publications. I would spend many hours developing and producing these, with many nights and weekends spent with pen and pencil outlining ideas and finalising a growing folio of graphics depicting women at work in a wide variety of community and development activities.

The Convener of the NGO Forum Committee, Elizabeth Palmer (formerly General Secretary of the World YWCA in Geneva) had also asked that IWTC undertake a core program at the forum, one that would provide ongoing assistance with resources and networking for women coming from every region of the world. The ongoing event organised by IWTC was called *Vivencia* – a Spanish word meaning 'experience'. Vicky Mejia, our Latin America Program Coordinator from Colombia, had put forward this title and it was perfect. A wing of the Amager University was set aside for the program which included a resource centre for publications, areas for small group activities, a space for ongoing sign and banner production, special events, organising and strategising spaces, all booked and publicised in the daily Forum newspaper. Networking lists were hung from the walls, and women added their names to a growing number of issues and concerns.

From these lists, networks were formed, many of which remain to this day. A special issue of *The Tribune* would be produced once we were back in New York to give information of these networks, with contact persons and addresses.

IWTC staff at the NGO Forum, besides myself, included Vicki Semler, Vicky Mejia, Joanne Sandler, Vanessa Davis, and Martita Midence. One of the reasons for my arriving a week early in Copenhagen was, at the request of Elizabeth Palmer, the NGO Forum Convener, to paint all the banners for the Forum. These were to hang high on both the inside and outside walls where the Forum was held. With the help of a local Danish artist, Annelise Hansen, we found a loft space with a large concrete floor, and stretched out bolts of cotton material for me to outline all the banner titles freehand, and then supervise the filling in by a band of volunteers. It was backbreaking work, but we got all the banners finished in time for the Forum opening.

Our IWTC team for Vivencia also included two Fiji YWCA members, one of whom was Joan Yee, who went on to become the director of the University of the South Pacific Library in Suva. Another volunteer was Dot Jackson from the USA, a long-time friend and supporter from my Fiji days in the 1960s, when she and her husband came out to visit Nan and Leyton Zimmer working in the US Peace Corps. Dot and I had become close friends. She was a great community activist and would put her hand to anything that she felt progressed the rights of women in the world and she was a great supporter of IWTC's work.

The UN World Conference for Women and parallel NGO Forum brought 10,000 women to Copenhagen. They came to meet other women and groups fighting for the same rights, the same concerns, the same desperate needs. They wanted action from their governments and they wanted it now! Foremost amongst the activists at the Forum were those fighting against female genital mutilation and gender violence of all kinds, for water, environmental, food, agriculture, education and health needs; and for equality, development and peace in every region. Amongst these activists was Domitilla Barrios de Chungara, long time Bolivian social activist, feminist and mine union leader. The organising of what became known as Domitilla's March from the NGO Forum to the official world conference took place in *Vivencia*. Domitilla held the floor for days surrounded by crowds of women painting banners, T-shirts, posters, and whatever else was needed for the march.

The day of the march was unforgettable. Tiny Domitilla led the way in full Bolivian attire, holding high a banner demanding human rights for miners in Bolivia. Thousands of women streamed behind her, singing, chanting, waving banners. Demands had been expanded to include women's human rights, labor rights in general, calls for nuclear disarmament, and more rights that women worldwide wanted to be included in the document being forged by UN Member States at the world conference.

At the Convention Centre heavily armed police and militia met us. Scuffling broke out as the police and militia attempted to stop the marchers from reaching the doors to the official meeting underway. Then Lucille Mair (Jamaica), the Secretary-General of the world conference, appeared before the crowd and with much shouting and cheering from the crowd, agreed that Domitilla and three others could go into the plenary meeting and place the demands of the march before the delegates.

The march was a major step in forging a greater role for civil society in global decision-making, and followed in the tradition established in 1975 when women's NGOs, led by US feminist writer Betty Friedan, marched across Mexico City from the nongovernmental IWY Tribune to the official UN IWY Conference to demand more participation by NGOs in the conference.

Out of the UN World Conference on Women came another Declaration and a Program of Action. United Nations Member States and Agencies, other international agencies and NGOs again committed themselves to the implementation of programs that would raise the status of women. Many also signed the Convention on the Elimination of All Forms of Discrimination

Against Women (CEDAW), a treaty for women's rights that had been developed over many years by the UN Commission on the Status of Women.

On our return to New York from Copenhagen, we found our hands full once again. We were faced with a flood of new ideas, tools, technologies, and contacts. Bridges had been built between communities of women activists and those of women scientists and engineers. These were exciting years that led us into many new paths and opportunities, and the growth in women's networks and women and development activities in general took an enormous leap forward.

We were now also working on a Latin American projects development manual in Spanish, while concurrently involved in follow up to an appropriate technology materials development project in the South Pacific. Vicki Semler and I had gone to Fiji in August 1979 to conduct a workshop for the South Pacific Commission Community Education Centre (CETC) in Suva, and were now developing materials for use at the centre and across the Pacific. We were also planning another workshop at CETC in Suva for April 1981. Vicky Mejia would be joining me to run that. Out of these workshops we hoped to be able to develop materials on appropriate technology for women in every world region.

The South Pacific workshop in Suva with the SPC Community Education Training Centre in April 1981 was attended by 40 women from South Pacific countries and was a great success. For me, it was wonderful to have yet another opportunity to be back in the South Pacific where I had lived and worked for almost 11 years 1962–1972. The 1981 workshop was a first visit to the region for Vicky Mejia and she revelled in the extra excursions we took in canoes up rivers, and out to isolated villages to meet women and to take part in traditional ceremonies.

From Fiji, Vicky flew on to Colombia, via Chile and Peru, to meet with women's organisations, joining up with Joanne

Sandler to conduct a one-week workshop with the National Federation of Coffee Growers, Women's Division. Out of that workshop, IWTC was to develop and produce a highly visual, Spanish-language manual for women undertaking business and marketing venture in Latin America. Entitled *Movilizando la Mujer*, it became one of our most requested manuals in the years to come.

These years were some of our most productive. We introduced our first computer into the office, a CPT Word Processor, and some of the staff underwent training in how to use it. I included myself in the training offered by CPT so that I could understand a little of the intricacies, even without possessing any real typing skills. The computer had not yet taken over our world but was soon to do so!

In the midst of everything else, we continued the development of *The Tribune*, each edition focused on a specific women and development issue – and now being published in English and Spanish. Titles included 'Women and Media', 'Women, Money and Credit', 'Women Organising', 'Women and Small Business', 'Women's Centres', and 'Women and Natural Resources'.

One of the new programs we instituted was the staff exchange/internship program and requests poured in from all over the world. The program was based on training experience in four areas: (1) establishing resource centres; (2) organisational development and administration; (3) low-cost media production; and (4) networking locally, nationally, regionally and internationally. The first three interns who worked with us were Zoila Ellis and Kaye Veron from the Belize Committee on Women and Development, and Lesley Barrow, Communications Officer with the Women and Development Unit in Barbados.

In late December 1981 I flew home to Australia to spend time with my mother and family and also to visit development and funding agencies in Canberra. The visit with the Australian

International Development Assistance Bureau (AIDAB) was successful and we received small grants from them for the next three years, mainly to support our workshops in the South Pacific. I also heard of the setting of up a new women and development group within AIDAB. Its major purpose was to 'to set up a clearing-house of development information 'like the International Women's Tribune Centre', but at a national level', to educate the Australian public on the needs of women in Third World countries. They also planned to lobby the Australian government for more funds to be allotted towards women's projects, to assist women in funding agencies to be better recognised within those agencies and for women to be promoted to decision-making positions. I was delighted that this was happening and promised to remain in close contact with developments at the new group.

During this time in the life of IWTC, we were in regular contact with two UN women's organisations that came out of the IWY World Conference in Mexico City, 1975. We had all begun at the same time, with IWTC coming from the non-governmental IWY Tribune, the other two coming from the UN governmental world conference. One group was the International Research and Training Institute for the Advancement of Women (INSTRAW). The other group was the UN Development Fund for Women (UNIFEM). With INSTRAW setting up in the Dominican Republic, and UNIFEM based at UN headquarters in New York, it was UNIFEM staff with whom we became close working colleagues, particularly the director, Margaret Snyder. We at IWTC felt that we could provide the information and resource materials being sought by women the world over until such time as UNIFEM was up and running and would take this over from us. Such was the thinking at the time. In fact of course, UNIFEM had a very different mandate, involving the raising of funds from UN Member States and allocating them to women and development projects as specified by those Member States, with a priority for government projects.

In later years, UNIFEM did become one of the few UN departments that increasingly took an interest in the essential work of NGO women's groups.

The early 1980's were particularly busy for all of us at IWTC. We undertook women and marketing workshops in Colombia and Costa Rica, work with WAND in Barbados on plans for a Caribbean women's conference, a women and disarmament conference in New York, a media skills workshop in Kenya, a project development workshop in Zimbabwe and a feminist media conference in Washington DC, the latter with the Women's Institute for Freedom of the Press. An important organisation set up during this time was the Association for Women in Development (AWID) of which IWTC was a founding partner. I travelled to Racine, Wisconsin for AWID's inaugural meeting, along with academics, researchers and feminist activists from all over the USA. AWID has since grown into a global organisation and one of the preeminent women's rights networks in the world.

During this time we also had more interns at IWTC, including Pauline Onsa, Provincial Minister for Women's Affairs, Bougainville, and Mallika Dutt, feminist activist from India, at that time studying at Mt Holyoke College, Massachusetts. Mallika was to go on in future years to found Breakthrough, a global human rights organisation working to end violence against women and girls. Many of our interns went on to be part of women's rights groups all over the world.

Pauline spent much of her time identifying resources and resource groups with whom she could work in PNG. She also created information materials to take back with her. One of her projects while she was with us was to translate and adapt into pidgin language the IWTC slide-tape set 'The Issue is Women', retitling it 'Tok Tok Bilong Ol Meri'. It was the beginning of the development and production of many such materials in PNG after she returned home.

9

'The Invisible Work of IWTC'

Planning for the next UN world conference on women and NGO Forum in 1985 was already underway, and there was a difference in understanding between some members of the Board of Directors and the staff on what part IWTC should play in planning for the Forum '85. The Board President felt that IWTC should be the secretariat for Forum '85. The staff –Vicki Semler, Vicky Mejia, Martita Midence, Joanne Sandler, Vanessa Davis and myself – were cautious about taking on that role. We were deeply immersed in developing and producing essential women and development information materials, and committed to sharing skills in low-cost media, fundraising, project development and proposal writing with women in every world region.

Traditionally, these nongovernmental forums had been organised by a committee of international NGOs in consultative status with the UN and not by any individual NGO. We agreed with this system, and wanted to be able to support such a committee in any way possible, but not by being the secretariat. This caused some angst and disruption between our Board and staff but was finally resolved. We went on to work with and support an appointed committee of international NGOs in the organising of Forum '85, Nairobi for the next two years.

In December of 1983, another major upheaval took place at

IWTC. Our landlords suddenly informed us that they would not be honouring our continuing five-year lease and we would once again have to move. After a search for new office space, we accepted an offer from the Church Centre at the United Nations (CCUN), directly opposite the UN. It could not have been a more perfect location for us. IWTC was proudly secular and had many non-Christian women's organisations amongst its constituency but we were assured that there were other NGOs in the building with no religious affiliations and so accepted the invitation.

It was not an easy move however. With limited space on the 12th floor of CCUN until the 3rd floor became available, most of our equipment and materials had to be stored in a warehouse in New Jersey. It was a move that Vicki Semler directed in my absence since it took place at a time when I needed to fly home to Melbourne to be with my family.

My mother was becoming increasingly frail and had been moved to an aged care facility. A family member was with her every day to make sure she had all she needed. December and January are summer months and school holidays in Australia, and my sisters and brothers all had children. I came home to give them some family camping time and to be with my mother. I was eternally thankful that I had done this as it was to be the last time I was to see her.

After a month with my mother, I met with agencies in Canberra before flying back to New York, with stops in Noumea to spend time with Amelia Rokotuivuna who was working with the South Pacific Commission on a consultancy, in Suva to meet with former YWCA colleagues, in Papeété to stay with Bendt and Marie-Therese Danielsen and discuss anti-nuclear testing activities in the South Pacific, and in Santiago via Easter Island. In Santiago, I stayed with Adriana Santa Cruz, founder and editor of FemPress, a Latin American network of feminist activists. Adriana and I had met at the feminist media conference in Washington DC in April 1982.

While in Santiago, I was able to visit and meet with many other feminist activists in Chile, and to get a better impression of what was happening in that part of the world. I returned to Santiago several times in the years ahead, each time marvelling at the strength and persistence of the opposition to the Pinochet rule and the incredible resourcefulness and energy of Chilean feminists.

Back in New York, much was happening in the new, temporary offices of IWTC. We were being overwhelmed with requests for information materials in the lead up to the next UN world conference on women and NGO forum in Nairobi, July 1985, and work was almost complete on IWTC Working Notes No. 2: Regional Resource Materials for Women: Prospects and Possibilities for Collaboration and No. 3: A Communications Tool for Sharing Information and Skills Related to the Decade for Women.

Funds were coming in from a variety of funding sources: from the Ford Foundation, the American Association for the Advancement of Science, from Canada, Denmark, the Netherlands, and Norway was showing signs of interest. I would be setting off for Vienna soon to attend the UN Commission on the Status of Women's Preparatory Committee (PrepCom) for the UN women's world conference in Nairobi. There were plans for me to travel on to France and Belgium afterwards to meet with development agencies in those countries to try and raise further funds for our French-language proposal.

We were struggling to meet the demands of not only our primary constituency of women in developing countries, but were increasingly being asked for information materials and workshops for the so-called 'developed' countries, e.g. Europe, North America, Australia and New Zealand. Vicki Semler, IWTC's lead staff member on the development and writing of most of our program proposals and reports, presented to the Board a plan for more development education information materials, both visual and written. These would help to inform people in developed countries about the needs and concerns of women in other regions of the world; something that we all felt was desperately needed.

Plans were also formulating around a major activity to be known as 'Tech and Tools', to be undertaken by IWTC at the upcoming Forum '85 in Nairobi. Nita Barrow from Barbados – a long-time friend from the 1960s when she was President of the World YWCA – had been appointed as Convener for Forum '85 and was giving strong support to the project. She had already been in touch with Eddah Gachukia, Chair of the Kenya NGO Forum Organising Committee, who was also very supportive.

'Tech and Tools' was planned as an exhibition of appropriate technologies for women with accompanying demonstrations, workshops and panels involving women from all world regions who had related knowledge and experience. IWTC would be collaborating with the World YWCA in the initial planning stages, specifically with their director of appropriate technologies, Ruth Lechte, my former colleague in the Fiji YWCA. We were soon joined in the planning process by the newly formed Kenya Appropriate Technology Advisory Committee.

In June 1984, after extensive renovations to the 3rd floor space at CCUN, we moved our office there and were to stay for the remainder of the life of IWTC. Following the move, our activities shifted into a higher gear. In quick succession, we developed and published bound volumes of *The Tribune*, each on a specific development issue. We also produced three issues of a new series entitled 'Decade for Women Information Resources' and sent them off to women in every world region.

In August 1984, the midst of all these activities, I received a call from my brother Robert in Melbourne that our mother had died. Even though it was expected, it still came as an enormous shock and I flew home immediately. It was a dramatic trip, with engine failure on the big passenger jet that saw me stranded in Honolulu for hours before another plane could take us on our way to Sydney. I filled the time writing a eulogy for my mother as I had been asked by my siblings to do this. Ethel Walker was so many things to so many people and I worked hard to try and cover all the different facets of the life of that extraordinary woman.

The time at home was hard, but as a family we needed that space in all our lives to be together. I flew back to New York after a week and once again threw myself into the activities of IWTC.

In October of 1984, I was again in the air, flying to Canadian and European funding agencies with the three-year IWTC project proposal for 1984–1987, along with a detailed program report of all IWTC activities for the past year. We were on a major campaign to raise the funds needed to undertake all that was planned for the UN World Conference on Women and Forum '85 in Nairobi, and for all the other important projects that would deliver much-needed development information materials into the hands of women worldwide.

I first flew to Ottawa, to meet with the Canadian International Development Agency (CIDA) and the International Development Research Centre (IDRC). CIDA was considering a request for further funding assistance for our French-language program and IDRC had expressed an interest in our Micro-Computer Networking Workshop proposal. Then on to Oslo, to meet with the Ministry of Foreign Affairs (MFA) and the Ministry of Development Cooperation (MDC). The MFA had set up a special fund for UN Decade for Women activities and we thought the Tech and Tools proposal would interest them and the MDC seemed interested in our general program, which was encouraging.

My next stop was Stockholm, for meetings with Karin Himmelstrand of SIDA. Karin was very supportive of IWTC and promised to present our program proposal for consideration for funding in 1985. Then to The Hague in the Netherlands, for meetings with Laetitia van den Assum and Jose van Hussen at the Ministry of Development Cooperation. It would be true to say that IWTC would not have been still functioning without the support from these women and their colleagues at the MDC in The Netherlands. These development cooperation agencies in Europe were undoubtedly the life-blood of so many women and development organisations in these important years after the UN world conferences on women in Mexico City (1975) and Copenhagen (1980).

On my return to New York I reported to the IWTC Board that the Organisation for Economic Cooperation and Development/ Development Assistance Committee (OECD/DAC) Women and Development Experts Group had called a meeting to discuss how all these donor agencies could collaborate more around the area of women and development. It was to be held in Paris from 28 to 31 January 1985, and I was invited as a resource person. It was agreed that I should attend as it would give us an opportunity to discuss future funding issues that were being faced by all women and development women's groups worldwide.

In November 1984, we held our first Micro-Computer Training Course at IWTC, to share some of our computer learnings with four staff members of international, regional and national women's groups. There would be another training course in January 1985 when four more staff members of women's groups would be coming to New York from regional media networks. We were beginning to see just how important computers could be in our work.

Plans for Tech and Tools, other programs at Forum '85 and the United Nations World Conference on Women were proceeding well and we now had additional staff members. Alice Quinn became our Financial Coordinator and Sonia Mills (Jamaica) our Network Coordinator.

In the lead-up to the meetings in Nairobi, I flew to Halifax, Canada, to be part of a women and peace meeting at St Mary's

University. Women peace activists had gathered from all world regions for discussions leading up to Forum '85, with workshops and meetings planned for the Peace Tent at the Forum.

Nairobi 1985: UN Third World Conference on Women and Forum '85

In 1983, Nita Barrow of Barbados had been chosen as the Convener of the Forum'85 Planning Committee. Her task was to shepherd the many representatives of women's international non-governmental organisations that were part of the UN Decade for Women Committee, through a planning process that would ultimately result in Forum '85 in Nairobi. It was a mammoth undertaking, but Nita Barrow was the right woman at the right time. Nita had been President of the World YWCA for a record eight years and had led this global network of 25 million members into a new era of progressive thinking and policy around racial diversity and program outreach.

Key to Nita's success as Convenor of the Forum '85 Planning Committee was her ability to extend support and encouragement to networks and organizations when they came up with new initiatives and ideas for the forum. She was particularly excited about Tech and Tools. With IWTC and the Forum '85 Planning Committee both situated at CCUN, we were able to closely coordinate all of our activities with those of the other NGOs taking part.

Joanne Sandler and I travelled to Nairobi two weeks ahead of the rest of the IWTC staff, to work with our local Africa staff person, Amina from Ethiopia, and with the Kenya Appropriate Technology Advisory Group, in building the huts and various stands on the sports grounds of the University of Nairobi. The buildings were all to be constructed using only recycled and natural materials.

In the months leading up to the Forum, we had forged close working relationships with not only the Forum '85 Planning Committee in New York and Kenya, but also with Kenyan construction experts and with transport and technology contacts. Even so, it was a mammoth undertaking to set the whole 'Tech and Tools' exhibition up and we spent many late nights struggling with construction and equipment needs and the painting of all the banners needed for each building.

Every day during Forum '85, 'Tech and Tools' was packed with appropriate technology demonstrations, with action panels, with music and dance. Wangari Maathai, later to be awarded a Nobel Peace Prize for her work in environment, development and peace, chose 'Tech and Tools' to set up a plantation of trees with her Green Belt Movement for Women. They were on a mission to plant a million trees across Kenya but far exceeded that target in later years. Ruth Lechte of the World YWCA gave daily demonstrations on how to build smokeless stoves along with other simple technologies for village women. Kenyan women beekeepers made pots of honey and gave them away. Messages were sent out on solar-powered computers. Food was prepared on simple solar-powered stoves. Water conservation techniques and all manner of household saving and burden sharing ideas and technologies were demonstrated. A wheel-along barrel for carrying water was particularly popular.

Forum '85 was above all else an African event, with women from all parts of Africa filling the halls, classrooms, and open spaces at the University of Nairobi. There was a sense of excitement that was palpable as Africans on their home turf met with women from Asia, the Middle East, Europe, North America, the Pacific, the Caribbean and Latin America, and shared experiences in workshops and plenaries. And all joined in occasional, usually spontaneous waves of dancing and singing, adding greatly to the feeling that this was indeed an African event.

The President of Kenya, Daniel Arap Moi, was brought to the 'Tech and Tools' exhibition in the second week of Forum '85. He had been informed by the Kenyan Forum Planning Committee that it was in fact the main Forum, as they were a little anxious that he might disapprove of some of the activities taking place on the main campus (e.g. the display and informal discussion group set up by Lesbian Researchers each morning that was pulling large crowds). Whatever the case, he was delighted with what he saw at 'Tech and Tools' and his visit was broadcast far and wide via radio and TV.

The next day we were almost overwhelmed with people. Busloads of village women began to appear wanting to see smokeless stoves, water pumps, drum ovens, beehives, hand-washing machines, solar ovens and cookers, and all the other things they had heard about on the radio. The end of the day saw women leaving with stoves and solar cookers balanced on their heads as they made their way to waiting buses to take them back to their villages.

In the women's international NGO world, Forum '85 became known as 'the action forum', with a focus on action strategies and appropriate technology that would help to ease the burden on rural women, and provide legal and other human rights for women. Organisations and action networks that evolved from Forum '85 included the international network of Global South feminist scholars and activists known as Development Alternatives for Women in a New Era; the Africa Women, Law and Development Network; the Asia and Pacific Women, Law and Development network, both set up as regional bases of Women, Law and Development International; and the International Women's Rights Action Network originally set up by Arvonne Fraser and based at the Hubert Humphrey Institute at the University of Minnesota.

Across town at the Nairobi Convention Centre in downtown Nairobi, official delegates from every Member State of the UN gathered to discuss the advancement of women, and to follow up on the outcomes of the first and second world conferences on women in Mexico City (1975) and Copenhagen (1980). The official outcome of that conference, under Secretary-General Leticia Shahani of the Philippines, became known as the Forward-Looking Strategies for the Advancement of Women to the Year 2000 (FLS).

An action-oriented document, the FLS was fully supported by NGOs worldwide. Building solidly on the two preceding documents that were the outcomes from the world conferences on women in 1975 and 1980, the FLS outlined strategies for addressing the needs of women in very specific areas.

Back once again at IWTC in New York, we immediately began work on *The Tech and Tools Book*, a manual containing graphics and descriptions of the technologies displayed at Forum '85 and where they could be obtained. *The Tech and Tools Book*, co-sponsored with the Intermediate Technology Development Group in London, was also developed in French. The resulting French edition, entitled *Guide Mondial des Techniques et Outils*, along with *The Tech and Tools Book*, proved to be invaluable as tools for introducing women to technologies created, developed and utilised by women, with a heavy emphasis on food production and processing technologies.

In the year immediately following Nairobi, we created an additional program at IWTC that allowed senior level staff from organisations around the world to come and spend an extended time working with us on sabbatical from their own organisation. The first woman to take up this opportunity was Irene Santiago, a founder of Kayayag Foundation in the Philippines and an active member of the Asian Women's Research and Action Network. During her year with us, Irene made contact with many of the international NGOs who were active at the UN, and went on to become the Convener for the NGO/CSW Planning Committee for the NGO Forum in Beijing in 1995.

We were also able to bring on a French-language consultant,

to work on the preparation of several IWTC publications for translating and adapting into French for African, Asian and South Pacific French-speaking countries.

In December 1985, I participated in a women and development conference at the Rockefeller Foundation Bellagio Conference Centre in Lake Como, Italy. Women leaders from every world region met to discuss strategies for the future of the global women's rights in development movement.

From Lake Como and Milan, I flew to Santiago for three months long service leave. My time in Chile was an opportunity to become more proficient in Spanish now that our Latin America program was growing steadily. I undertook intensive language training with a tutor and did become somewhat more proficient, certainly able to assist with final production of Spanish-language materials, and to converse at a basic level with visitors to IWTC. But most of all, the three months in Santiago was a wonderful time to renew and strengthen friendships, to become more familiar with the work of sister feminist networks such as FemPress and Isis Internacional, and to bask in the sunshine of that beautiful country. I returned refreshed and ready to take on the steady growth in requests for our materials, workshops and consultancies.

Back in New York the external evaluation of the work of IWTC was proceeding. One country from each of five world regions had been selected for the in-country evaluation: Jamaica; Colombia; the Philippines, Zambia and Papua New Guinea. In each country, a national women's organization staff member had been chosen to disseminate the survey forms and undertake interviews as necessary. In addition, a one-page questionnaire had been sent out as an enclosure to all IWTC recipients of the 'Peace is a Women's Issue' edition of *The Tribune*. We were already receiving some of these back and the initial responses were very encouraging.

The questionnaire was being translated into Spanish with some adaptations made in view of the nature of the training and technical assistance activities that had been carried out in Latin America in recent months. Both of these one-page questionnaires and the more in-depth survey forms from the selected countries would all be collated and studied by an outside consultancy firm who would then produce a final overall evaluation of the work of IWTC.

Thankfully, a Resource Coordinator had at last been identified to fill the post held by Martita Midence for almost ten years. And we heard that Vicky Mejia, our Latin America Program Coordinator, was returning to New York in April after living in Paris and then Venezuela with her family. I was able to visit Vicky, John and baby Sara when I stopped for a few days in Caracas on my flight back to New York from Santiago. The Caracas visit was an opportunity for me to experience one of Latin America's most vibrant, and colorful countries. IWTC was preparing for a marketing workshop in Venezuela to be undertaken in collaboration with CESAP, a regional training institute working in the area of women and small business, and I was interested in seeing and meeting women from these communities.

Soon after my return to New York, we undertook a variety of activities with UNIFEM during the Special Session on Africa at the UN. I worked with Grace Jung, IWTC's graphics assistant, on the graphics for several posters and postcards. We also produced a series showing the work of African women farmers and these began to appear throughout the main UN buildings. IWTC co-hosted, with UNIFEM and United Nations African Mothers (an NGO we had worked with over many years), a reception for delegates to the Special Session, along with other international NGOs. Close to 400 participants came to the reception and we were able to spend much time discussing with African delegates and NGOs working in Africa the requests being received by IWTC from African women's organisations and how we could work together on these.

Through all of these events we continued to develop and

produce information materials, including *Images of Nairobi*, a manual of outcomes from Forum '85 and the UN world conference; more issues of our series entitled 'Decade for Women Information Resources'; and an issue of *The Tribune* on 'Women and Funds', with more issues underway on trade unions, food production and housing. All of these areas of interest came from requests received from women in the regions and indicated the range of issues being faced by women everywhere.

In 1987, our activities in Latin America grew substantially, with a business and marketing workshop planned for March in Lima and another workshop planned with women's groups in Uruguay. The Uruguay workshop would this time be in collaboration with GRECMU, a women's research action group in Montevideo. Marketing materials, first developed at a workshop in 1986 co-sponsored by IWTC in Venezuela, would be field-tested and adapted for final production of a training manual on marketing, and two participants at the Venezuelan workshop would be participating at the Lima workshop. Joanne Sandler and Vicky Mejia from our staff were providing the technical expertise for all of these workshops and for the development of the marketing materials and manual. IWTC was building a solid reputation for working alongside women's organisations in several Latin American countries, and our Spanish-language information materials were becoming very popular.

Our African contacts and programs were also expanding, and we were combining our efforts with women's global and regional networking groups whenever possible. One such group was Isis International, and its sister organisation Isis-WICCE (Women's International Cross-Cultural Exchange). Isis-WICCE was currently based in Geneva but soon to transfer to Kampala in Uganda. In 1987, we happily accepted a Zambian intern, Beatrice Chileshe, for three months from that program. We were to have several Isis-WICCE participants with us at IWTC in the coming years.

IWTC was also developing a highly visual community action guide on the *Forward-Looking Strategies for the Advancement of Women to the Year 2000*, the outcomes document from the UN World Conference on Women in Nairobi in 1985. This was part of our vision from the very beginnings of IWTC, to make the most important documents produced by the UN on women's empowerment more readable and useable. We shared some finished pages of the guide, entitled *It's Our Move Now*, with the IWTC Board which represented women from most world regions, some working at the UN, some with other international NGOs or organisations. They became very excited about the guide and began making suggestions. It was clear they wanted this to have a much wider dissemination than with just women's groups.

And so this manual was sent to government Women's Bureaus around the world with a letter suggesting that it be shared with other ministries and departments in each country and region. It was also disseminated to women parliamentarians; members of the Third Committee of the UN Economic and Social Committee, delegates to the UN General Assembly, and all UN Country Missions. It was suggested that the publication be launched in conjunction with the tenth anniversary celebrations of UNIFEM.

During these months, we were also working on developing and producing 'Derechos de la Mujer', the Spanish edition of our booklet on the UN international conventions and treaties related to the rights of women. And we were moving into a new computer age of desktop publishing, transferring our typing, cut and paste skills and hand-drawn graphics onto the screen and onto page layout programs. These were all new skills to be learned, and as we had done in all of our past media training workshops, we shared our new skills with other women's groups, who learned desktop publishing along with us.

On 8 March 1988, we celebrated International Women's Day

(IWD) with a combined reception at our offices in collaboration with the UN Department of Public Information We had taken part in IWD celebrations and marches in other years but this would be our first IWD reception. The invitation list was long. It included all UN Country Missions; women's organisations; UN agencies; the development community; and many NGOs with an interest in development and women's rights.

It was the first of many such receptions at IWTC in the coming years. Women's rights organisations mingled in our space with representatives and delegates from the UN, government officials, NGOs, development, peace, human rights and all manner of other activists groups. It was a place to meet and discuss important and urgent issues in warm and hospitable surroundings. We became widely known as an international focal point for women's rights issues and concerns and a centre for global organising around women, peace, equality and development rights.

We now had two Apple Classic Macs in the office, purchased with funds from our friends and long-time supporters Doris Hess and Rose Catchings from the United Methodist Church, Board of Global Ministries, Women's Division. We named our little computers 'Rosendoris' in honour of these two remarkable women who had worked with and for women in developing countries for decades.

Both Rose and Doris supported our vision of collaborating, co-sponsoring and sharing with other women's groups that had become hallmarks of our activities in these years. IWTC had become a core part of the expanding global women's rights movement, most especially in the development and dissemination of women and development information throughout the world. They especially approved of our efforts to develop UN and other official documents into highly visual, simple language workbooks and manuals.

We were able to maintain these collaborations and co-sponsorships by participating in all manner of outreach programs. In 1987 for instance, along with IWTC co-sponsored workshops in Uruguay and Ecuador, we participated in an international seminar organized by the International Council on Adult Education in Montreal on 'Feminist Challenges to Adult Education' and prepared an annotated bibliography and mounted an exhibit of materials related to women and small business at an OECD/CIDA meeting in Ottawa; I participated in a seminar hosted by the Friedrich Ebert Foundation of Germany on Women and Development and assisted with the final report.

At our own offices, we hosted three informal meetings on housing, one with 6 international participants who had attended a housing conference run by the National Congress for Neighborhood Women, and the others with women from Pakistan and Indonesia who had participated in a Women and Management course at the School for International Training (SIT), Brattleboro, Vermont. The issue of housing was becoming a matter of considerable urgency with women, most especially the need for low cost housing for women and their families, and for the millions of refugees around the world.

A highlight of 1988 was a computer desktop publishing workshop that IWTC undertook for the United Methodist Church in Harare, Zimbabwe. It was undertaken as a personal thanks to the United Methodist Church of the USA who had given the funds for our first Mac computers. They had also given a Mac desktop computer and printer to the staff at this church and now wanted us to assist them in learning how to develop and print their own publications.

While in Zimbabwe, I visited several women's organisations, including the Zimbabwe Women's Resource Centre, the Zimbabwe YWCA and the Zimbabwe offices of UNIFEM. The Director of the Zimbabwe YWCA drove me out to several YWCA rural women's projects, including an early childhood centre in a small village, a solar-powered kitchen producing meals for farm workers and women's craft marketing activities. These in-country experiences were important to all of us at IWTC. They impacted our work in many different ways, most especially in the development and production of workshops and information materials that were appropriate and developed in a participatory way.

Within a month of returning from Zimbabwe, I flew to Europe for another visit to funding agencies in Sweden, Norway, The Netherlands and Finland. I was travelling to these countries much later in the year than usual, and the weather turned very cold and I was not prepared for the blizzard that met me in Stockholm! In fact, with totally unsuitable clothing and no snow boots, I was stuck in the small hotel for some time until the roads became passable for vehicles.

The main purpose of this funding trip was to share some of the results from the IWTC external evaluation with our major donor agencies. It was also to open up talks with FINNIDA, the Finland government development agency. I had not returned to Helsinki since my hitchhiking days back in 1960 and it was great to visit this very beautiful – though very cold – country again. We were hopeful that, in light of the very positive results from the in-depth and lengthy evaluation of our work, they would be interested in funding some of our projects.

It was a disappointing trip in many ways, as the donor agencies had decided that they would all get together in 1989 to strategise around future funding to women's networks and to prepare their own evaluation of women and development project funding. This meant that there would be a halt to all funding until after this meeting.

These European funding trips, although often exhausting, served many purposes in addition to seeking funds for IWTC activities. They were also opportunities to discuss with the women and development staff in each agency, some of the new programs in the regions, particularly newly active women's groups and networks, where resources and support services were most needed. I was always careful not to evaluate or give preference to any specific networks, but to try and give an overview of where things were happening and where support was needed.

In later years, when funding became more and more difficult to find for IWTC activities, many wondered why we had been so generous with our knowledge and support of other women's groups when talking with these donor agencies. But we were always first and foremost a support service to women and development groups in the regions. If they were to become stronger and more financially viable than us, then that would be fine.

In preparing for the next Board meeting, the staff put together some statistics on the work undertaken in 1988. We entitled it 'The Invisible Work of IWTC', and shared some of our findings with our Board at the December meeting. They included 4,000 requests for information during the year; the maintenance of the IWTC mailing list of over 14,000 names (that list was to grow to 28,000 women and women's groups worldwide); meeting with more than 800 individuals and groups from countries around the world; and the hosting of numerous informal gatherings of people and organisations. These activities were all additional to our primary work of running media workshops in the regions, developing and producing women and development manuals, posters, slide-tape sets and *The Tribune* newsletter.

1989 saw many new activities for IWTC. Worldview International Foundation (WIF) in Norway requested that IWTC undertake a two-day low-cost media workshop for representatives from Nepal women's organizations in Nepal in March-April 1989. I flew to Kathmandu to undertake this workshop, and then continued on Bangkok to serve as a resource person for the second of three workshops for the Women's Information Network for Asia and the Pacific (WINAP) at the UN Economic and Social Commission for Asia and the Pacific (ESCAP).

Following the Bangkok workshop, I flew to Kuala Lumpur, where I had been asked to run a four-day workshop with staff members of the Women and Development Office of the Asia and Pacific Development Centre. It was great to see the continuation of the work started in Teheran by Elizabeth Reid.

It was in Kuala Lumpur, that I received a phone call from Vicki Semler informing me that my apartment building in Long Beach, NY, was closed after a fire in one of the apartments. I had moved out of Manhattan just a month before, into my first ever property purchase. Now I had no home in New York. Then began two years of moving from sub-leased apartment to sub-leased apartment, a time when I got to know parts of Manhattan I had never seen before. I lived out of a suitcase, and did more of the overseas workshops and meetings than ever before. I returned to my Long Beach apartment in 1991, and sold it in 1993, moving back to a rental apartment in the East Village.

In 1989, IWTC again organized a reception for International Women's Day, having seen how effective it had been in bringing together the women and development community at the UN the year before. Under the leadership of Vicki Semler, and in conjunction with the Group on Equal Rights for Women at the UN, IWTC hosted over 200 people, representing the UN, international agencies and women's groups in New York. A special poster was produced for the occasion, along with postcards, and these were sent to women's organizations worldwide. Messages and reports came back to us from all over the world of activities being undertaken by other women's groups. International Women's Day was seeing a massive revival.

But the core of our work continued to be the development of media materials, either by us or by the participants in our workshops that would be of use by women in their own countries. Whatever the materials, they had to be in a language appropriate to their needs. We continued to use graphics widely and the feedback we were receiving, both personally and through the ongoing external evaluation, was telling us that graphics were all important. It made an enormous difference for women to see themselves portrayed in a positive way, at work, in their home, in the field, in any professional capacity, and always an important and vital part of their community and the world around them.

Through 1989, we developed and produced issues of *The Tribune* entitled 'Women Using Media to Effect Change', and 'Making Connections: Economics and Women's Lives'. A major achievement was the completion of 'Droits de la Femme', the French version of the IWTC workbook on the rights of women as outlined in major UN and international conventions and declarations. Other issues of *The Tribune* were another one on 'Women and Water' and 'Women and Legal Rights'. A training manual entitled 'Communicating Appropriate Technology with Rural Women' was a much-needed follow-up to our Tech and Tools Book following the Nairobi Forum '85. And the development and production of a marketing manual was a collaborative undertaking with women's groups in Latin America, resulting from a series of workshops undertaken by IWTC over the past three years. This marketing manual was greatly assisted by three women representatives of groups in Ecuador, Peru and Venezuela who came to New York to work with us at IWTC in its final production.

However, in terms of financial stability, these were worrying times. It had become increasingly clear that without a UN World Conference on Women and parallel NGO Forum planned for 1990, donor agencies and UN agencies were not under the same pressure to report on implementation of resolutions passed at previous meetings and had turned their focus elsewhere. It was such an ironic turn of events for IWTC as the now-completed external evaluation of our work over the first ten years of operation (1976–1986) was overwhelmingly positive and supportive of the organisation and its activities.

As an immediate cost-saving measure, we reluctantly decided to reduce the materials produced in French and the time of our part-time personnel. However, we continued developing all the planned materials in English and Spanish, hoping that funds would arrive so that we could go ahead with the final printing and dissemination.

As the year progressed, we began to get word from donor agencies in Canada, Sweden and Norway, and from the Ford Foundation, that funds would be forthcoming. Our fundraising efforts were succeeding! And we were able to complete and disseminate all of the planned materials before the year was out. Such was the roller coaster ride that was our funding status during these years.

In November 1989, I flew out to undertake the final of three workshops on media materials for women's groups with the Economic and Social Commission of Asia and the Pacific (ESCAP), this time with their Pacific Operations Centre in Port Vila, Vanuatu. I flew across the International Date Line on 8 November, arriving in Port Vila on 10 November, completely losing 9 November which was the day the Berlin Wall came down. In listening to the news on my little shortwave radio on the night of 10 November in Port Vila, it took some time for me to completely understand what had happened.

The workshop took place on the Port Vila campus of the University of the South Pacific and was a wonderful opportunity to again meet up with friends and colleagues from the South Pacific. Elizabeth Cox, (known in the Pacific as Sabet), had worked for decades with women's groups in PNG. She worked alongside me as a trainer in low cost media materials on women's issues. Fanaura Kingstone of the Cook Islands was the ESCAP/POC Social Affairs Officer for the whole of the South Pacific and along with her grassroots knowledge of the region, brought music, dance and laughter to the group. Janet Hunt of the Australian Council for Overseas Agencies (ACFOA) gave in-depth analysis of women and development issues, and ways in which support could be given to the groups with whom we were meeting. Together with the 30 women representatives, we developed and produced a wide variety of media materials for use by women's groups across the Pacific.

While on the campus of USP in Port Vila, I discovered the use of satellite communications amongst women in the Pacific. There was a 'downlink' meeting room on campus where representatives of Vanuatu women's groups met and discussed plans and programs with representatives of other women's groups across the Pacific, utilising the PeaceSat satellite taken over by USP when it was no longer of use to the US military. I took part in one of the discussions and marvelled at the ease with which these women communicated verbally across the vast reaches of the Pacific Ocean.

From Vanuatu, I flew down to Melbourne to spend Christmas with my family after quite a long stretch of time away. It was good to see them all again and catch up on what was happening in their lives. I no longer stayed in the 'house across the road' from the school, where Mum had lived and where so many of the family had also lived at various times in our lives but with my sister Frances and her growing family.

Back at IWTC, Vicki Semler undertook a consultancy with the staff of the Centre for Documentation and Information on Women in Jakarta, Indonesia. The focus of the consultancy was in the area of development and production of media materials for use by rural women fieldworkers in Indonesia. IWTC staff was much in demand for consultancies and we were accepting more of them since our financial crisis in 1989. Joanne Sandler participated in a World YWCA workshop on Women and New Technologies in The Netherlands as a leader and rapporteur, and we co-produced a special issue of *The Tribune* as a 52-page manual on this subject. We also were developing more marketing and small business for women in Latin America.

Of great importance during this time was the IWTC internship program, with an intern from India, Sharmila

Ribeiro working with us during the summer and three interns spending three months as part of the Isis-WICCE exchange program. A consultant with UNIFEM, Ipek Illkaracan from Turkey, also worked with Shamila Ribeiro and IWTC staff in organizing the Communication Appropriate Technologies with Rural Women seminar that IWTC ran collaboratively with UNIFEM in July 1990. Out of this seminar came a series of four workshops undertaken in Harare, Zambia (November), in Dakar, Senegal (December), and in Bangkok, Thailand (January 1991) by UNIFEM and IWTC.

Maria Negroni, working with us as a consultant in the Spanish language program, assisted on the next issue of *La Tribuna, 'Mujer et Ley', and* on the development of new Spanish productions, including posters and postcards which were becoming increasingly popular. Maria also represented IWTC at the Fifth Encuentro Feminista for Latin America in Buenos Aires, Argentina, October 1990.

In 1991, IWTC lost two of its long-time staff. Joanne Sandler, IWTC's Special Projects Coordinator was leaving to work as an independent consultant, and Vicky Mejia, IWTC's Latin America Director was moving to Brussels with her husband and daughter. In future years, both were to have distinguished careers, Joanne with UNIFEM (later UN Women), and Vicky as the Colombian Ambassador to Belgium, Germany and Sweden.

Meera Singh joined our staff to take over the Resource Centre and work alongside the IWTC team in all manner of administrative and program matters. We were busy developing and producing an IWTC Women and Development Catalogue, IWTC Brochures in English and Spanish, and developing and producing Issues of *The Tribune* on women's rights, violence against women and women and en vironment in English, Spanish and French.

In early 1991, I flew to Japan, mainly to visit with the staff of JICA (Japanese International Cooperation Agency) and to give a presentation on the work of IWTC in the area of women and development. At IWTC, we had prepared a special slide-tape presentation with a Japanese audio script for the seminar and it was very well received. While in Japan, I also conducted a one-day communications workshop and a one-day seminar at Yokohama Women's Centre for staff and city officials. Meetings were arranged by JICA for me to meet with various government ministries including the Ministry of Women's Affairs, the Ministry of Agriculture, the Ministry of Foreign Affairs and the Ministry of Economic Aid. And I also met with a group of women's organizations.

There was considerable interest in collaborative ventures between IWTC and Japanese women's organisations, including organising a meeting that would include women from developing nations. All expenses would be covered by Japan. I was to return to Japan several more times in the coming years, always received with enthusiasm. Unfortunately however, IWTC was never to receive any funds from the Japanese government. But we did develop close relationships with Japanese feminists and activists.

After the Japan visit, I flew to Australia, spending one day of my time there in Canberra meeting with officials at the Australian International Development Assistance Bureau (AIDAB) and with staff at ACFOA. Amongst NGOs in Canberra, principally those represented on ACFOA, there was some consternation when they discovered that Australia no longer funded any of our South Pacific programs, principally the media and networking workshops, and that we would in fact have to stop undertaking these through lack of funds. ACFOA staff committed themselves to lobby AIDAB on our behalf as they had seen how much the workshops we had conducted had assisted in supporting the work of women's networks in the Pacific.

Throughout all of this, IWTC had continued its work in sharing computer skills with desktop publishing and networking workshops. In 1991, we hosted ten women from women's organizations in Latin America, Africa, the Caribbean, Asia, the Pacific and the Middle East, all with some computer skills and already involved in the publication of newsletters and journals. A Norwegian TV Action program that raised money each year for women's organizations had provided funding for the workshop.

We also collaborated with the Pacific Regional YWCA in the organizing and facilitating of a month-long regional communications workshop in Fiji. IWTC staff member Alice Mastrangelo acted as facilitator and trainer and flew to Fiji to work with the regional Pacific YWCA and the newly formed Pacific Women's Regional Network (PAWORNET). She ran several workshops in low-cost media production, computer skills and networking strategies with the National Information Officers from that network. It was to be our last South Pacific workshop.

IWTC's Women, Ink. marketing service for publications on women and development issues was also progressing well. We had taken this service over from UNIFEM some years earlier, with Alice Quinn in charge. Women, Ink. made it possible for us to get women and development publications from a wide variety of organizations and women writers into the hands of women activists throughout the world.

At this time we saw the beginnings of several new international women's organisations, foremost amongst them a group formed around women and environment issues. Bella Abzug, former US Senator and well-known US political activist, had called together leading women activists from Africa, Asia, the Pacific, Latin America, the Caribbean, Europe and North America to form an International Policy Action Committee (IPAC). The purpose was to plan for an international meeting to discuss a women's environmental agenda that could provide a much-needed gender perspective to Agenda 21, the policy document that would to come out of the UN Conference on

Environmental Development (UNCED), to be held in Rio de Janeiro, 1992. IWTC had become the initial meeting place for this new organisation which, by the time the meeting, entitled 'Women for a Healthy Planet', was held in Miami November 1991 had become the Women, Environment and Development Organisation (WEDO).

This role as initial meeting place was an early service of IWTC, in recognition of the need to provide structural support to fledgling groups if they were to have a chance of surviving. Other groups who used IWTC as an organizing start-off point were Development Alternatives for Women in a New Era (DAWN) and SAKHI – a South Asian women's support group based in New York.

Bella added many valuable political strategising skills to the activities that took place in Miami, and IWTC and many women's networks around the world were the beneficiaries. There's no doubt that our planning around advocacy and lobbying activities would be far more effective in the years to come, especially at the world conferences being organised by the UN through the 1990s.

But IWTC was not only engaged in preparations for UN world conferences. We welcomed more summer interns from Thailand, India, Turkey and Colombia. We continued with our development of information materials, including an issue of *The Tribune* on 'Violence Against Women: Invisible Barriers to Development', in English, Spanish and French, and a special issue for the Miami women and environment conference on 'Women and Environment' that became a valuable information tool for all participants.

Amongst the most important conferences during this time were the AWID International Conferences, held every three years. These conferences brought women together from around the world regularly, filling the ten-year gap between Nairobi 1985 and the planned meetings to be held in Beijing 1995.

Alongside our workshops, the outside conferences, the preparations for UN World Conferences and NGO Forum, the visits of UN staff, European development agencies, women from every world region, nothing ever stopped the development and production of information materials. We were all kept busy with the research, writing and graphics needed for every publication. Women from every world region were sending us copies of their own materials, many of them full of IWTC graphics. This always pleased me as it meant the drawings were indeed reflecting their realities.

Once we had fleshed out an issue, work would begin on translating often very difficult professional language into what we termed 'spoken language'. Finally would come the graphics and the final layout. The whole process took many days, nights and weekends.

UN World Conferences in the 1990s

The first of the UN world conferences in the 1990s was the UN Conference on Environment and Development (UNCED) in Rio de Janeiro in 1992. IWTC had been asked to organise a day of activities on information and education regarding environment as part of a 12-day series of events to take place in the Women's Tent at the Global Forum, the non-governmental meeting to be held parallel to the world conference. The request came from a coalition of women's organisations in Brazil who were asking several international and regional organisations to each coordinate one day of activities on a specific issue.

This coalition of environmental activists was just one of many feminist activist groups forging a more decentralised and equal partnership around other emerging issuesff that included women's human rights, violence against women, women in armed conflict situations, peace, and equal access to information. Amongst the many women leaders of this movement was Charlotte Bunch, now the Director of the

Center for Women's Global Leadership (CWGL) at Rutgers University in New Jersey. CWGL brought together women leaders from every world region each summer to work on strategies for action around women's rights issues.

It was from one of these annual global seminars that the idea for 'Sixteen Days of Activism Against Gender Violence' was born. From 25 November (International Day for the Elimination of Violence Against Women) to 10 December (International Human Rights Day) 1991, IWTC would join forces with CWGL in organizing a rally Against Violence Against Women. Large banners were prepared and a wide variety of speakers, exhibitors, supporters and press would gather at CCUN and at Dag Hammarsjkold Plaza opposite the UN. Demonstrations of self-defence and poetry readings by women activists would be highlights of each demonstration. The '16 Days if Activism Against Gender Violence' is now held every year across the world with millions of women taking part.

In 1992, following the Expert Group Meeting of representatives from the International Fund for Agricultural Development (IFAD) in Fiuggi, Italy the year before, I participated as a Resource Person in the International Conference on Nutrition in Rome. At this conference, First Ladies from developing countries met to discuss a program to combat poverty in their countries. With women and poverty a core issue from the very beginnings of IWTC, and with our long-term focus on food, agriculture, appropriate technologies and labour saving devices for women, I felt the meeting would be a valuable way to find out what international agencies were planning to combat these root causes of poverty.

It was a meeting that felt surrealistic in many ways, held as it was in a magnificent palace complete with marble floors, crystal chandeliers, satin drapes, exquisitely woven and expensive tapestry-covered seats. One sumptuous feast followed another. All this luxury and grandeur jarred with the stories of extreme poverty from the developing country delegates.

I was therefore happy to continue on afterwards to Turkey, where my brother Robert was teaching. He took me on a train trip deep into the Turkish countryside where we stayed with friends of his in the small village of Sultanhisar. Here, I was able to meet and talk with several women and get a much better idea of the problems and issues that rural women in that part of the world face.

Back in New York, we were busy planning for the next world conference, the International Conference on Human Rights in Vienna, 1993. IWTC, in collaboration with CWGL, had begun the process of collecting what we hoped would be tens of thousands of signatures of women worldwide on a petition to be presented to the UN Secretary-General. The petition, asking for violence against women to be included as a Human Rights Violation in the UN Declaration on Human Rights, was sent by mail and through the IWTC Global FaxNet. Piles of faxes piled up on the floor of the IWTC offices to greet us on arrival each morning. Some petitions were signed with thumbprints, others were translated by local women's groups into languages we had never seen or heard of before. In the end, the petition gathered 500,000 signatures, the first 75,000 of which were wheeled across to the UN from IWTC in a wheelbarrow, and presented to the President of the General Assembly.

In 1992, we responded to a request from UNFPA for IWTC assistance with a workshop with family planning personnel in Sarajevo. Vicki Semler, who had done extensive research on the subject of family planning communications for her doctoral dissertation at Indiana University, agreed to undertake the workshop. We were all somewhat anxious to say the least, as we had been reading of the civil unrest in that part of the world and feared for Vicki's safety. But after assurances from UNFPA, she flew to Sarajevo, where she spent a week with the women there, running a very successful workshop and forming many close friendships.

So it was with intense concern we began to hear of the terrible violence that had broken out there soon after Vicki's return. We began to receive faxes from women's groups in Sarajevo and Zagreb telling us of the horrific 'rape camps' and the gross violations of women's human rights taking place. We notified mass media outlets, which initially took little interest. But soon it became general knowledge. IWTC staff marched with thousands of others in the streets of New York City and gathered in Dag Hammarskjold Plaza to protest and try to raise the level of alarm at the UN.

In the three years leading up to the human rights world conference in Vienna, we had been working closely with CWGL and many regional women's human rights groups to get women's rights issues on the agenda at the UN International Conference on Human Rights. Using fax networks extensively, information was being shared with women activists everywhere. Tribunals were being held in each world region with women giving testimony to gross violations against their rights. Each region was selecting representatives who would come to Vienna to give their testimony before thousands at a Global Tribunal on Women's Human Rights.

To these women's human rights testifiers were added representatives from the women's activist groups in Croatia and Bosnia Herzegovina who had contacted us. They came to Vienna and lay down across the entrance to the World Conference on the first day forcing the arriving delegates to step over them. And that picture reached the world's press, bringing added force to their appeals for justice and compensation.

We were also planning a major exhibition area at the conference to be known as The Rights Place for Women. Alongside would be the hall where the Global Tribunal on Women's Human Rights was to be held. Tribunals had been held in every world region and women's rights testifiers from each of those were being brought to Vienna for the Global Tribunal. Meera Singh and I would represent IWTC and run the Rights Place for Women with the support of Isis International (Manila and Santiago). With many other groups, we would be displaying a wide range of women's rights materials and activities. Workshops and panels were planned for each day. It would be a major meeting place for women.

The Global Tribunal on Women's Human Rights was a major triumph. A panel of experts heard testimonies in five categories: human rights abuse in the family; war crimes against women; violations of bodily integrity; socio-economic rights; and political persecution and discrimination. The women who testified were from every world region. Delegates came and went from the upstairs official conference as word spread about the stories being told. Hundreds of people were crushed into the hall; it was standing room only.

That day at the International Conference on Human Rights became known as the Women's Human Rights Day. A feature of the day on the main floor was when the remaining hundreds of thousands of names on the worldwide petition were dramatically wheeled onstage and officially presented to the delegates during a plenary session.

The Rights Place for Women, undertaken by IWTC and Isis International, was also an outstanding success. There were many frightening moments however, when some anti-human rights activists attempted to intimidate women tribunal testifiers from their countries. Women human rights activists joined forces with Vienna security forces to give these women protection.

10

All roads lead to Beijing

The year before Beijing saw another revolution of sorts take place in the global women's movement. We had initiated a small fax network of 28 women's media groups following a DAWN/IWTC meeting of women's media networks in Barbados in 1993. This fax network had proven to be extremely useful as an immediate way of communication and we had expanded it when we sent out petitions on women's human rights prior to the Vienna human rights conference.

We needed urgently to keep women informed about the plans and preparations being made by both the United Nations and the NGO Committee on the Status of Women (New York and Geneva), through the recently set up NGO Forum '95 office. We were already providing a variety of services to help build the infrastructure for this NGO official planning team. Our support included access to copies of relevant IWTC mailing lists and databases, equipment, business contacts for printers, mailers, distributors, media contacts; and we offered space for informal meetings and facilitated meetings as needed.

At IWTC, we had new staff members to help us with all our preparations and plans. Rosemary Kalapurakal from India was with Women, Ink. Joan Ross Frankson from Jamaica was working on the Once and Future Pavilion exhibits and events. Pauline Tamesis from the Philippines was handling the mailing list and much of the administrative logistics,

Tina Jorgensen from Trinidad and Tobago was assisting with layout and design of information materials, Laurel Douglas had joined the graphics team to ease some of that load, and Stephanie Banuelos and Lourdes Vasquez were assisting with administration and Spanish language materials. Additional part-time staff supported the team in logistics, bookkeeping, handling visitors and much more. These included Maria Angeles Molinero Roldan, Karen Bishop, Meera Singh, Carminia Avecilla, Chi Kwok, Sima Saran, Monica Mehta and Maria Negroni. It was the largest the IWTC team had ever been.

In 1994, Alice Mastrangelo and I flew to Bangkok for a women and media conference called Women Empowering Communications, organised by IWTC, Isis International (Manila) and the World Association for Christian Communication (London). This important meeting brought together more than 400 media women to strategise for collective action on media issues at the 1995 UN Fourth World Conference on Women. The final document was entitled The Bangkok Declaration: Women Empowering Communication and it was to serve as the basis for our intervention at a UNESCO meeting on women and media, also held that year, out of which came the UNESCO Toronto Platform on Women and the Media. All of this activity came about following the inclusion of Women and Media as one of the 12 Critical Areas of Concern in the upcoming Beijing Platform for Action.

I continued on from Bangkok to Manila for the UN Asia and Pacific women and development conference, the regional meeting held in preparation for the 1995 Beijing NGO Forum. From Manila on to Beijing to speak at a women's seminar at Peking University and to take the opportunity to tour the Workers Stadium and surrounds where the NGO Forum was due to be held in July 1995.

On my return to New York, I drew up maps of the Beijing Workers Stadium and surrounds to let women know what the possibilities were for workshops and activities that they might be planning. We prepared special issues of *The Tribune* and introduced a new occasional newsletter called Preview '95 along with other graphic materials and sent them out by mail and via the new faxnet. All seemed to be progressing well and we were excited by the possibilities. It was especially reassuring to know that the planned location for the NGO Forum was within easy access of the official UN Fourth World Conference on Women.

So there was great consternation when the news arrived in March 1995 that the Chinese Government had decided to move the NGO Forum out of Beijing to Huairou, a town 40 miles away. The news came at the final UN Preparatory Committee (PrepCom) before Beijing, held at UN headquarters in New York. At IWTC, we sent the news immediately to women's media networks in every region via our expanding fax network. They in turn sent the news to their local and national networks. We knew that by throwing the non-governmental forum 40 miles out of town, the Chinese Government had, with one sweeping action, removed NGO women from close proximity to the UN World Conference on Women, thereby limiting our ability to lobby and advocate on a daily basis.

The morning after the news had been faxed worldwide to media networks, IWTC was flooded with letters demanding action. We developed a suggested letter of protest with the fax numbers of the UN Secretary-General in New York and the China Organising Committee in Beijing and this was faxed out.

Within 24 hours, hundreds of copies of protest faxes were pouring into our office. We placed them into a large binder, and Joan Ross Frankson and I carried the binder across the road from the IWTC office to the UN PrepCom and personally handed them to Gertrude Mongella (Tanzania), the Chairwoman of the UN Fourth World Conference on Women and therefore also of the PrepCom. She met with us and listened to our concerns, expressing sympathy with what had happened.

Our IWTC fax network grew and grew. Women in every region found themselves contacted by their local media requesting that they be added to the network. Did we achieve our goal of remaining at the Workers' Stadium in Beijing? No we did not. But we did make the UN and the Government of China sit up and take notice of the fact that women are a force with which to reckon. It was clearly an enormous surprise to find that we could organise and mobilise women in so many countries with such speed and solidarity.

Then the problems around visas began, especially for representatives from NGO groups in countries not officially Member States of the UN, such as Tibet, Taiwan and Hong Kong. There were also NGO groups of which the Chinese government did not approve. All of these women had intense difficulties in finding accommodation in and around Beijing and Huairou. IWTC became the last hope for many struggling to cope with all these bureaucratic difficulties.

The titles of some of those faxes that circled the world in the months leading up to the Beijing meetings in August–September 1995, tell their own story. They included: 'Petition and Urgent Appeal to the United Nations and the Government of China re Forum site change', 'Campaign Update to Petition Signing Groups', 'Follow-Up Action to Forum Site Change', 'NGO Facilitating Committee Rejects Huairou Site', 'Government's Rally Behind NGOs', 'Call to Secretary General of the UN to Take a Stand on Behalf of NGOs', 'Activists Pressure Tactics for New Beijing Forum Site Start Paying Off', 'UN Under Secretary General Goes to China for Last Minute Negotiations Over Site', and finally 'Organizers Gain Major Concessions for NGO Forum'. As the fax network grew, we formally renamed it IWTC Global Women's FaxNet.

Of course, what all of these faxnet titles do not say is the ways in which we had to get around the increasingly bureaucratic and impossible obstacles being placed before women everywhere. At one point, I took my own hotel and visa application forms, copied them, whited out my details, then copied them again and sent them to women in countries where they were just not available. Yes, it caused difficulties in Beijing and we had to double up on hotel rooms, but we did help to get 35,000 women and some men to the NGO Forum in Beijing. It also meant we IWTC staff members were met at Beijing airport by security officers and thoroughly searched before we were escorted to our place of residence, miles away from the Huairou township and Forum grounds.

Meanwhile, back at our offices in New York, the fax machine was breaking down. We needed to find a new way to reach women quickly and effectively. So we turned to the newly emerging world of e-mail and set up the IWTC Global WomeNet. Within a month, the IWTC Global Women's FaxNet and IWTC Global Womenet lists had grown to 1,500 groups and individuals. It was obvious that a whole new way of communicating had arrived.

Beijing 1995: UN Fourth World Conference on Women and NGO Forum

The UN Fourth World Conference and NGO Forum drew 50,000 women and men. Never before had there been a UN meeting of this size. The NGO Forum alone attracted 35,000 participants who came to take part in what was largely seen as a once-in-a-lifetime opportunity to gather, organise, strategise, and mobilise.

IWTC, in collaboration with the World YWCA and the Intermediate Technology Development Group and working with a coalition of more than 60 women's science and technology groups from around the world, undertook a major program at the NGO Forum, housed in what we called the Once and Future Pavilion.

It was not an easy task preparing and running the pavilion. We found the building allotted to us in a far corner of the Huairou compound, piled to the ceiling with rubbish. It was a backbreaking task clearing it all out and it meant missing the extravagant opening ceremony put on by the Chinese government at a stadium in Beijing. Because we were billeted far out of town, it also meant very early starts to each day and much transporting of books and supplies in suitcases from the buses that dropped us each morning at the front gates.

The Once and Future Pavilion featured an Alternative Media Space; the Women, Ink. Bookstore of women and development materials; the Beneath Paradise exhibition put on by Pacific women; appropriate technology exhibits; science and technology demonstrations; radio skills workshops, and much more. Women from every region came and shared their discoveries, their publications and writings, their hopes and dreams for the future.

Next door to the Once and Future Pavilion was the Media and Communications Centre, organised and run by the Association for Progressive Communications/Women's Networking Support Program. There, women learned about the Internet, most of them for the first time, and discovered e-mail and the World Wide Web. In fact, it was from the Media Centre that I was able to type up editions of the IWTC Global Women's Faxnet and Women's GlobalNet each morning, and email them back to the New York office for sending out to our networks. These two technology pavilions with their discussion groups, exhibits, training and workshops were to change the face of women's communications in the years to come. Thousands of women passed through the doors and tried their hand at learning new skills.

I stayed on for the last week of the UN Fourth World Conference following the NGO Forum, moving from our rather spartan Huairou accommodations into a comfortable Beijing hotel. At the official conference, I joined forces with several NGO task forces lobbying to get action statements and resolutions into the final Platform for Action, the resulting document to come out of the conference. Issues for which we were advocating, in addition to strengthening the women and media section, included actions on behalf of women's human rights and reproductive rights, against violence against women, protections for women living in conflict areas, recognising rape as a war crime, women to be included in peace negotiations, and women, science and technology. I met and discussed these issues with government delegates from Australia and Fiji amongst many others.

The Australian government delegation had come to the conference with a plan to focus on one specific issue so that they could get maximum benefit from specific funding and government support. The issue selected was the fight against domestic violence and the need for prevention activities and refuges for women and children facing violence. Australia led the way in championing one major issue while supporting the whole Platform. They encouraged each member state to choose a pressing issue in their own country and do the same.

11

The years after Beijing 1995 for IWTC

Out of the conference in Beijing came the Beijing Platform for Action (BPFA), a document that owed more to the activities, advocacy and lobbying of the global women's movement than any previous UN document. Women's media activists played an important role in first getting Women and Media as one of the twelve Critical Areas of Concern in the PFA, and then in working tirelessly on the resolutions and actions within that area.

At Beijing, activists for the other eleven critical areas of concern also worked hard to make sure the very real demands of women would be heard and included in the BPFA. Because of this, and with the feeling that this document was indeed the result of their own lobbying and advocacy, women played an enormous role in monitoring and measuring its implementation.

The IWTC Women's GlobalNet became an increasingly valuable tool in the sharing of Beijing Platform for Action information, and its outreach steadily grew as more and more women and women's groups became part of the newly emerging electronic networks. Immediately following the Beijing conference, the IWTC network grew to include 3,000 'multiplier' groups, each group sending material on to their own networks in every region. At one point it was estimated that the IWTC Women's GlobalNet was reaching tens of thousands of women activists, all in a matter of seconds. This ability to reach women with breaking news, almost instantaneously, was a dramatic change in the way women organised and strategised.

IWTC however continued to develop and produce simple, highly graphic workbooks and manuals, deeply conscious of the fact that the vast majority of the world's women, especially those in rural and low-income areas, did not have access to computers and the internet, and probably would not have that access for many years to come. Out of the Beijing meetings we produced Platform for Action workbooks, slide-tape presentations, and *The Tribune* newsletters, focusing on important women and development issues and the importance of the PFA within each world region. As much as possible, *The Tribune* continued to be produced in English, Spanish and French.

Another advantage of the new digital age was our ability to have a computerised mailing list of 26,000 individuals and groups, simplifying things enormously. We now had a method of sending *The Tribune* and other IWTC publications to global regional mailing points, bypassing New York's Grand Central Post Office where there had been many delays in the past. From these regional points, the publications were mailed to individual addresses. This did sometimes cause some confusion, with our regional, national and local constituencies believing IWTC had moved out of New York! In Australia for instance, IWTC publications arrived with a Hong Kong postmark. In Africa, they were postmarked Paris.

In 1995, the 50th Anniversary of the United Nations, IWTC was honored to receive the *We The Peoples: 50 Communities Award* in recognition of our contribution to 'creating common unity'. Sponsored by the Friends of the United Nations, the purpose of these awards was to identify and document models that demonstrate success in areas important to the United Nations' agenda and that bring forward the practical experience of innovative communities and citizen's initiatives from around the world. The Award was overseen by an independent International Panel of Advisors, co-chaired by Dame Nita Barrow, now Governor-General of Barbados, and Dr. Pierre Marc Johnson, former Premier of Quebec, Canada. It was presented to IWTC at an Awards Ceremony at the Cathedral of St John the Divine in New York City, 24 September 1995.

In September 1996, IWTC celebrated the launching of its twentieth year of working with women around the world. For two decades we had been involved in the building of networks of support for women and community activists fighting for justice, equality, peace and sustainable development in their countries and regions. We celebrated the expansion of our information networking with new information technologies that meant we could now reach tens of thousands of women in the blink of an eye. We shared these experiences through publications and workshops, and expanded the outreach of our Women, Ink. publications marketing service. The outreach of Women, Ink. publications marketing service was also supplemented with a workshop for African women writers and publishers at the Zimbabwe International Book Fair in collaboration with Kali for Women (India).

IWTC also participated in the Association for Women in Development's Seventh International Forum 'Beyond Beijing: From Words to Action' in Washington, DC. As a collaborating partner of AWID, IWTC helped develop the program, assisted in publicising the event and facilitated the participation of representatives of key women's organisations from the Global South. We also assisted the expansion of information technology expertise amongst women' groups with a cyber café computer centre and electronic outreach workshops.

IWTC took part in two panels at the AWID Forum. The first

one entitled 'Information and Power' explored women's use of communication techniques and tools for empowerment and brought women involved in popular education and participatory media at community level in Jamaica, Uruguay and Papua New Guinea to take part.

Following the AWID forum, IWTC undertook a three-day consultation on popular education and participatory media with these three media specialists. The second panel, 'Scientific Literacy: New challenges, approaches, programs' brought together educators from Ghana, Malawi, the US, Trinidad and Tobago and India to explore innovative programmes that challenged perceptions of science and technology and redefined literacy.

As at previous AWID forums, Women, Ink. ran a bookstall and sold women and development publications. The Women, Ink. bookstall was always a wonderful way to meet women from every world region and find out more about what women were involved with in their own countries.

Back in New York, IWTC co-sponsored, with the UN Department of Public Information and the UN Division for the Advancement of Women, an event called 'One Year After Beijing' in which over 1,000 people participated. We took the opportunity to celebrate our own 20th anniversary at a reception held in conjunction with this event, and honoured nine women from international NGOs who had worked on furthering women's rights issues at the UN for 50 years. We called it our 20/50 celebration. It was important to us that these women be recognised for the work they had done over five decades, recognition frequently ignored when awards are handed out. IWTC's original Board members, Mildred Persinger and Rosalind Harris, were among the nine women honored that day. When the UN Secretary General, Boutros Boutros-Ghali, heard of the event, he provided bound volumes on the history of the United Nations, each personally signed by him, to be presented to the nine women.

As much as possible during these years, IWTC staff continued our active participation on several boards and management committees outside of the work at IWTC, as part of our ongoing efforts to collaborate wherever possible with other women and development groups. I was elected to the Board of AWID that met in Washington, DC, and was made Chair of the Board of Isis-WICCE in Kampala. I was also designated Chair of the Working Group on Information Dissemination, Telecommunications Content Development and Awareness Raising, one of the six working groups of the International Telecommunications Union (ITU) Gender Task Force in Geneva. And I flew to the Philippines for a week of Isis International board meetings in Manila each year, usually staying on the top floor of the Isis meeting-house built in a suburb of Manila.

We were increasingly being consulted about issues and concerns relating to serious transition situations being encountered in many international women's organisations. Frequently, the problems were connected with the workload faced by small, dedicated teams of women who had seen their activities grow and expand in ways not anticipated when they began. Sometimes this situation had been caused by the intense activity during the years leading up to the Beijing meetings, and the feeling of exhaustion and lack of focus in the year after Beijing. We at IWTC could empathise with their problems, and worked hard to find ways in which to support them.

The years after the 1995 Beijing meetings had seen a dramatic drop in finances at IWTC and a subsequent downsizing of the organisation. From a program staff of twelve at the time of the Beijing meetings, we were now operating with only six staff. The need to collaborate with media groups worldwide in the production and dissemination of information was therefore paramount.

New staff had joined our team as former staff had left to take up other positions. Leonora Wiener became publications editor, Yolande Hatiye-Atwater was now our part time bookkeeper and Tina Johnson acted as part time layout and design expert for Women, Ink. The core management team remained myself, Vicki Semler, Alice Quinn and Vanessa Davis

As global media networking grew and developed, it became clear that many of us who had been working closely together for years needed to come up with bolder strategies for the future, utilising the new technologies now available. With this in mind, in 1998, following the second Know How Conference on Women's Knowledge held at the International Archives for the Women's Movement (IIAV) in Amsterdam, IWTC organised a meeting with the three Isis groups that were the result of the work of Jane Cottingham and Marilee Karl, the founders of Isis International in 1974. (Isis took its name from Isis, the ancient mother goddess, who symbolises creativity, knowledge and women's power.)

Over the years, IWTC and the Isis networks had worked together closely to develop strategies to reach out to women activists wherever they were. We recognised that in many ways we were the glue that had held the movement together through these 24 years of world conferences and forums, and we needed to combine our efforts in a more strategic and productive way.

Isis International was now set up as three autonomous organisations working out of three world regions: Isis International in Manila, servicing both the Asia/Pacific region and the world; Isis Internaçional in Santiago, servicing the Latin American region; and Isis WICCE (Women's International Cross Cultural Exchange) in Kampala, which brought together an international group of women every two years to develop skills and expertise in a specific issue area. After three intense days of meetings in Amsterdam, we came up with a Women's Global NGO Communications Plan of Action that combined and supported the strengths of each of the four networks. This plan became the basis for an expanded project that emerged six months later.

During these years, IWTC's work in the human rights arena was more and more focusing on the issue of women and armed conflict. In the 1997-1998 program year, we served as co-convener of the NGO Status of Women Task Force on Women and Armed Conflict for the 42nd session of the UN Commission on the Status of Women. As part of The Hague Appeal for Peace Gender Task Force, we collaborated with Women's International League for Peace and Freedom in 'Raise Your Hands or Peace' at the Hague Appeal for Peace convention in The Hague, May 1999. This major event transformed the convention hall meeting areas with women's peace messages from more than 500 women in 32 countries. The messages were mounted onto large, brightly colored hand cut outs and placed on long sticks in flowerpots. In this way, women who could not be present at the negotiations and meetings could make their presence felt through words of peace.

We also participated in a campaign to get more women involved in peace negotiations in areas of armed conflict and internal disorder. 'From the Village Council to the Negotiating Table' was initially organised by International Alert (UK) and was a worldwide effort that became very much a part of our strategising and information outreach. These activities all became part of a more focused campaign to get a women and peace resolution passed at the UN Security Council. WILPF, IWTC and several other NGO women's organisations formed a group known as the NGO Working Group on Women, Peace and Security.

Meeting regularly at IWTC, the NGO Working Group focused its efforts initially on bringing women who were involved in peace activities in their own countries to New York to testify before the Security Council. With the support of UNIFEM, the lead UN agency working with the NGO Working Group on this project, we were able to do this. Never before had grassroots women activists stood before the UN

Security Council to speak, and certainly never before had women talked of gender-based violence, situations of rape being used as a tool of war, and other extreme violations of women's human rights during conflict situations at a Security Council session.

United Nations Security Council Resolution 1325 on women, peace and security was adopted unanimously by the UN Security Council on 31 October 2000. It was the first formal and legal document from the Security Council that required parties in conflict to prevent violations of women's rights, to support women's participation in peace negotiations and on post-conflict reconstruction, and to protect women and girls from sexual and gender-based violence in armed conflict. The resolution has since become an organising framework for the women, peace, and security agenda.

In March 1999, for use at the first UN/CSW Preparatory Committee for the planned UN Beijing Plus Five meeting in 2000, IWTC prepared a pocket guide called 'CSW '99 Book of Days'. It consisted of 62 pages of UN official meetings and names of delegates, NGO task forces, groups convening meetings, resources available, workshops and other events. It was laid out giving equal space and appropriate graphics for UN and NGO information. On one side of each double page spread we listed the official UN meetings; on the other page NGO activities. We wanted the official delegates to give NGOs equal consideration and to see some action on implementation of all the resolutions and actions agreed to in Beijing.

As part of these efforts, a group of women's media groups got together to discuss ways of improving communication outreach among women involved in plans and preparations for Beijing Plus Five. We recognised that governments around the world appeared to be losing interest in women's rights and the momentum gathered over 25 years of activism needed some serious strategising.

Out of these meetings came WomenAction 2000 (WA2000),

an NGO Women's Global Communications Network. WA2000 undertook a workshop in October 1999 at the SookMyung Women's University in Seoul, Korea. Forty young women gathered on this beautiful campus to strategise, learn new skills, and discuss ways to inform, communicate and train media networks in women and development issues and concerns. We were serious about women's human rights and wanted action at government and NGO levels.

Led by trainers from APC Women's Network Support Group, IWTC, Isis International (Manila), IIAV (Amsterdam) and SookMyung University, we learnt about web construction and regional online dialogue facilitation, how to build networks, and most importantly, how to train a new generation of women media professionals who would work together with us in informing the world of women about the Beijing Platform for Action and the urgent need to see its actions implemented. All of us returned home to our regions to train others. Within the space of a year, a dynamic, interactive network was formed, beginning with a global website and regional websites in Africa, Asia/Pacific, Latin America/Caribbean, Europe and North America.

At IWTC, while enthusiastically supporting the construction of websites and online dialogues around issue areas, we were still very aware of the fact that most women in the world did not have access to the Internet. We continued to focus our efforts on repackaging workshops and skills training into easy-to-access manuals and workbooks which were developed as print materials. We uploaded many of these print materials onto the newly developed IWTC website so that those with access could download the information and make it accessible for those without access.

We remained committed to working with low-income and rural women in the Global South as we had throughout the three decades of IWTC's existence. These grassroots women were challenging the status quo in their struggle to create viable communities and we had worked hard to build a complex communication infrastructure as well as a solid set of working relationships with their networks and organisations. Throughout, we sought to function as a supportive practical task force for groups fighting to bring change on the frontlines.

At the Beijing Plus Five UN General Assembly Special Session in June 2000, WomenAction 2000 undertook an unprecedented level of media activities, including two daily newspapers – one with a focus on Africa; an Internet café where women could keep in contact with their groups back home; webcasts for radio and TV, and a daily media caucus. The two daily newspapers were uploaded to the web and used by regional focal points, which printed and disseminated them locally and nationally.

A Global Media Project brought 20 women writers from every world region, sharing journalism and other media skills. The group sent daily articles on the UN Beijing Plus Five Special Session back to their home papers. All of these activities were mainly organised on the Internet via e-mail conferences, list-serves and one-on-one online dialogues. There was also a good amount of print and graphic material developed and disseminated. The complexity and degree of detail needed for each activity gave added credibility to the notion that the world of women's organising had been dramatically strengthened and changed with the coming of the Internet and the subsequent global growth of women's media networks.

Alongside the WomenAction 2000's activities at the Church Centre in New York, the Communications Consortium Media Centre (CCMC) out of Washington DC also set up an action base. CCMC disseminated daily press releases and set up interviews for newspapers, TV and radio reporters. Their summary of global media reports, alongside the activities of WomenAction 2000, showed a level of reporting from Beijing Plus Five far above any seen previously.

Out of Beijing Plus Five came an Outcomes Document, which was intended to review, strengthen and expand efforts to implement the actions called for in the Platform for Action developed out of the Beijing meetings. There were mixed feelings as to whether this goal was achieved. A concerted effort by religious fundamentalists to move back the gains made in Beijing had been launched at this Special Session, with more than 300 right-wing activists lobbying to have PFA paragraphs withdrawn. This was especially the case with groups opposed to actions agreed to in the PFA on issues such as reproductive rights, inheritance rights, and the more inclusive definitions of family.

Women activists became increasingly concerned that if the BPFA were to be opened up and revisited, there would be losses of hard-won women's rights. This led to a strong campaign by NGOs that actively resisted any such suggestion. To combat some of the well-funded campaign mounted by the right-wing activists, who had arrived with glossy brochures and professionally produced buttons and banners, women's groups gathered each morning at IWTC to handprint banners, badges, brochures and other handouts in preparation for each day of lobbying and advocacy.

The Beijing PFA, after extensive discussion, was not reopened. This meant that other issues that we felt were important, and that had been left out of the Beijing document, could not be added. These included issues surrounding the rights of the Lesbian, Gay, Bisexual, Transgender and Intersex (LGBTI) community; climate change and other environmental crises affecting women's lives directly; rape as a war crime, and more, all needing to be strengthened and broadened in the original BPFA. But overall, it was more important at the time to stop the attempts of religious fundamentalists to undercut hard-won gains.

One significant response to the UN Beijing Plus Five Outcomes Document came from the NGO Linkage Caucus, which met daily throughout the Special Session to combine the efforts of the task forces and caucuses on each critical area of concern. This is the final statement from this caucus:

> While there have been positive aspects to this review process, we want to register our disappointment with the Outcomes Document agreed to by governments at the United Nations today.
>
> We appreciate the hard work that many have put into this process and applaud those delegations that have fought to defend and advance commitments to women. However, we regret that there was not enough political will on the part of some governments and the UN system to agree on a stronger document with more concrete benchmarks, numerical goals, time bound targets, indicators, and resources aimed at implementing the Beijing Platform for Action.
>
> It is women's movements that have placed women's empowerment and rights on the world's agenda over the past 25 years ... and it is women who will continue to take the leadership in working for these goals. We will not be turned back. We welcome support and partnership with men, with governments, the United Nations and other institutions as we continue the struggle to realize economic justice and all human rights for all women in all our diversity in the next decade.

With the end of the UN world conferences on women, the development agencies of UN Member States became less and less interested in giving financial support (our support came mainly from European development agencies). They had supported IWTC throughout the years of the conferences, stretching from 1975 (Mexico City) to 1995 (Beijing), perhaps in part because they needed to give regular reports on the implementation of promises made by their countries at each world conference and we were able to assist them in doing this. Each year, the UN Commission on the Status of Women had been meeting to review progress made in each country towards achieving actions on which each member state had agreed. The work of organisations such as IWTC had been critical in disseminating and receiving information about such progress.

Now the world conferences were over and the focus on the review process seemed to have become of less importance within the member states. Funding became increasingly difficult to find. Added to that was the rise of more conservative and right-wing governments across Europe.

However, for IWTC, our work was becoming even more important as women everywhere were realising that they had rights and wanted to be part of the movement towards achieving those rights. From its beginnings, IWTC had sought to reach out to rural and low-income women – in Africa, Asia and the Pacific, Latin America and the Caribbean – with information, communication, technical assistance and training that would support their work for and on behalf of women's rights.

In many ways, we welcomed the opportunity to work more closely with these women's groups now, and not to be sidetracked by major world conferences. IWTC had been intimately involved in informing, organising and mobilising for each of the world conferences and NGO forums since Copenhagen in 1980, and the original UN/NGO committee that had organised the Mexico City 1975 IWY Tribune had launched IWTC. Yet our major focus had remained on reaching out to rural and low-income women.

With this in mind, we welcomed the approach made to us by the Canadian International Development Research Centre (IDRC) office in Kenya in 1999, who, under the leadership of Eva Rathgeber, were asking the following questions: Can rural women in Africa benefit from new information and communication technologies (ICTs)? Is it possible to develop ICT-based resources that are relevant to the needs of women with limited education opportunities? Is it realistic to expect rural African women to speed along the so-called Information Superhighway?

IDRC had supported the development of rural telecentres in Uganda, and Eva in particular was concerned that they were not being utilised by the women who lived near them. Many of the women had only basic education, if any at all. Some had been taken out of school at an early age to work in the fields. But they were amongst those most in need of information and resources as they were the breadwinners and main support for their families.

I had been travelling to Kampala, Uganda every year for some years as a member of the International Board of Directors of Isis-WICCE (Women's International Cross Cultural Exchange) in Kampala. At the conclusion of the 1999 board meeting, I took the opportunity of visiting one of the telecentres in a village called Nakaseke, about an hour outside of Kampala.

For this first visit, a mistake was made in the time of the meeting with a group of local women, most of them farmers from the area. When I turned up in the early afternoon, I found to my dismay that these women had been waiting for many hours in the blazing sun, in their best clothes, just to meet with me and discuss ways in which they could use the telecentre. It demonstrated a very real interest and I was impressed.

We sat and talked for hours, with an interpreter in the local Luganda language assisting with the conversation. In what area did they need information? Did they want to know how to use a computer? The driver of the Isis-WICCE van who had driven me out to Nakaseke village had told me on the way out that he thought the idea was crazy. He couldn't imagine village women using computers!

But it was not crazy to these women, who were delighted at the thought they might be able to use the computer, and full of ideas about the kind of information they would find of use.

Of most importance to them was information on how to start small businesses, using what resources they had.

And so we began to work on a program for these women. With IDRC/Kenya, and in partnership with the Uganda National Council for Science and Technology; Media One (Kampala); community groups such as the Council for Economic Empowerment of Women/Uganda, Isis-WICCE and the Uganda YWCA, we developed a new information tool to be used on basic computer systems at rural telecentres. It was planned as something that would require minimal technical know-how to operate, and would not rely on access to the Internet. This was important, as Nakaseke had limited Internet access due to dependence on a power generator that often broke down.

The educational requirements were that the content material be accessible to an audience with little or no reading skills, be seen as having immediate value and be in the language of the community. Furthermore, and from a practical perspective, the new tool needed to be affordable in cost and adaptable into other languages to ensure widespread replicability and viability.

An underlying premise of the project was that the audience for this new information tool would be first-time users of computers. It was also assumed that a rural woman's initial experience in using this new information tool would be important in determining whether she became a repeat user of facilities in the telecentres. In short, the new tool was expected to deliver not only useful information but also a positive experience.

The end product was a CD-ROM entitled *Rural Women in Africa: Ideas for Making Money* that used a simple browser navigating system with graphic interface and spoken text. The content for the new CD-ROM was drawn and adapted from two primary sources: *From Boardroom to Burning Sun: Interviews with 75 Successful Entrepreneurs in Uganda* by Margaret Snyder, which offered a wealth of information on best practices of successful entrepreneurial women; and the small business training manual *Marketing Strategies,* developed by the Overseas Education Fund and field-tested extensively among low-income women in Africa. The CD-ROM was produced by IWTC in English and Luganda language versions.

In developing this computer program with the local women at Nakaseke village, taking care to field-test each section with these women at every stage of development, IWTC had moved into a new area of information communication technologies with enormous potential, especially in reaching rural and low-income women with information suited to their needs. The CD-ROM was a great success and was the only program for rural women available at rural telecentres in Africa. IWTC began talks with IDRC/Kenya to adapt and translate that program into several languages, initially for Uganda, then for the other four countries in the IDRC Acacia program (Tanzania, Senegal, Mozambique and South Africa).

Unfortunately for IWTC, IDRC changed leadership in its Kenya office and decided to focus their efforts totally on research. There was to be no more funding support for the CD-ROM project.

IWTC then began a partnership with the World YWCA to develop another program for telecentres, this time with four African YWCAs (Kenya, Benin, Sierra Leone and Ghana). IWTC undertook a scriptwriting workshop in Accra, Ghana with two staff from each of the YWCAs. We developed sections and the basic outline for a CD-ROM program for community activists and young people to use at Internet cafes, telecentres and community organisations in Africa. The focus was to be on the prevention of HIV/AIDS.

Planning for the future of IWTC

In addition to the new information communication technologies becoming available as tools for making knowledge more accessible to rural and low-income women, IWTC had also been deeply involved with the discussions amongst women's non-governmental organisations around the need for actions to support women in conflict situations. War and its effect on women was becoming a very real concern in many countries, most especially in Africa.

The NGO Working Group on Women, Peace and Security was formed in 2000 and met regularly at IWTC to formulate lobbying actions and draft resolutions for inclusion in United Nations discussions that would put women at the core of peacemaking, peacekeeping and peace plans and programs worldwide. With leadership from the Women's International League for Peace and Freedom and other NGOs working for women's peace and human rights, funds were raised to bring women from conflict situations to speak at a special UN Security Council session. Their testimonies were to prove key to the deliberations of the Council.

On 31 October 2000, United Nations Security Council Resolution 1325 was adopted unanimously. This Resolution was the first formal and legal document from the United Nations Security Council that required parties in a conflict to prevent violations of women's rights, to support women's participation in peace negotiations and in post-conflict reconstruction, and to protect women and girls from sexual and gender-based violence in armed conflict. It was also the first United Nations Resolution to specifically mention women.

IWTC began to focus more of its programs around this vital area, with a specific emphasis on women in Africa. This Africa focus was not something new to IWTC's overall strategy, coming after many collaborative projects and programs in the decades prior to 2000 that had focused on African women's needs and concerns. These included collaboration with the Kenya Appropriate Technology Action Committee, a coalition of African technology groups, in the organising and undertaking of Tech and Tools at the Forum '85 in Nairobi, and support for a church community group in Zimbabwe in the development of their capacity to produce educational materials for their community and schools.

Then in 1992, two women from regional and national women's organisations in Africa joined women from other regions in the Global South in an intensive two-week desktop publishing workshop at IWTC in New York. Working closely together, the women gained tremendous insights into the types of publications being produced around the world, the ways in which information was retrieved and utilised, and techniques in using sophisticated word-processing, graphics, database and page layout programs. Women, Ink. staff travelled to Zimbabwe to undertake workshops at the International Book Fair there to encourage African women writers.

Thus, in the years leading up to the 1995 Beijing conference and forum, IWTC played a major role in seeing that these two important gatherings were more inclusive of women everywhere, and most particularly women from Africa, in the setting of the agenda and in the developing of policies and plans. IWTC had served as a first line of information and support for groups in Africa. All of these Africa-specific activities undertaken were in addition to the total activity program of IWTC that focused on Africa, Asia and the Pacific, Latin America and the Caribbean, Central and Eastern Europe.

It was therefore with some confidence that IWTC laid out its plans and proposals for the coming years. It would be a decade focused on tackling the growing problem of poverty amongst women and children, building strong communities and wherever possible, supporting women, especially in Africa, in the use of new information communication technologies in the prevention of HIV/AIDS.

We would throw our efforts even more strongly behind global policies that brought about transformative action on women's human rights, human security and the inclusion of women at all levels of the peace-building process. And we would expand our creative use of information, networking, capacity-building and knowledge-sharing, including the expansion of Women, Ink. to enhance women's access to information and new global perspectives.

And then, everything came crashing down on 11 September 2001.

12

New York under attack: 11 September 2001

On a bright, sunny morning in September 2001, a passenger plane flew into the South Tower of the World Trade Centre in New York City. I was finishing my breakfast and preparing to leave my downtown apartment, situated quite close to the World Trade Centre. Suddenly, a silence on WNYC, my local radio station. Then a confused and slightly faltering announcement. 'It would appear that a plane has flown into the side of the World Trade Centre, which must have been an accident, though early reports seem to indicate it might have been a passenger aircraft. Which seems impossible on such a beautiful day ...'

I turned on the TV, in time to see the second plane heading for the North Tower. And I watched in disbelief as it crashed into the side. This was no accident.

I called several staff members who travelled the subway underneath or close to the World Trade Centre. I couldn't find them. So I left the apartment and set out for the office. Everything was at a standstill. There were no buses. There were no underground trains. So I walked the two miles to my office in mid-town Manhattan, opposite the United Nations. An eerie stillness had descended on the Eastside of Manhattan. People were watching the skies and pointing as more and more helicopters filled the sky above us. Sirens split the air with an increasing urgency as emergency vehicles raced down Second

Avenue, all heading for the World Trade Centre.

Finally I reached the corner of Second Avenue and 44th Street. And that was where I was stopped. East 44th Street was cordoned off with National Guard and NYPD officials on guard. Crowds were gathering as more and more offices and surrounding residential buildings emptied out into the street. I joined other colleagues from my office building, the Church Centre at the United Nations, situated directly opposite the UN. Cora Weiss from the Samuel Rubin Foundation was there, a close friend and colleague of many years and a tireless peace activist. We stood and watched as the tragedy unfolded on the streets of Manhattan. I was desperately worried about staff members who were still trying to get to work. Cora said, in a soft voice, 'Things will never be the same again', words of prophecy deeply felt and proven to be so right.

Before I left the East Village I had seen one of the towers crumble to the ground with devastating effect. On my walk uptown, the other tower unbelievably had also collapsed. We all stood in silence trying to comprehend what had happened. I would be lying if I didn't say we were scared. Any sounds above us were frightening. No-one knew what would happen next. Rumours abounded that the UN building, standing so tall and bold beside the East River, would be the next building to be hit by aircraft. The UN staff had been evacuated from the building and were crowded around us on the streets.

After a couple of hours, it became clear that the roadblock around our offices would be staying in place as more and more military personnel arrived to guard all streets leading to the UN. I decided to walk home. Mobile phones were not working because the main antenna for lower Manhattan had gone down with the North Tower. I needed to be home where I could use my phone and try to track down the IWTC staff. Where were Alice Quinn, Vicki Semler, Yasna Uberoi, Mary Wong, and all the others dependent on subway trains, some of whom went under the World Trade Centre? Alice was of particular concern as she was disabled and had a driver who drove her over an East River bridge each day to work and/or doctor's visits. Where was she?

I began the long walk down Second Avenue, through thousands of mostly silent, grim-faced people. They seemed more aware of each other than I had ever seen before on the streets of Manhattan. There were wary smiles. If someone bumped into you, they apologised! Many asked for help finding their way in the total absence of buses and subway trains. All bridges and tunnels across and under the East River had been closed off. I looked to the skies, thinking what easy targets we were at that moment. Tens of thousands of people were in the streets, too scared (or not allowed) to return to their offices in the skyscrapers around us, not able to catch public transport. I helped an elderly woman who had collapsed in tears, not knowing what was happening. Where are the buses? she was calling out. Where are the cars? Why is everyone walking in the middle of the streets? We walked together all the way to 14th Street and I saw her safely into her apartment.

Back in my own place, I found messages from my family, including my brother Robert and nephew Duncan Mok, up late at night in Melbourne, Australia and watching in horror as the tragedy unfolded on TV in the middle of the night on the other side of the world.

The next day, I walked to the office, being one of the only staff who lived near enough to be able to walk to work. The following is the note I sent around the world that morning from my computer, via the IWTC Women's GlobalNet:

> September 12, 2001 Special note to readers of IWTC Women's GlobalNet the day after New York and the US were attacked
>
> Firstly, our heartfelt thanks to all of you who have written or called with your thoughts and concern since the surprise attacks on the World Trade Centre (WTC) and surrounding buildings in downtown Manhattan Tuesday morning, September 11. It was to have been not only the UN World

Day of Peace but also a day of voting by the people of New York City for the Democrat and Republican candidates for the next Mayor. Those events have been postponed until a later date.

Everyone here at IWTC is fine though shaken. Our building was evacuated soon after the planes crashed into the WTC twin towers, with officials worried that the United Nations building would be the next target. As many of you know, IWTC is in a building that is opposite the UN. And our acronym of IWTC for International Women's Tribune Centre sometimes gets confused with 1WTC (One World Trade Center), further concerning those who thought we might be housed in one of the WTC towers. We are not.

At 8.45 am yesterday however, the two towers were filled with working people just like us, all of whom had done nothing wrong that day except to turn up for work. This city is now filled with families of all kinds whose lives have been changed irrevocably by the loss of parents, wives, husbands, sons, daughters, brothers, sisters, partners and friends.

I walked with thousands of New Yorkers down Second Avenue on my way home yesterday, the sky ahead of us filled with massive clouds of billowing smoke, fighter aircraft and helicopters. The only sound in a stunned and silent city was the scream of piercing sirens on ambulances, fire engines, police cars and buses. It was a surrealistic and frightening scene. Yet New York rose to the occasion and there were countless instances of people going out of their way to help others. With all tunnels and bridges closed, the famed Circle Line cancelled all tours and ferried thousands of people from Manhattan to New Jersey. Anyone with a boat, big or small, ferried people across to Queens, Brooklyn, New Jersey. And at the call for blood donations, city hospitals and clinics were jammed with thousands of people lining up to give blood.

New York is still a shocked, stunned, and unnaturally quiet city today. It feels a bit like the day after a nuclear holocaust except those of us out of the line of fire are not physically injured.

New York will survive, the towers will be rebuilt, and life will go on. But it will be a different city and country in many ways, with many questions to answer and many solutions to find. It behoves us all to think through the ramifications of this event and to work a little harder at conflict resolution and peace in our time and in all of our countries and regions.

Again, our thanks for your thoughts and concern, which are deeply appreciated.

In the days following the attack, IWTC was swamped with letters, phone calls, emails and faxes. Two days after, I wrote the following to all the readers of the IWTC Women's GlobalNet:

September 14, 2001 A note of thanks to Women's GlobalNet readers

To the hundreds of people from every world region who have written to us with their support and concern, all of us at IWTC extend our heartfelt thanks. Seeing on television the global surge of support for New York, Washington and the US in general has been overwhelming. In this age of instant communications, the experience has been a revelation of how the world can think and feel together as one. Imagine what could be done if we harnessed some of this energy and strategised for peace!

Here in New York, the traumatic events of Tuesday September 11 continue to reverberate through all of the activities and routines of each day. The morning commute for those of us who can walk to work takes us by thousands of photos of missing family members that paper the outside walls of hospitals, the interiors of bus-stands, the sides of phone booths, lamp poles, tree trunks and even some trucks and vans that are travelling through the city. Fathers and mothers search desperately for sons and daughters, daughters and sons search for mothers and fathers, brothers search for sisters, friends search for friends.

The names of the missing speak of Asian, African, Latin

American, Middle Eastern, European, Pacific, Caribbean origins. They represent Muslim, Jewish, Buddhist, Christian, Hindu and many other religious groups. Most of the photos show smiling, happy faces, many are family group shots. Some represent company workers from the many financial firms that rented space in the World Trade Centre. A huge number are waitresses, security guards, janitors, cleaners, floor managers, shopkeepers, cooks, dishwashers, teachers, and firefighters, police officers, chaplains, medics, workers who were first on the scene to help trapped people get out.

I looked in awe last night at the mountains of flowers, letters and candles that now cover Union Square, near where I live. The memorial apparently began with a poem taped to a tree by a New York University student. Another student stood up on a soapbox and began shouting out a list of things needed by rescue workers. Residents living around the Square were arriving with bags and parcels of goods. Other students rushed off to the shops, coming back with bags of goods that were loaded into vans and raced downtown. The power of one was palpable.

The days following the attack were ones in which I was to have flown to Europe to visit some of our long-term development agency funders. This of course became impossible as all flights in and out of JFK were cancelled. So I wrote a letter to friends in SIDA, NORAD, DANIDA and the development assistance agencies of the Netherlands and Brussels, all of whom had written to IWTC with their concerns:

Thank you so much for your letter of today. Your thoughts and concern at this time are very much appreciated.

Regarding my planned trip to Europe next week, things do not look good at the moment with the airports in the New York area again closed to all airlines. We are also being told that when they do re-open, they will only be open to American airlines. My flights are all booked on SAS.

However, even without this information, it has been a week of such trauma and enormous sorrow in New York that when I met with the staff yesterday, it became clear that no-one wanted me to go anywhere. There is such a need for security and stability and I do understand how everyone is feeling. We each travel to work through streets plastered with the photos of missing people, photos that cover bus-stands, phone booths, lamp poles, trees, the outside walls of hospitals and even some trucks and vans. Families are desperately trying to find their loved ones. Yet we all know that the chances of finding any further survivors are now so slim as to be virtually impossible.

So I have cancelled my trip, which was to have departed tomorrow evening for Norway, at least the visits to donor agencies in Nordic countries, the Netherlands and Brussels. I still hope to be able to participate in the ITU/Task Force on Gender issues in Geneva 27–28 of September, and I will try to organise a visit to donor agencies in late October if that would be convenient to you.

Two weeks after the attacks on New York, I wrote the following:

September 25, 2001 Hear the voices of women

The photos of smiling families and individuals – all victims of the September 11 attack on the World Trade Centre twin towers – are beginning to disappear from the walls, phone booths, bus stands, light poles, trees and vans in downtown New York City. Some have fallen because of rain. Others are being taken down and collected by city officials for a possible memorial collage. Yet families and friends keep hoping that someone will be found in the mountains of rubble. They hold onto hope with quiet desperation.

Against this background, I sit at my corner desk looking out at a very subdued United Nations building, reading through hundreds of emails from women in every world region. And what I hear are women's voices calling for restraint, calling for the use of a system of global justice already in place that utilises international and national courts of law. And calling for military force not to be used against more innocent and defenceless victims.

Most comment on the need for immediate and long-term solutions in an unequal world capable of producing such violent acts of rage. And they all reflect the growing determination of women to be part of the decision-making processes that will shape our next steps.

1977: Fiji. Adi Cakobau School. YWCA Pacific Regional Conference.
Amelia Rokotuivuna leading a group. Jewel Graham, World YWCA President, seated in front

1978: Teheran, Iran.
Asia and Pacific Women and Development Institute,
Anne S Walker and the Director, Elizabeth Reid

1979: Fiji. South Pacific Commission Community Education Training Centre (CETC), Nasese.

IWTC low-cost media workshops with women from the Pacific. Front row, l. to r.: Anne S Walker, Mee Kwain (CETC Director) and Vicki Semler

1979: Fiji. SPC/CETC.

IWTC low cost media workshop. Anne S Walker with Vicki Semler and workshop members

1979: Fiji. SPC/CETC.
Vicki Semler leading an IWTC
low-cost media workshop

Left

1979: New York.

Anne S Walker at anti-apartheid protest march for jailed political activist South Africans

Below

1979: New York. IWTC.

Anne sorting IWTC publications on floor

1980: New York. IWTC headquarters.
Planning for the Information and Communication Networking (INCONET) workshop. L. to r.: Jacqui Starkey, Vicki Semler, Anne S Walker (at the whiteboard)

1980s: New York. IWTC headquarters.
Vicki Semler and Anne S Walker

1983: Fiji. SPC/CETC.
IWTC staff are taken on a visit to a rural village on a put-put (canoe with motor). Vicky Mejia with our hosts, Esiteri and Jo Kamikamica

1983: Peru. Encuentro Feminista.
Adriana Santa Cruz (Fempress, Santiago), Anne S Walker and Ximena Charnes (Isis Internacional, Santiago)

Left

1985: NGO Forum, Nairobi.

Anne S Walker painting the banners for the Tech and Tools exhibition on the Sports Grounds of the University of Nairobi

Below

1985: IWTC headquarters on our return from the NGO Forum in Nairobi, with a hand printed fabric artwork gift from Kenyan women.

Anne S Walker and Vicki Semler

1985: NGO Forum, Nairobi.
Tech and Tools exhibition. Anne S Walker welcoming participants to the exhibit

1985: NGO Forum, Nairobi.
Anne S Walker painting banners

Above

1985: NGO Forum, Nairobi. Tech and Tools exhibition.

Ruth Lechte leading an appropriate technology group on how to build a smokeless stove

Left

1985: NGO Forum, Nairobi, Tech and Tools.

Ruth Lechte demonstrating how to build a smokeless stove

1985: NGO Forum, Nairobi.
Anne S Walker at one of the Tech and Tools buildings under construction

1985: NGO Forum, Nairobi, Tech and Tools.
Anne S Walker talking with Kenyan feminist activist

1985: NGO Forum, Nairobi, Tech and Tools.
Anne S Walker showing Canadian Minister Flora MacDonald around the exhibit

1985: NGO Forum, Nairobi, Tech and Tools.
IWTC staff members Joanne Sandler, Vanessa Davis, Vicky Mejia with banner

1985: NGO Forum, Nairobi, Tech and Tools.
Joanne Sandler leading a group

1985: NGO Forum, Nairobi.
Anne S Walker writing workshop numbers on helium balloon to float above workshop group areas at Vivencia!

1985: NGO Forum, Nairobi.
Joanne Sandler and IWTC Kenya Tech and Tools programme assistant Amina

1985: NGO Forum, Nairobi.
Planning Group with Anne S Walker

1986: Papeete, Tahiti.

With the anti nuclear activists Marie Therese and Bengt Danielsen (Bengt was also an original Kon-Tiki crew member) on my trip across the Pacific from Australia to Chile. Marie-Therese and Bengt on the far left. Anne S Walker on the right

1989: Bangkok, Thailand.

ESCAP/IWTC low cost media workshop for women from Southeast Asia. Anne S Walker with participant drawing simple line facial expressions

1990: New York. IWTC headquarters.
Anne S Walker at her desk

1991: Turkey. Riding the Pammukale Express to Sultanhisar village.
L. to r.: Ahdinal, Robert Walker, Anne S Walker

1992: New York. IWTC headquarters at CCUN.
Feminist strategy meeting in progress with several IWTC staff members and other women leaders. IWTC staff, l. to r.: Meera Singh, Mary Wong, Grace Jung, Vicki Semler (head of table), Alice Quinn (seated at back), and Alice Mastrangelo (far right in front of bookshelves)

1992: New York. United Nations.

Women demonstrate outside the UN against Bosnia/Herzegovina/Serbian rape camps and Korean sex slaves in WWII ('Comfort Women')

1992: New York. United Nations.
Women demonstrate outside the UN against Bosnia/Herzegovina/Serbian rape camps and Korean sex slaves in WWII ('Comfort Women'). Gloria Steinem, Charlotte Bunch, Anne S Walker

1995: NGO Forum, Beijing.
Anne S Walker painting anti-nuclear test banners for demonstration at Huairou

1995: NGO Forum, Beijing.
Anne S Walker meeting with US feminist author and activist Betty Friedan

1995: New York. IWTC headquarters.
Anne S Walker with Dame Nita Barrow, Convenor of the NGO Forum in Nairobi 1985 and Governor General of Barbados

1995: NGO Forum, Beijing.
Betty Friedan and Anne S Walker with a group of Chinese feminists and Ford staff at Ford Foundation offices

1995: NGO Forum, Beijing.
Anne S Walker being greeted on arrival at Beijing airport

1995: NGO Forum, Beijing.
Anne Walker Ruth Lechte putting up banner at the Once and Future Pavilion

1995: NGO Forum, Beijing.
Anne Walker showing Senator Carmen Lawrence of the Australian delegation to the UN World Conference around the Once and Future Pavilion

1995: Beijing. Once and Future Pavilion.

The original Fiji YWCA staff meets up again! Anne S Walker, Amelia Rokotuivuna and Ruth Lechte

1995: NGO Forum, Beijing.

Painting banners. Vicki Semler and Anne S Walker

1995: NGO Forum, Beijing.
Pacific 'Beneath Paradise' Display at the IWTC Once and Future Pavilion

2000: Uganda, Kampala.
Anne S Walker with Uganda YWCA members on way to visit women's appropriate technology projects

2001: Uganda. Nakaseke Community Telecentre.
Anastasia Namisongo, the first to try out the test 'pages' of the IWTC/IDRC CD-ROM 'Rural Women in Africa: Ideas for Earning Money'

2001: Uganda. Nakaseke Community Telecentre.
Anne S Walker with the group of village women who tested the first 'pages' of the new IWTC/IDRC CD-ROM 'Rural Women in Africa: Ideas for Earning Money'

2001: Uganda. Nakaseke Community Telecentre.
A group of young village women testing the first 'pages' of the new IWTC/IDRC CD-ROM 'Rural Women in Africa: Ideas for Earning Money'

2002: Mexico, Guadelajara. AWID International Conference.
The IWTC/Women, Ink. bookstall with Rita Mijumbi (IWTC Uganda Programme Officer) and Anne S Walker holding the finished CD-ROM, and Yasna Uberoi, IWTC/Women, Ink staff

2008: New York. IWTC headquarters at CCUN.
L. to r.: Vicki Semler, Mildred Persinger and Anne S Walker

13

IWTC and the years after 9/11

There can be no doubt that the events of that fateful morning in New York changed the world in many vital ways. It certainly changed the focus of the work at IWTC. We had already begun working more in the area of women, peace and security following the momentous passing of UN Security Council Resolution 1325 in October 2000, but now we also had the voices of women crying out for a different way of thinking that would work against the prevailing thoughts of revenge, retribution and conflict. Issues of poverty and hunger, inequality, the HIV/AIDs crisis, the environment, gender equality, girls' education and the uneven spread of information in northern and southern countries called for creative use of ICTs and low-cost and easily accessible media that would bring women and girls everywhere into the new millennium.

And we now also had the United Nations Millennium Development Goals, articulated in the year 2000 and extending to 2015. Reaching these goals, particularly the first, demanded women's action to resolve conflict and spur reconstruction. Late 20th century armed struggle had exacerbated extreme poverty and hunger not only in the developing regions, including middle-income countries, but societies in transition in Central and Eastern Europe. International and civil strife had swelled the AIDS crisis to pandemic proportions in many areas; for a variety of reasons, women were particularly vulnerable, but also shouldered staggering responsibilities in AIDS-stricken communities. Conflict had also damaged or destroyed their environmental bases of health, sustenance and productivity. As to universal primary education, child mortality and maternal health, (respectively Goals 2, 4 and 5), suffice to say that in a number of strife-torn countries, women constituted as much as 60% of the remaining productive population, many of them heading families that included traumatised, sick, maimed children who were not their biological offspring.

And so in 2001, the team at IWTC sat down to plan for the coming three-year period. We mapped out our core programs, focusing on advocacy, skills, tools and resources to achieve best outcomes. In our office we were small in number yet our outreach was enormous. How could we best respond to all the requests for support, information, resources and technical assistance?

We mapped out the major emerging issues facing women in the world, with a now even greater emphasis on women, peace and security, and women's use of new media information technologies. Upcoming issues of the IWTC Women's GlobalNets were planned, the IWTC website would be developed to broaden its outreach and include such things as online planning for NGOs around the world to take part in major UN meetings such as the Commission on the Status of Women. We would develop regional as well as international interactive sections on the website so that women everywhere could have input with their activities, plans and proposals.

But our major purpose would remain that of developing, producing and disseminating information in usable and readable formats that would help to translate UN and other policy resolutions and statements into words and actions that would make a difference in women's lives. Prominent amongst these policy areas was the UN resolution on women, peace and security. But there were many other issues about which we were being asked for information, such as the environment and climate change and how that affected women, appropriate technologies to support rural and low-income women, training for women in community radio and TV, violence against women, women working in HIV-AIDS affected communities and with issues of child mortality and maternal health. We were also involved in follow-up work around science and technology that had arisen from the Once and Future Action Network that came out of the Beijing NGO Forum.

We worked on benchmarks, targets and indicators for all these issues, with all of our sister networks and forums around the world. The depth and breadth of global partnerships and networks we had cultivated over the decades was impressive. Looking back, we were probably overreaching our capacity to implement all our plans. But the need seemed so great and we were determined to do all that we could to reach out to women everywhere as they moved forward in their fight for development, equality and peace.

IWTC, with its experienced, hard-working and professional staff of women, headed by Dr Vicki Semler, was now a globally recognised women's information, communications, technical assistance and training entity with links to global, regional, national and local women's networks. We had played an enormous role in making it possible for women from every country to be involved in global gender policy activities that affected them and their families at all levels. We had seen rural, low-income women from some of the poorest countries on earth take their place at the policy table along with the high and mighty, and speak out in their own voices about the problems they faced on a daily basis.

We were not to know that a dramatic change would be taking place in the ensuing years, related to a decidedly conservative political swing in North America and Europe, affecting dramatically the priorities of the development agencies within those countries, agencies that had been

IWTC's chief supporters for decades. More than likely, the September 11, 2001 attacks on New York City and the resulting attacks by the USA and its Coalition partners on Afghanistan and Iraq played a part in the conservative swing. But whatever the reasons, IWTC was to face severe financial problems in the years ahead. Gender and development activities were to become low funding priorities as the 'developed' world geared itself up against new adversaries.

These concerns were very far from my thinking: I was preparing to leave IWTC and go home to Australia after 44 years away. Why was I leaving? I had always told my family that I would return one day, not that they had ever really believed that! I had been Executive Director of IWTC for 26 years, far longer than I had ever imagined and certainly longer than was the case with most leaders of similar organisations. And I had been part of a team for all those years with Vicki Semler as Associate Director. It was definitely time for Vicki to become Director.

Some people believed at the time that I must be leaving because of the events of 9/11. In fact I had been planning my departure for some years, even putting a deposit down on an apartment in Melbourne in 1999. Things were changing for my family. I had lost a niece to breast cancer, a brother-in-law to Parkinson's Disease and now we had found out that my brother Evan had the same dread disease. I had a very real sense that it was time to go home.

And so on 22 December 2002, I boarded a Qantas plane for the long flight across the Pacific. It seemed strange to be leaving it all behind, but I was confident the future of IWTC seemed secure and I knew that I could keep in close touch as needed via the internet.

After my return to Australia, I went back to New York several times in the following years, usually at the time of the UN Commission on the Status of Women (CSW), working with IWTC and other international and national non-governmental organisations to fight for the implementation of the decisions made in Beijing at the UN Fourth World Conference on Women in 1995 and endorsed at the Beijing Plus Five Special Session in 2000. I was a speaker at the CSW in March 2003 when the Women and Media section of the Beijing Platform for Action was discussed, meeting again with colleagues and friends from all of our women's networks worldwide.

We women activists found ourselves increasingly faced with a rising tide of right wing fundamentalists at each of these meetings, led by a determined group of mainly fundamentalist Christians from the USA, with a growing group of hard-line Catholics and Islamists from other countries. There was increasing opposition from conservative governments that had become politically powerful in many member states of the UN.

It was becoming clear that progress being made in the area of gender and development was working. It was threatening the established order, especially in the critical areas of concern raised in the Beijing PFA: women and poverty; women and health (in particular, reproductive and sexual rights); education and training of women; violence against women; women and armed conflict; women and the economy; women in power and decision-making; institutional mechanisms for the advancement of women; women's human rights; women and the media; women and the environment, and the girl child. This last critical area of concern was added by women from Africa at the final CSW planning session before Beijing.

IWTC continued for a decade following my departure, continuing to function as a resource centre and information base for women worldwide, and as a home base for women leaders coming to New York to participate in UN and NGO meetings. As armed conflicts and serious tensions rose steadily in Africa and the Middle East following the attacks on the US in September 2001, IWTC program activities became increasingly focused on women, peace and security activities.

Implementation of Security Council Resolution 1325: Women, Peace and Security, passed in October 2000, became a priority concern. The resolution reaffirmed the important role of women in the prevention and resolution of conflicts, peace negotiations, peace-building, peacekeeping, humanitarian response and in post-conflict reconstruction, and stressing the importance of their equal participation and full involvement in all efforts for the maintenance and promotion of peace and security.

One would think that this focus by IWTC would be supported and strengthened by development agencies, but in fact this was not the case. Development funding went increasingly to government and/or UN global and regional organisations to deal at government and corporate levels on these issues, essentially cutting out the smaller funds for NGOs working with women on such community projects as women in armed conflict. I became President of the IWTC Board of Directors in 2006 and returned to New York each year for meetings as we struggled with this new reality.

Whatever the cause, we were having increasing difficulties making the case for funding to more and more conservative governments in Europe and Canada. IWTC did continue stoically until 2011, when the decision was made to close down. We had never been in debt and did not want to break that tradition. Also, there were now many more women's activist networks, particularly in the regions where we had worked for more than three decades. In fact you could say that we had achieved our main purpose which had always been to support local, national and regional women's networks.

However, there was considerable distress when IWTC closed its doors. Letters were written from women in every world region expressing their sadness and thanking us for our support for their activities. I think it's true to say that the work of IWTC over 35 critical years played a very real role in supporting the activities of women and in making it possible for them to represent themselves at the UN and other policy-making tables. There are now women's activist organisations and networks in every world region, all fighting for women's human rights and for the implementation of the Beijing Platform for Action.

I know that all my life experiences played a role in preparing me for the 26 years I spent at IWTC. Whether it was the early years growing up in Melbourne, the training and experience as an early childhood educator, the years travelling and working my way around the world footloose and fancy-free, the decade in Fiji as both an early childhood educator and a women and development leader/communicator, or the critical decision to return to study instructional systems technology, international affairs and development communications at a major USA university. No doubt all of these experiences led to New York, the founding of IWTC and working with women worldwide. They indicate that great opportunities are there for anyone who is prepared to take risks and jump into the unknown. I am thankful I did that on many occasions, and am above all grateful for the love and support of all those who took the jumps with me.

14

Reflections: New York 1976–2002

Thinking back on those 26 years in New York, there is much of my personal life that has been left out in the previous chapters. I began my Manhattan sojourn in September 1976 in a small studio apartment in an East 44th Street multi-storied apartment building that turned out to be a regular place for sex worker dalliances! I had wondered why rather embarrassed men and amazingly dressed women often did not speak or look at each in the elevator of a morning. I then moved to a loft apartment in Turtle Bay Towers on East 46th when Vicki Semler joined me from Indiana University in 1977, and it was there that we lived for the next ten years.

That apartment was within walking distance of the IWTC offices, initially based in the old Carnegie Building on the corner of East 46th and UN Plaza, When the Carnegie Institute moved to Washington DC, we moved our office to the Albano Building directly opposite Turtle Bay Towers and were there for five years. Finally, we found a more permanent home for IWTC at the Church Centre at the United Nations (CCUN) on the corner of East 44th Street and UN Plaza in 1985.

It was always great to be able to walk to work, and to have an apartment where women from around the world could easily visit for drinks or meals or for more informal discussions about their activities, hopes and dreams. Often, women from less developed parts of the world, sometimes overcome with anxiety at being in New York by themselves, would spend a few days at our place while they acclimatized.

Then I made the decision to move out of town for a while and, in October 1988, bought an apartment out at Long Beach on Long Island. It meant a train commute from Grand Central Station each day but I saw it as a chance to enjoy a beautiful beach in the summer and a place to relax from the noise and busyness of Manhattan. I also thought it was long past time for me to own something!

My Long Beach apartment was close to friends who ran the Foundation for Peoples of the South Pacific, most especially Father Stan Brown and Betty and Maurice Silverstein. Betty was a former Australian film star who had married Maurice when he was Vice-President of MGM. They met while Betty was starring in *Forty Thousand Horsemen*, filmed in Australia and Southeast Asia in the 1940s. Betty was a great supporter of IWTC and most especially of our collaborative work with women in the South Pacific.

My move out of Manhattan was not to be a success. Within months, I was exhausted by the daily commute and the inability to spend time with women from around the world in the evenings and weekends. No-one was eager to travel out to Long Beach! And then, unexpectedly, my plans to live in my own place all came crashing down.

In early 1989, I flew to Kathmandu, Nepal to run a workshop with women leaders, and then on to Kuala Lumpur to meet with Noeleen Heyser and others at the newly formed Asia Pacific Development Centre Gender and Development Unit. This Unit was the successor to the APCWD Women and Development Unit in Tehran where I had worked with Elizabeth Reid in 1978. They were forced to flee due to the Islamic revolution in 1979. First to Bangkok where the UN regional office for Asia and the Pacific is situated, and then to Kuala Lumpur.

After KL, I flew to Bangkok to run a workshop at UN/ESCAP (UN Economic and Social Commission for Asia and the Pacific). It was while I was there, preparing to return to New York, that Vicki called to tell me there had been a fire in my apartment building at Long Beach and the building was now closed indefinitely.

To say I was taken aback would be putting it mildly! I was flying home to New York City after weeks away with nowhere to stay. And all my belongings were now locked up in my apartment out at Long Beach with no access allowed.

So began two years of my life in New York City sub-leasing apartments, using the notice board at the United Nations where staff and others posted availability of their places for periods while they were on overseas assignments. I lived uptown, downtown, on the west side and closer to the office on the eastside. I came to know parts of that incredible city that I had never known before.

I also took on almost all of the overseas assignments during that time, travelling to Africa, Latin America and Asia running workshops and meeting with women's groups. I went on a speaking tour of Japan, travelling to extraordinary women's centres and meeting many remarkable feminists and activists. I also spent weeks on fund-raising trips in Europe, meeting with development agencies in Switzerland, Germany, The Netherlands, Denmark, Sweden, Finland and Norway.

And I became very accustomed to living out of a suitcase. On my return from each assignment, I would check the UN notice board and assume another sub-lease of an apartment in a different part of Manhattan. One friend, Pam Silverstein, made her apartment available to me on the Upper West Side on more than one occasion. Then another good friend, Jane Katz, (now renowned author Jane Summers) informed me she was moving from her little apartment in the East Village and maybe I could sub-lease that from her. I jumped at the offer, moved in and later assumed the lease for myself. And there I lived for the remaining eleven years of my time in New York.

Eventually I was able to sell my place at Long Beach, when

finally the building was reopened after repairs, but at a great financial loss. I was very happy to be back in Manhattan. I was later to purchase and sell three other apartments as investments, two in Manhattan, one in Queens, following the stock market crash of 1992. It was in this way I was able to recover some of the losses made with my Long Beach venture. I had become a New Yorker, more money-wise and savvy!

Life in New York and at the Tribune Centre was always full. With friends, such as Lynda Wismer (McNeur), Vicki Semler, Joanne Sandler, Jacqui Starkey, Ros Harris and so many more, I saw numerous great opera, drama, musical, and comedic performances both on and off Broadway. Vicki, Ros and I formed a Manhattan Theater Club team and subscribed to their productions year after year. I subscribed to the Metropolitan Opera and was privileged to see and hear singers such as Dame Joan Sutherland, Luciano Pavarotti, Jose Carrerras, Beverley Sills, Placido Domingo and more. Lynda knew the art world like no other and we took in art galleries, museums, outdoor performances, concerts, plays and many an evening just enjoying a meal and/or drinks on the sidewalk absorbing New York life and culture.

And at the Tribune Centre itself, our days were filled with visits from women from every region of the world. It was our enormous pleasure to provide a base for women coming to the UN for meetings, discussions, and to gain information on resources and funds available for their activities back home. We met new generations of activists year after year and encouraged them in any way possible. Just having a home base was sufficient for many of them to be able to overcome their anxieties at the prospect of facing government officials from their own countries at the UN, meeting with foundations and development agencies, or just finding their way around the United Nations labyrinth.

Every year, we would throw an IWTC Holiday Party to celebrate the end of another year, the beginning of the next year, and the Christmas Season. These parties would bring together all those with whom we worked and plotted during the year. The invitation list was long and wide and encompassed people from the United Nations, non-governmental organisations, foundation personnel, family and friends. The parties became widely known and were events to which many looked forward. In fact, we discovered some women were changing their travel plans to make sure they would be in New York for the IWTC Holiday Party!

We also had regular Book Parties during the year. Women, Ink. – the IWTC women and development marketing service –, would celebrate new publications and authors by inviting publishing firms interested in women's publications, UN and NGO personnel, friends far and wide, so that they would be kept up-to-date with new writings by women.

All of these added to making the Tribune Centre – or 'The Trib' as it was affectionately known – a meeting place and home away from home for literally thousands of women both in New York and worldwide. It was in fact sometimes quite difficult to get our work done with an office full of visitors and friends. And it meant many late nights, sometimes right to closing time at 11pm when the building staff would arrive and throw us out so they could go home.

On one memorable Friday night, the building staff member on duty came up to our floor and did not see me. I was working at another staff member's computer, not at my own desk. The man decided there was no one there and he would therefore leave early, effectively locking me in. At 11pm, on realizing the building was locked, I spent a half-hour roaming around trying to find a way out, or a way to contact someone. Finally, I forced open an outside steel door, setting off the alarm. Thinking the police might come and I would have to spend the night explaining myself at a police station, I ran up East 44th Street to catch a bus to the East Village down Second Avenue.

I arrived on Monday morning to be met by the supervisor

of the building staff who showed me security tapes of my search for a way out on Friday night and gave me news of the disgruntled people sleeping rough in the park next door. The alarm apparently ran all night and no one ever came. Then he apologized and told me that the young man on duty would be sacked. I was able to stop that happening, explaining it was my fault for not being at my desk when he came to inspect. And the building soon installed new security measures, with sensors that showed if someone was still in the building and an alarm system that actually alerted security personnel when it went off.

So much else happened in those 26 years it is impossible to speak of it all. There were the marches I took part in with women demanding action against violence against women, against the rape camps set up in Bosnia and Hersegovina, against apartheid in South Africa, in support of the environment, in support of those protesting US actions against Afghanistan following the 9/11 World Trade Centre plane crashes and many more.

And then there was the memorable time Universal Studios used IWTC's offices to film scenes from a movie called *A Perfect Murder*. (It was a useful way to earn some money when we were particularly low on funds, probably awaiting a cheque from Europe to arrive.) The main woman character, played by Gwyneth Paltrow, was an official at the US Mission to the UN, but Universal were unable to film there, for obvious security reasons. When the movie was released, the staff at IWTC waited for me to return from a funding trip across Europe so that we could all go to a Manhattan cinema and see it together. And we all whooped when our office came up on the screen.

At a later time I was woken halfway across the Pacific on a visit home, and looked up at the big screen above me to see Gwyneth Paltrow seated at my desk in New York overlooking the UN! I wanted to turn around and shout out to all the other passengers on the flight 'Hey! That's my desk!' but luckily for them I did not.

I moved out of my little studio apartment in the East Village in June 2002, having sorted all my belongings into three piles: one sent to Australia, one given away and one thrown away. I had packed a suitcase for my final six months in New York and with that, I moved uptown to sub-lease an apartment of a friend, Marilyn Carr, in an apartment block near the United Nations at Mitchell Place. From there, I could walk to the office in five minutes. My cat Orlando, who had lived with me in my studio apartment in the East Village, went to stay with Ros Harris, and then with an IWTC staff member, Yasna Uberoi. (I returned for the Commission on the Status of Women in March 2003 and Orlando was flown home to Melbourne then).

For my last day in New York, I spent one night in the Beekman Hotel in Mitchell Place. There I held a 'soiree' for all the IWTC staff and many friends, enjoying one last evening of laughter and memories. The next morning, 22 December 2002, Vicki and I left for the John F. Kennedy airport in a hire car. Vicki accompanied me to say farewell and bid me good luck on this next stage of my life. We had shared so much together, at Indiana University for four years, and almost 26 years working together at IWTC. It was hard to say goodbye but I knew we would be seeing each other often in the future. And I knew that IWTC was in a safe and experienced pair of hands.

Part Two: Women's Voices, Women's Stories

Introduction

The International Women's Tribune Centre in New York, of which I was Executive Director from 1976 to 2002, functioned more as a task force than an organisation, with a small staff and a vast outreach mission. Much of our time was spent working with women in Africa, Asia and the Pacific, the Middle East, Latin America and the Caribbean. We supported regional, national and community networks with information, communication, technical assistance and training in women and development issues.

As part of the IWTC team I travelled widely, mostly running workshops on low-cost media techniques so that women could produce their own media materials in their own languages. There were also large conferences mixed in with small gatherings in remote villages. My luggage was always packed with manuals, newsletters and other information materials on women and development issues to hand out as requested. During these travels I met thousands of women from all walks of life, in cities, towns and rural areas.

I saw first-hand the conditions in which women lived in these countries and learnt of their needs for improving those conditions. Through IWTC we were able to help in many ways, usually through supporting efforts the women and their communities were already making. We were often able to put them in contact with international and regional funding and resource development agencies. Importantly, we heard their stories and helped them to make their voices heard throughout the world.

My experiences on those journeys covered the whole gamut of emotions, from elation to despair and my memories are still vivid. These stories recount some of those experiences. I hope they will give a small taste of the issues faced every day by women around the world, and show their strength, determination and courage.

Strange happenings at the IWY Tribune Mexico City, 1975

We were finally installed in our little rooms high above the noisy streets of downtown Mexico City. It was 1975 and the United Nations International Women's Year Conference and non-governmental parallel IWY Tribune were about to get underway.

Vicki Semler and I were graduate students at Indiana University in Bloomington, Indiana. We were finishing our doctorates in Instructional Systems Technology in the School of Education, and had heard of these two groundbreaking meetings through my contacts in Fiji and New York. I was joining up with colleagues from the Pacific who were coming to the IWY Tribune to speak out against the French nuclear testing in the Pacific. We had a little funding from the organisers of the Tribune and with that were able to get ourselves to Mexico, living cheaply in a somewhat crumbling but quite charming pensione.

During the last week of the Tribune, a nuclear-free Pacific panel was held at the non-governmental IWY Tribune. I donned a hat and taped PRESS on the side so that I could go on stage and take photos. There had already been much comment on the fact that all the journalists and photographers were men, so I thought I'd even out the perception a little. I also wanted to get slides of my Pacific activist friends and colleagues as they spoke at the meeting.

Amelia Rokotuivuna from Fiji was one of the speakers

on the panel. Amelia, Ruth Lechte and I had started the Fiji YWCA back in 1962 and had all been actively involved in the protests against the nuclear testing that had been taking place on Mururoa Atoll in French Polynesia since 1968. Amelia was now the General Secretary of the Fiji YWCA. Alongside her on the panel were other anti-nuclear activists including Seán MacBride, winner of the 1974 Nobel Peace Prize, and Noel Brown, from Jamaica. I placed myself towards the back of the stage ready to take photos of the speakers and the crowd once the meeting had begun.

Suddenly, there was some kind of commotion in the meeting hall. Photographers rushed to the front of the stage. I couldn't understand what was happening. Then two women jumped on stage and grabbed one of the microphones and stood up on the table where the panellists were seated, positioned at front of stage. One of the women was blonde, one was a brunette. They were shouting loudly in Spanish.

Amelia leaned forward and tried to negotiate between the women. She suggested calmly that they speak one at a time and reached out to hold the microphone. Then suddenly, flashbulbs went off from the floor as a dozen or more photographers took their shots. Three women fighting on the stage!

And then, just as swiftly as it had taken place, the women left the stage and the photographers walked out of the room.

With the meetings over, Amelia, Vicki and I were on a plane heading for Houston USA and then on to our homes: Vicki and I to Indiana University, Amelia to Fiji. I had picked up a copy of *Time* magazine to read on the plane.

I turned to an article on the UN Women's Conference. It was headed something like: 'Women from all over the world fight in Mexico City!' and there, large and clear, was the picture from our nuclear-free Pacific panel. Apparently the two women, both Mexican government officials as it turned out, and Amelia from Fiji were being used to represent Latin America, Europe and Africa, and they were all fighting.

We were pretty shocked, particularly Amelia who felt it was terribly unfair that she should have been used in this way. And the organisers of the IWY Tribune were stunned that their efforts to bring women together in what had been termed 'the largest consciousness-raising session of women ever held' should be characterised in such a way. Yet that photo, so unrepresentative and so staged, became the enduring image of the meetings in Mexico City.

And it could not have been more wrong in its characterisation of the Mexico City meetings. In fact, women came together in a miraculous way, forming alliances, networks, making contacts that have endured. It was the beginning of a new day for women of the world, and within a year of International Women's Year the UN recognised this by declaring a UN Decade for Women 1976–1985.

International perceptions at the US IWY Conference Houston, 1977

Two years had passed since the 1975 Conference and Tribune in Mexico City. Not many American women had participated in those meetings, mainly as a result of a decision made by the NGO organisers of the IWY Tribune. They believed it would be impossible to cope with the numbers that might come to Mexico City from the US and Canada. Therefore there was little publicity for the IWY meetings within North America.

So it was that the US organised its own IWY Conference in Houston, Texas, from 18 to 21 November 1977. Vicki Semler and I accompanied a group of international women leaders to this major event to develop a US Plan of Action.

Beside the Astrodome in Houston where the main plenary sessions were held were several other halls where exhibitions were staged by women's organisations and where spaces were available for informal group meetings, coffee and sandwiches, etc. We spent much time in these halls with our international group of YWCA women and they enjoyed opportunities to sit and discuss what was happening.

It was on one of these days that we noticed on the closed circuit TV feed from the Astrodome that there was an upcoming vote on a very contentious resolution on sexual preference. Amongst the delegates meeting in the Astrodome was a strong group of conservative, right-wing delegates from across the US who were determined to see this resolution fail. Vicki and I thought it would be good for the women to be in the balcony overlooking the floor of delegates when this was discussed and the vote taken.

As we walked the short distance over to the Astrodome, we passed groups of young women holding hands, waving rainbow flags and holding aloft helium balloons with WE ARE EVERYWHERE printed on the side. Some of the couples were kissing.

To be honest, Vicki and I thought things were fairly obvious regarding the resolution. There had been considerable discussion within our group. And we were pleased that by and large this fairly conservative group of older YWCA women from traditional cultures were being extremely broad-minded and progressive and were eager to see the resolution take its place in the Plan of Action.

We took our seats in the balcony just up to the right of the platform and watched and listened to the heated arguments being presented by delegates below. At the back of the Astrodome, high up on the middle balcony, crowds of young women were holding the balloons we'd seen outside. They were waiting anxiously for the discussions on sexual preference to come to a conclusion. They were not delegates and had no say in the final vote.

Then the vote was taken and the result announced. The sexual preference resolution had been accepted! It was 1977 and equal rights for same sex couples was in the National Plan of Action. The back of the hall erupted in dancing and singing and WE ARE EVERYWHERE balloons took flight across the great ceiling of the Astrodome.

Then to our utter surprise, Vicki and I noticed that all of our group were also on their feet clapping and cheering. Yes, they had seemed progressive and broad-minded earlier, but essentially this was a group of fairly conservative women and we were not expecting this show of enthusiasm. But it was just great, and especially so because they were dressed in their traditional costumes, very visible to the delegates in the hall below and were giving an extremely positive international flavour to the occasion.

Then we all sat down and things quietened. I turned to the woman beside me, representing an African YWCA, and told her how terrific it was that the group had given support to this really important vote. 'Why of course', she said. They had all discussed it in their hotel the night before. And everyone agreed that all women should have the right to decide whether their baby was a boy or girl!

Should I have corrected her? Should we have discussed the issue more? I guess so. Yet an international group of women had seemingly supported probably the most contentious and progressive resolution in the USA 1977 National Plan of Action and joy was abounding throughout the Astrodome. I left things as they were.

Working in Iran: lost on the first day Teheran, 1978

As the plane coasted through the clear blue sky, I looked down on the vast dry plains below. Ancient Persia, home to the mighty Shah who sat on the Peacock Throne. I remembered being at an opera at Covent Garden many years before when the Shah and his royal party arrived and were seated in a central box overlooking the theatre. I was high up in the 'gods' but had a good view of it all. Brightly coloured peacock feathers adorned the ornate box and the royal men in the party were dressed in military uniforms with decorations and sashes. The women were in flowing ball gowns and glittering jewels.

Now here I was beginning the approach to Teheran Airport. I was to be met in a UN van and driven to the newly established Asian and Pacific Centre for Women and Development (APCWD). Elizabeth Reid, formerly Adviser on Women's Affairs to the deposed Prime Minister of Australia, Gough Whitlam, had invited me to come and spend some time working with her and her staff on a resource kit of information for women's groups in the region.

Suddenly the scene below the plane window began to change and I saw ahead of me a vast black cloud. I asked the flight assistant if we were approaching a storm? No, she responded, that was just Teheran's pollution. Not a great beginning.

Amongst the chaos of the airport arrival area, I spotted the UN driver and thankfully boarded the dusty van. We drove into Teheran, a city of 10 million designed for 4 million as it was explained to me. It had once been a showpiece amongst cities with wide boulevards, clear water streams running alongside the roads, boutique fashion shops, parks and gardens, but the flood of people coming in from the countryside had overwhelmed the infrastructure and things had gone downhill.

We drove through impressive gates into the walled compound of which APCWD was a part. It was a government compound and the APCWD had taken over the former headquarters of a major government women's organisation, headed by Princess Ashraf, sister of the Shah. That organisation had been relocated and Elizabeth was now ensconced in the lavish offices once occupied by the Princess. After my long journey from the Philippines, I was happy to be seated on plush cushions sipping a cup of tea and eating a slice of bread and butter with Vegemite (of which Elizabeth had a secret stash in her massive desk).

We discussed in general what I would be doing during my stay and I met some of the staff. I was allotted a small office with desk and chair. Then I met the young Australian woman with whom I was to share lodgings. She and two other Aussies (young men) were sharing a house quite some distance from the compound and they had an extra bed for me. Before we left for this place, I asked for someone to write down the exact name of the compound, with address and phone number, in Farsi, in case I got lost. I was assured that would be done for me the next day.

I left for my lodgings, accompanied by the young woman with whom I would be staying. She was spending some weeks at APCWD as a volunteer.

The next morning, she put me on a bus with what seemed like clear instructions as to where I was to get off : a bus stop 'very close' to the government compound.

The bus wove around Teheran in an amazingly complex way, completely disorienting me, which wasn't difficult as I'd only arrived the day before and had never done this trip before. I saw what I thought was my stop approaching and got off. Away went the bus. I couldn't see the walled compound but thought it was just around the corner. In fact, I had got off the bus too soon. No problem I thought. I decided to walk around the corner. But the walled compound wasn't there. I kept walking. Nothing seemed to be familiar. Then again, I had only arrived yesterday and the walled compound was the only place I'd been.

Then I felt the presence of people gathering behind me. Initially in small numbers, but definitely gathering. The day before, over that cup of tea, Elizabeth had told me of a bad experience she had had when she first came to Teheran and was walking the streets alone and uncovered. Men had begun to follow her, gathering stones in their hands as they walked towards her, and she had found herself trapped in a street with nothing to defend herself. The men had angrily thrown stones at her and she was only saved from serious damage by a passing policeman. She could very well have lost her life. Such was the growing anger against uncovered, foreign women in Teheran in June 1978.

For some months, the mullahs had been preaching religious fanaticism and calling for a return to Islamic law. Khomeini, in exile in Paris, was sending regular audiotapes that were played every Friday in the mosques. Opposition to the Shah and his progressive ideas was growing rapidly. I had read about daily demonstrations in Teheran's city squares in *Time* magazine on the plane. In fact, my copy was quickly picked up and read by Elizabeth and all at APCWD as news of that kind was heavily censored within Teheran.

Now here I was walking uncovered and very foreign in the streets of Teheran and being followed by a growing group of men who were clearly not friendly. I knew instinctively that I should not stop and ask directions. That would not have been helpful anyway as no one spoke English and I did not speak Farsi. All street signs were in Farsi only, as were names on the front of buses. Even if they were more readable, I would not have been helped because I did not have the address of the walled compound, nor the address of the place where I was staying. All not good in this situation. And even if I'd had a phone number, which I very much wished I did have, these were pre-mobile phone days and there were no phones in sight.

As I walked, more and more rapidly, I began to list in my head the things I could and could not do. I could not stop and ask the men following me where I was. I could not ask anyone for an address or place because I didn't know any address or place. Was this the place where I was going to disappear forever? What could I do? I kept making mental lists. Where would I be most likely to find someone who could speak English? And then, what would I ask them?

A bank. A big bank where there was a Foreign Exchange desk. Surely they would have to speak English. Okay. Now what would I ask them? Ah. Got it! I would ask for directions to any United Nations office in Teheran. No good asking for APCWD as it was new and well hidden in a walled unnamed government compound.

I came to a city circle with a huge statue in the middle. Placed to one side was a large stone building with sweeping steps leading up from the footpath. Maybe a bank? I climbed the stairs. My followers melted away. Yes, it was a bank and I stepped up to the Information Desk. They searched for an English-speaker and finally found someone. I asked for help in finding any UN office in Teheran.

After much discussion among themselves they came up with a UNDP office. I asked for the address to be written in Farsi so I could show it to a taxi driver. Then I changed some US dollars into local currency and sallied forth, back down the stairs. A taxi was at the kerbside and I climbed in. The driver looked at the address and nodded his head.

Then off we went. But it was the kind of taxi that only goes up main roads and picks up endless passengers who then get off at intersections somewhere near where they're going. I found myself buried under more and more people. There must have been about eight in that mini taxi by the time they threw me out, all waving cheerfully and pointing across the road and up the hill. I knew I was very far from the walled compound and APCWD but was thankful for their combined help.

Over the major highway and up the hill of shops I went. I could not see anything resembling a UN office and the feeling of panic began to descend again. I tried going into a couple of crowded little shops that seemed to have only women inside but no-one could understand me nor I them. Then, as I walked, I glanced down a small lane. There, halfway down the lane was the blue UN flag dangling from its flagpole. Never was I more happy to see that flag than at that moment, and in all the years I sat in my office opposite the UN in New York, I would look at that flag with enormous gratitude.

My journey was still not over, however, as the staff at reception spoke only Farsi. Then I noticed the UN phone book on the counter and reached across to get it. Inside I found the number for APCWD and called Elizabeth. She was relieved to hear my voice as my non-arrival had caused some concern. She spoke to the UNDP Resident Representative upstairs and someone came down and took me for a cup of tea and something to eat while we waited for an APCWD car to come and collect me.

I was very far across town and many miles from where I was supposed to be. But I was safe at last and would never be without an address or phone number again in the six weeks I worked at APCWD.

We did indeed develop and produce a Resource Kit for women and women's organisations throughout Asia and Pacific and were able to disseminate it across the region using the offices of UNDP. And when Elizabeth Reid and the staff of APCWD had to flee Teheran in 1979 because of the Islamic revolution, they headed for Bangkok with that manual as a starting point for reorganising.

The boxes full of files and organisational materials from APCWD, including all the names and addresses of country and regional women's organisations, training institutions, resources etc. so painstakingly collected by the staff, were confiscated by the revolutionary militia in Iran and never forwarded to Bangkok. All of that was lost. The Resource Kit was therefore the main basis for reorganising APCWD in its new home in Bangkok as part of the UN Economic and Social Commission for Asia and the Pacific. After a few years based in Bangkok, APCWD moved on to Kuala Lumpur and became the Gender and Development section of the Asia and Pacific Development Centre.

A UN water project gone wrong in Kenya
Nairobi, 1979

Often after a meeting or a workshop, I stayed on in the country or region to visit women's projects, especially those that were relevant to an upcoming issue of *The Tribune*, the IWTC newsletter that focused each edition on a specific women and development issue. We were gathering information on women and water projects in 1979 and had heard that several such projects were being undertaken by a UN agency in slums outside Nairobi.

One project was being carried out in a notorious slum community known as Mathare. Hidden behind hills that shield this community from the eyes of travellers driving along the highway to the Nairobi Safari Park, Mathare was a sprawling heap of shanties amid piles of reeking garbage.

With the UN agency project officer, we headed out in a van to see the much-talked about water project that seemed to be a spark of hope in this depressing scene. A water pipe had been laid underground to carry fresh, clean water to a central square where a tap had been installed giving slum dwellers easy, direct access. This would obviously be of enormous benefit, particularly to women, the main providers of water, who walked great distances with pots or tin cans on their heads to collect water that was unclean and disease-laden.

As we crossed the hills that hid this community from the highway, in front of us appeared an enormous reservoir of water, stretching almost as far as the eye could see. I was surprised. Wasn't this a community that had no access to water?

Yes indeed, replied the UN agency person. It was a community without access to water because this reservoir was only for official residents of Nairobi. Mathare residents were not allowed to use it.

Somehow, watching someone water-skiing on the reservoir behind a shiny white speedboat seemed to bring home to me even more sharply the contrast between those who have and those who have not.

Then we arrived near the community square and stepped out to see the women and water project. In front of us was a long line of people, mainly women and children, all waiting in the oppressive heat with their pots, pans, kettles and containers of all kinds. We walked up the hill beside them towards the tap that had been provided by the UN.

There in front of us was seated an enormous Kenyan woman with a guard on either side of her. In her hand she had a large bag into which she was dropping money from each person before they could put their containers under the tap. If the person receiving the water complained that the container was only half full, a guard would step up and muscle them away.

I was taken aback. Wasn't this a UN project provided with UN funds for the good of the people of Mathare? Well yes it was. Then why were they being charged exorbitant fees for the right to have that water? The charges worked out to be significantly higher than the water rates for the citizens of Nairobi.

It was then explained to me that this was a good arrangement set up by the large woman as it did provide a certain amount of order for the project. Surely this could be categorised as a successful example of entrepreneurship?

I found myself standing near a woman who had collected her water and was heading back to her shanty. I asked, 'Why don't you just get water from the reservoir in your container?

What's to stop you just walking down the hill to the water's edge and filling up?'

She looked nervous at first and drew me away from the large woman, the guards and the UN person. If any of them went anywhere near the reservoir, she said, they would get shot. Just a few nights before, a neighbour's son had gone down at 2am and they hadn't seen him since. But they had heard the shot. Soldiers patrolled the edges of the reservoir night and day, and all the residents lived in terror.

We drove away from the 'successful' water project in silence. It's hard to be critical of something that is indeed providing water where before there was none. But is it not possible to provide a little clean water for people in desperate need without them being blatantly taken advantage of like that?

A workshop in Liberia. Lost again! Monrovia, 1979

It was very late at night when the big Pan Am plane landed at Roberts Field Airport, Monrovia, Liberia. The scene in the customs shed was chaotic. Crowds of returning Liberians who had boarded the plane in New York seemingly calm and dignified had turned into a screaming, excited mob who couldn't wait for their luggage and to get outside into the sultry night to be with their relatives. One woman ahead of me at the customs counter was angry that they wanted to open her enormous cases and look inside. She argued with the officials and tried to stop them. Finally they opened them only to find stacks of toilet paper rolls, all promptly confiscated. What did this mean? Was there no TP in Liberia?

At last I was outside, looking for the women who were to meet me and take me to the hotel where the workshop was to be held. I looked around hopefully. In an instant, two small boys grabbed my case and disappeared into the night. The case contained pretty well everything for the coming weeks in Africa, including workshop materials, so I dashed after them into the blackness. Being fairly fit at that time, (and the boys were carrying a heavy case) I caught them and reclaimed my luggage. I'm told I took an enormous risk doing that because even small boys in Africa often carried weapons. But I reacted without thinking and all was fine. Except that I had missed whoever was waiting for me and was stranded a long way from where I needed to go. And it was very deserted and very dark.

Roberts Field airport is 50 miles or so from Monrovia, and the road is desolate and dangerous. Or at least it was in October 1979. There was much political upheaval in Liberia at the time. I had been invited by two very good friends, Thelma Awori (Liberian) and Elizabeth Okwenje (Kenyan) to participate in a Women and Media workshop in Monrovia on my way through to Lusaka, Zambia where the United Nations was holding the Second Africa Regional Conference on Women. The governments of Africa were preparing the African Platform for Action as part of the lead-up to the UN Mid-Decade Conference on Women in Copenhagen, 1980.

I had a letter from Elizabeth and Thelma with the name of the hotel where the workshop was to be held and where all the participants would be staying so I felt fairly confident I could make my way there. Except there were no taxis available. A Dutch couple offered me a seat in a car that they had hired to take them through town to a rubber plantation where they lived. I gratefully accepted. We set off into the pitch darkness. It was dusty, there were strange sounds all around. We talked. The couple had lived there for some years but were clearly a bit frightened and I didn't know why.

Then the car stopped. We seemed to be in the middle of nowhere. There were no lights, no buildings. Just a couple of soldiers or at least two men in old and torn military uniforms. The driver wound down his window and began shouting at the men. The Dutch man seemed to understand a little of the language and began bargaining with them. He pulled out his wallet and money was exchanged. Still we waited. Then the driver stepped on the accelerator and we zoomed away. I was damp with perspiration – yes it was incredibly humid, but it was mainly fear. Not a nice feeling and the stomach takes a while to recover.

The couple dropped me off at the hotel where the workshop was to be held. It must have been about 1.30 in the morning. It was a ramshackle building and poorly maintained. The heat was palpable even though it was so early in the morning. I rang and rang the bell on the front desk. Finally a very sleepy old man appeared. He had no idea about a workshop, nor about a booking for me but allowed me to check in for the night and ushered me to my room. There was a bed and a basin and I was grateful for that. I washed a little of the day's grime off and fell onto the bed.

The next morning I began my search for Elizabeth and Thelma and the workshop that no one seemed to know anything about. I initially made the mistake of walking out onto the road with my camera visible and was instantly mobbed and almost mugged. Mainly small children, dressed in rags, bare-footed, clearly hungry and badly malnourished. All around were signs of great poverty, and the stifling heat made walking almost unbearable. So I retired back to my room while I tried to develop a plan of action. First, find where the workshop was to be held.

It was a Saturday and the woman who was the main organiser of the workshop was a secretary at a local church. I asked for a phone book but apparently there was no such thing available in my small hotel. I walked the streets searching for a newsagent or bookstore that might have a map. No luck. I happened upon the church, but it was all locked up.

On Sunday, walking alone through the streets was no fun. I became aware that I was being followed by bunches of children. I could find no one who spoke English or who wanted to talk with me. There was much tension in the air. The crowd was building and I felt very unsafe. The workshop started on Monday.

Monday morning, and I entered a place I thought might be able to help as it had many people inside and there was air-conditioning. I could hear the very old, rusty and shaky machine from the middle of the street. It looked like a respite from the heat and flies, and my followers. The darkness inside revealed itself to be a bar and I turned to leave. Another Dutch man called out to me and offered to buy me a drink. To be honest, I was dreadfully thirsty and a cold lemonade seemed like paradise so I accepted. He was a salesman for Nestlé, selling milk powder to impoverished women who could not afford to mix the full measure for each feed and were basically starving their babies. They were being told it was better (and more civilised) than their own breast milk. Then, to top it off, he had a Liberian mistress who was sick to death of him and he began asking me to help him persuade her to stay with him for another night before he flew out back to Europe to his wife and children. I headed for the door.

Then I saw a phone book, across the bar. I reached over and pulled it towards me. I found several listings of the surname of the conference organiser and asked for the phone. I began making my way through the list and finally found a relative. I called him on the phone. He was surprised to find where I was and told me to leave there immediately. I said I would return to my hotel and get my things. He knew where the workshop had been moved to and sent a car to fetch me.

Arriving at the much grander hotel where the workshop was being held, I made my way to the room where the welcome to participants was underway. I found a back seat and looked around. There were Thelma and Elizabeth at the head table, giving the welcome speech and explaining that their overseas speaker from New York was missing. I put my hand up and rose to my feet.

I thought for a minute that they were going to pass out. There was cheering and shouting and I was literally carried down to the front. Apparently, the workshop had been moved from the hotel I had gone to because they realised it was not a nice place, and was situated in a very dangerous part of town. Someone had neglected to inform me before I left New York, and when they couldn't find me at the airport, they just thought I'd missed my flight.

The workshop went well. I shared some tips and skills

on how to develop and produce low cost media (manuals, newsletters, slide/tape sets etc) on women and development issues with women from all over Africa and met and got to know some wonderful activists and leaders.

We were taken to meet heads of government in beautiful air-conditioned offices, travelling always in large air-conditioned vehicles, a wholly different vision of Monrovia from the one I seen for my first couple of days. We had afternoon tea in the home of the head of the Anglican Church, situated by the sea with a gorgeous white sand beach. I only knew this because during tea, I pulled back the heavy drapes and looked outside for an instant. The excessive heat – and as I found out later – the need for security, meant that the house was closed up tight and in darkness with the air-conditioners always on. For an Australian used to letting in the light and opening up to the view and the outside world whenever and wherever possible, all this seemed sad and strange. But the people we met were exceptionally generous and overwhelmingly kind to all the participants in the workshop.

Shortly after I returned from Africa it was with horror and regret that I saw photos in the *New York Times* of some of those gracious government and church people tied to poles on the golden beaches of Monrovia. They had been shot to death in the revolution that took place in Liberia just weeks after I flew out in October 1979. Clearly, the tension and anger that I felt in the mean streets of Monrovia as I walked around in the heat and dust that weekend so long ago was very real and about to burst. And burst it did in a violent and horrific way.

In 2006, Ellen Sirleaf Johnson became President of Liberia. She had previously been with UNDP and the World Bank and was a highly respected peace, development and women's empowerment activist. I met and talked with Ellen while she was still with UNDP, at a rooftop drinks party thrown by Peg Snyder at her New York apartment near the UN. I told Ellen about my 1979 visit to Monrovia and how I had found myself totally lost for that rather frightening weekend while I searched for my workshop. We talked about the poverty I had seen and the work of women activists trying to build something new and sustainable in the midst of such need.

Of course, neither of us knew what was ahead of her and of the extraordinary position she would find herself in to be able to do something for her country. Ellen was the first woman to be leader of an African country and her years as President saw unprecedented progress. She brought Liberia out of an abyss caused by generations of war and unspeakable violence. She worked with market women and helped them build a sustainable future for their families. She welcomed a UN all-women police force from Nepal that had had unrivalled success in coping with domestic violence and other violence against women.

Liberia was the first part of Africa that I was privileged to visit and memories of that time are still very vivid.

Gathering information at the UN in Ethiopia Addis Ababa, 1979

The Africa Regional Conference on Women in Lusaka, Zambia was over and I was packing my bags to head towards Kenya and then Ethiopia. The regional meeting had been called to prepare the input from African countries into the final document to come out of the Mid-Decade Conference on Women to be held in Copenhagen, June 1980.

The development and production by IWTC of the Caribbean Resource Kit for Women and the Asia Pacific Centre for Women and Development Resource Kit had caused a lot of interest among other regions for similar resource kits. The Africa Centre for Research and Training in Addis Ababa, Ethiopia, had invited me to visit them following the regional meeting in Lusaka. After a few days in Nairobi, including a considerable amount of time confirming my air ticket to Addis Ababa and from there back to New York, I travelled to the Nairobi Airport.

I knew there would be a crowd as the meeting had brought women and government officials from every African country and we were all leaving. But still the crowd was over the top. The scramble to get through the check-in counter, then the customs area was intense, but I had finally made it. There we sat, hundreds of passengers in a vast waiting room at the gate. I looked through the picture windows and saw the plane being prepared on the runway. It seemed a bit small for this crowd but no matter. We were all checked in, somebody must have done the count.

The announcement came over the PA system: they were ready for us to board. A young man and I stepped to the gate to assist by holding open the door in the absence of anyone official. To our surprise, there seemed to be some kind of contest to get through the door first and the hustle and bustle of fighting passengers was something to behold. I looked across at the young man, and the realisation dawned on each of our faces at approximately the same time. Our tickets did not have seat numbers!

We dropped our helpful hands from the doors and ran for our lives and just made the last seats. Then a party of UN officials came aboard, including a young woman from the UK. No seats left. Furious, she stood in the middle of the plane and began to shout. 'I'm not leaving this plane. I won't let you drag me off. You have to find me a seat. I have an important meeting at the UN in Addis and I'm frankly not leaving!' There was a kind of silence that descended on us all. I guess I should have risen and offered my seat but I also had meetings at the UN in Addis. And a flight connection to make to New York.

Then the young African pilot appeared at the end of the centre aisle. He took the hand of the UN woman and they disappeared up front. Apparently they sat her in the co-pilot's seat though we were not informed of that. She told me when we met at the UN the next day. I'm happy I didn't know. I frankly like to think there are two pilots at the helm. But we landed safely in Addis.

In Addis I headed the next morning to my meeting with the Director of the ATRCW, Mary Tadesse, and we discussed the kind of resource kit they would like. With UNDP offices in every African country and women's groups requesting information, technical assistance and training in development issues, the need was acute. We mapped out the chapters for the kit, including names and addresses of all UN country offices and UNDP Resident Representatives, all women's organisations country by country, important UN resolutions and conventions on women's empowerment, and a final chapter that was to be a bibliography of available publications published by ATRCW and, if appropriate, by other UN departments at UN Economic Commission for Africa (ECA) of which ATRCW was a part.

Mary pointed me in the direction of a large wooden building outside the main building and told me I would find the publications there and I could have one copy of each. With these copies, IWTC would be able to write up a short bibliographical overview of each publication. I set off to collect the books. Maybe I could pick them up and be back at the hotel by lunch, then I could pack them in my luggage and take them back to New York.

With the key given to me, I opened the doors. This can't be right, I thought. In front of me as far as the eye could see were soaring piles of books, stacks reaching to the roof, pile after pile, literally thousands upon thousands of books. Surely this was a mistake? I looked around for someone to ask. Maybe this was some kind of manufacturers/publishers warehouse and the ECA building was somewhere else? There was no-one around. So I found a very tall ladder and climbed to the top of the first pile. It was an ATRCW publication on women and fishing. I took the top copy and carefully climbed down. I moved the ladder to the next pile. Another ATRCW publication, this time on women and small business. I took a copy and climbed down.

And so it went for the rest of the day. I climbed dozens of piles, taking the top copy and climbing down. By the end of the day, exhausted, I had a pile of around 30 specific ATRCW publications and another 30 or so ECA publications on relevant and appropriate development issues that women would find of use. Now what to do with this rather heavy collection of books?

I left the warehouse and walked across to the main building and found my way to the UN mail department. After some discussion with the very helpful person in charge, he agreed to help me pack all the publications into UN mail pouches which I addressed to myself care of UNDP/UNIFEM near my office in New York. I could not believe I had found such a treasure trove. And I couldn't wait to get back to New York and show off this extraordinary collection.

The books finally arrived in New York. We laid them out on the carpeted floor of the IWTC office. Then I got on the phone and called several UN friends working on women's issues. 'Come and check out what I've found in Africa', I told them. And across the road they came. Total amazement. Some publications they had heard of but not been able to get hold of. Most were totally new to them. Clearly we had a job to do to get the word out about this great collection of important information coming from Africa.

The work on the African Resource Kit for Women began and proceeded for the next months. With the help of UNDP in New York, we printed mailing labels for all of the UNDP centres across Africa and packed copies of the resource kit into UN mail pouches to be sent to each UNDP office, enough copies for every women's organisation in each country. We included printed labels with the name and address of each organisation from the IWTC mailing list. Such a distribution strategy had not been tried before, particularly with a manual produced by an NGO, though it was on behalf of a UN agency.

Some months passed. ATRCW had already asked us to begin on a French translation of the resource kit and we were well on the way with this, working with a UNESCO translator from Paris. Then my phone rang in the IWTC office. 'Please limit the number of publications each women's organisation can request on the order form in the French-language manual as we have completely run out of English-language books.' I literally fell off my chair: how could that be possible? I had brought back photos of the massive stacks of books and no-one had been able to believe there were so many in storage!

But indeed it was true. Our little NGO had worked out a dissemination strategy that had put our African Resource Kit for Women into the hands of almost every women's organisation in Africa. They had all jumped at the opportunity to be able to order publications on women and development being produced by the UN.

Those were pre-computer days, days when delivery of materials was difficult, when phone connections were poor across Africa, when travel was not easy. Things were to change dramatically in the years ahead and contact made much simpler. But the memory of those stacks of publications will remain with me forever. Along with the memory of clearing out that incredible warehouse in a matter of months!

Cleaning up after the Mid-Decade Conference Copenhagen, 1980

The UN Mid-Decade Conference on Women was in Copenhagen in 1980 and the NGO Forum was held parallel to the official conference, at Amager University. With the world of women now on notice since the first UN Conference on Women in Mexico City in 1975, we were expecting a large crowd.

Elizabeth Palmer, the recently retired General Secretary of the World YWCA, had asked IWTC to come to Copenhagen a week ahead to help set up the university for the expected invasion. One specific job I undertook was to paint large banners for the entrance and for each of the separate spaces allocated. With the help of a local Danish woman artist, Annelise Hansen, we found a studio with ample floor space, bought quantities of yellow cotton, lots of paint, and got to work.

Once hung up, the banners became very popular. As the two weeks of the NGO Forum went by, various local dignitaries signalled to the Forum organisers that they would like to have one of them. And so each was allocated well in advance of the end of the Forum.

IWTC was given one of the spacious dining areas at the university to turn into a Resource Centre. We called the area *Vivencia*, a Spanish word that means experience. On the walls near the entrance, we hung large sheets of paper and titled each page with a subject or issue area. Women wanting to make contact with other women and groups with a similar interest wrote their names under their area of interest. As the two weeks went by, the lists grew. In return for writing their name and address, we at IWTC promised to send each of them a typed copy of that list. We also thought that we could do a special issue of *The Tribune* on women's networks, and then special issues on each subject area. It was all still in the thinking stages but clearly an idea that was growing as each day went by.

We had started the NGO Forum in a clean, empty building at Amager University, and early on, as the walls began to be covered with posters, banners, lists, workshop ads, the resident supervisor of the building began to get frantic. We assured him that we would clean everything up and that he was not to worry. In fact we encouraged him to go home and stay there for the remainder of the time, worrying that he was about to have a nervous breakdown.

On the second last day of the Forum, an exhausted team of IWTC women stood looking at the job of clean-up ahead of us. We had promised the supervisor we would do that and we intended to keep our promise. But looking after the demands and interests of 10,000 women, many of whom had flocked in and out of our Resource Centre every day for two weeks, had left us totally drained and we could hardly stand on our feet.

The collective decision was made to go back to the little house that had been loaned to us for the duration by a group of Danish women, and have a shower and a good sleep and return early in the morning to clean up. But I was worried. I had been to previous meetings and seen things suddenly start to disappear as people took souvenirs. So I insisted that we remove all the precious networking lists of names and addresses and take them back to our house, plus any equipment belonging to IWTC. The rest we could collect in the morning, especially the large painted banners allocated to local dignitaries.

The next morning, bright and early, we arrived in our taxis

to begin the clean-up. To our utter surprise, there was nothing there. No banners, no posters, no announcements, demands, workshop ads, drawings, ribbons, balloons, nothing. The place was swept clean.

How had this happened? Perhaps the organisers had been there at the crack of dawn and done all this? But no, not so. Everything had disappeared, and not a single banner or poster was ever found. The local dignitaries certainly did not get the large banners. There have been several theories posited. Did a group of young people scale the walls and empty the place in the middle of the night? Did the nervous supervisor come and remove everything before dawn? No-one knows.

All we knew was that we were one of the lucky groups who actually took down the most precious things the night before, which in our case were the networking lists. Other groups had left things until the next morning and lost everything. It was a lesson we never forgot and from then on, at every large gathering of this kind, we packed up a day or night ahead of the end before the 'locusts' arrived and swept through taking all before them.

International Women's Day in Chile
Santiago, 1983

I had only been in Chile for a few days on my first visit to that country, so beautiful, so like Australia in many ways. Eucalyptus trees, beautiful beaches, a rugged coastline with a drive reminiscent of the Great Ocean Road in Victoria. And always, the kindness and generosity of people who welcomed me to their homes, and women's groups who took me to special events, concerts, galleries, picnics in the park. But it was a very big women's event on International Women's Day 1983 that will always hold a special place in my memory.

We gathered in our thousands to begin the march through the streets of Santiago. General Pinochet was in power and his military might was much in evidence. Women from every walk of life were lining up. There was much singing, chanting, and most were holding protest banners: Give Us Back Our Country. We Demand Our Rights. Democracy for Chile.

I had been put through some rudimentary training for the event, including instructions such as: run when they start throwing tear gas and hold a damp cloth over your eyes and nose and suck on a lemon; keep your eyes covered from the water cannons as there are chemicals in the water; drop to the ground if a soldier points his machine gun at you and cover your head.

It all sounded a little unreal. After all, I was just planning to take some photos, not to get too involved. I knew of plans for fake voting boxes to be placed at various parts of Santiago and everyone was going to have a protest, make-believe opportunity to place a fake vote for their choice of President and I particularly wanted to have photos of that.

So with a group of friends, I marched confidently down the main road of Santiago. It was kind of fun: lots of singing, lots of laughter, lots of bravado.

Then we saw the wall of soldiers across the road ahead. They were dressed in battle fatigues and their faces were painted with green and black as though they were camouflaged for a battle in the jungle. And they all had machine guns in their hands, at the ready. Camouflage! Battle fatigues! Machine guns! We were unarmed women holding banners and singing songs – what threat were they expecting from us?

I gave serious thought to turning back. I'm not accustomed to fighting a war and certainly not against armed military men. But then, neither were any of these extraordinary women marching beside me. Lawyers, doctors, nurses, journalists, artists, writers, shopkeepers, maids, cleaners, farmers, housewives, schoolgirls, university students. They just kept marching towards this wall of armed force in front of the Parque Forestal, across from the Bellas Artes Museum, and I continued on with them. One of the women marched right up to a soldier, stared him in the eye and said, 'Give me back my country!' Then all hell broke loose.

Tear gas canisters came flying towards us. I ducked for cover amongst some trees in the park. The gas rose up and hit me in the face. I struggled to get my moist cloth and lemon out of my pocket. For some insane reason, I kept taking photos – the results were quite surrealistic: wavy lines of gas, blurred images of running women. My eyes were burning and running freely. I could hardly breathe. Women were shouting for us to regroup in a nearby square. That was the plan: each time a crowd was broken up, we were to regroup in another designated place.

I had lost my friends in the chaos and wasn't quite sure where the next designated place was situated. I ran down a side street, and hands mysteriously came out of nowhere and dragged me inside a doorway. Someone told me to wait with them and then we would head off to this other place. I was happy to do as I was told. They couldn't believe I, a *gringa*, was in the midst of this very Chilean experience and were quite sure I would want to disappear to somewhere out of the firing line. But by now I felt so much a part of this extraordinarily courageous crowd of women protestors that I wanted to continue with them.

After a while, we left the safety of the doorway and headed off to a nearby square where large make-believe voting boxes, put together by the organisers of the demonstration to closely resemble real ballot boxes, were placed at various points in the square and women were bravely folding their ballots and slipping them into the slot provided. Hundreds of votes in a matter of minutes were stuffed into the boxes. Then the soldiers arrived. More tear gas. A large truck with water cannons aimed directly at us forced many of us to the ground. Those hoses are powerful and the force of the water was unbearable. We were all thoroughly drenched and stinging, eyes running. We ran for cover as the soldiers, brandishing machine guns and shouting, confiscated the voting boxes.

Again we regrouped some distance away, more make-believe voting boxes appeared from nowhere and women began to place their fake, protest ballots in them. Again the soldiers with their tear gas and water cannons stormed into the new space and confiscated the boxes. It seemed like many hours that this battle raged, with thousands in the streets being dispersed forcefully, regrouping, voting, then again being dispersed. It was a game of cat and mouse, quite incredible in its effectiveness and totally infuriating for the soldiers who never seemed able to totally control what was happening.

Unfortunately, the day ended violently when gangs of young men suddenly appeared and began more serious and damaging activities. Cars and piles of tyres were set on fire, amateur fire bombs thrown around, and soldiers were attacked with rocks and stones. Apparently, this happened often in Chile with even the most peaceful demonstrations. Whether these gangs were genuine protestors or government stooges intent on showing the population at large how dangerous any protest was, and how necessary it was to keep the dictatorship in place is hard to say. Most of the women were convinced of the latter and they were probably right.

That evening, on making it safely back to where I was staying, I was glad to sink into a bath. I can't say I enjoyed the day; rather it was a day of some terror and a lot of frightening moments. Yet to see the courage of those women as they tried to express their frustration at the complete loss of democratic rights in their country, a country that had been one of the first in South America to have won democratic rights, was a great privilege and an unforgettable experience.

Women sacrificing their daughters to get water
Peru, 1983

I was in Lima to participate at a regional feminist meeting. Known as Encuentro Feminista, it brought together women activists and leaders from every Latin American country. Through plenary sessions, small workshops, creative arts, film, dance and vibrant discussion, the meeting produced an action document outlining the needs and aspirations of women throughout that continent.

I was on another mission also, and that was to find women and water projects for a special issue of *The Tribune* on women and water. IWTC was continuing to highlight the fact that the inaccessibility of water in some parts of the world could totally dominate the lives of women. In what ways was this being recognised and how were women being assisted? Were development agencies really working with the community on ways to bring water to their homes? How were women tackling the problem? They are the ones who fetch and carry whatever water is available, sometimes from great distances and this daily essential task can be enormously exhausting and extremely detrimental to their health and life expectancy.

These were the things on my mind as I travelled to Canto Grande, a fast growing community clinging to a mountainside on the outskirts of Lima, with two women from the women's organisation Flora Tristan. Canto Grande was the first port of call for families leaving their villages and towns in rural Peru in search of work and a better life for their children. Houses were being hastily built to cope with the influx and services were rudimentary, or non-existent. All this I had been told before we set out, yet the reality was still confronting. Dirt tracks between overcrowded shacks, children scrabbling through mountains of garbage looking for food scraps and anything else they could use.

I wanted to take photos so that people back in New York could get a sense of this reality. But as soon as I produced my camera, the screaming started and mothers rushed from their homes to grab their children and disappear. Alarmed, I asked my friends what was the matter? One of them went in search of one of the mothers and talked with her. Apparently, people from 'adoption agencies' regularly visited Canto Grande, took pictures of the children, and then flogged the photos on the open market for the highest bidder. Once a bid had been accepted from overseas (usually the USA), they returned and kidnapped the child. I was horrified and swiftly hid my camera. My colleagues explained who I was and talked with the group who had gathered. We all parted on good terms.

From this experience we moved on to the water project. Arrangements had been made ahead of time for us to meet and talk with some women who had been able to set up a system whereby a water tanker visited their street once a week and filled up large pottery containers they had made and placed outside their houses. This had cut back the need to carry water long distances. It seemed a simple solution to their problem and I was happy to talk with them and take some photos.

However, I wondered how they were able to afford to have this regular service. And why were other streets denied water? Did these women have some source of income that the others did not? Was this a government service? Maybe the women in this dusty street were also making something and selling that at the market? Maybe they had husbands with jobs? All seemed possible, yet we were not getting any responses that seemed to indicate there was any source of income that would pay for these regular water tanker visits.

Finally one of the women broke down and began to cry. One of my friends drew her aside and talked to her. All suddenly became clear. Every week, a daughter from one of the families was offered up to sleep with the truck driver. This was the only way they could get water delivered.

From a successful water story, we were plunged into utter despair at the lengths to which these women went in order to survive. The thought of sacrificing their daughters for the common good was so awful I couldn't go on with the visit. Was there anything we could do in this situation? Nothing. We had no words of wisdom, just outrage and commiseration for their predicament.

Of course I could share the knowledge with important international agencies involved in water projects and I certainly did that over the next years. Maybe they stepped in and helped. I don't know. But I sure hope somebody did.

Getting information in the village
Kenya, 1984

We were driving into a very rural area in the foothills of Mt Kenya, to visit a women's group in a small village and talk with them about development issues that most affected their lives. I was part of a group of about ten women in three 4-wheel drive vans, my colleagues representing several women's groups in Nairobi, including the nationwide women's organisation Maendeleo Ya Wanawake.

We passed wide expanses of tea plantations with mainly women picking the leaves and placing them in bags on their backs. There were also large areas of bananas shielding coffee plants under their wide broad leaves.

Then we came to where the track ended and we all got out of the vehicles and began the walk towards the village, a muddy track over hills. In the distance, I could hear a strange sound, a little like many high voices trilling or calling. I asked one of my friends what it was but she didn't seem to know. The sound got louder and louder. There were indeed many voices involved and they were ululating, a vibrating high-pitched sound that is forever a sound of Africa.

Then over the hill came a crowd of women, all in bright, patterned long dresses with matching turbans on their heads. Many of them were waving a publication in their hands, from side to side above their heads. It began to look rather familiar. Then sure enough, I could see what it was. A copy of our little newsletter *The Tribune*.

The next thing I knew I was seated on a broad pair of

shoulders high above the crowd, weaving from side to side in time to the dancing crowd of women, all ululating and singing, many waving *The Tribune*.

As we approached the village, the crowd grew even larger. Word had spread and women from several villages and many huts nearby had gathered in the main village compound to greet and meet us. I was carefully lowered to the ground and seated in a chair along with my colleagues. Then the speeches began. All had to be translated; in short, they wanted to thank IWTC for finding them and sending them information that they had never received before. Yes, it was in English and only a few of them understood that, but they used all the graphics and knew what it was about and when they needed to, they got the local schoolteacher to come and translate the rest. Mostly, they wanted me to know that they had received our newsletter and would I please thank everyone who had contributed to putting it together, especially me because I drew the pictures.

I was deeply moved. I thanked them for their welcome and explained that they were the reason we produced our newsletters and manuals. I asked them to let us know what information was of most use for them and to send their requests to us via their women's group in Kenya if they couldn't send it themselves. After tea and biscuits, we headed back to our transport, surrounded by singing dancing women and children, the crowd growing larger by the minute. The children ran after the vans waving as we drove away.

So much hunger for information from the world outside. And in the end, it's not all that difficult to get information to them, with the help of local women's groups. It's the reason IWTC was set up. And no amount of World Wide Web or internet e-mail traffic will ever replace that little, highly visual, simple language newsletter we produced year after year and sent around the world by snail mail.

If it's not appropriate for women, it's not appropriate Nairobi, 1985

It was an amazing scene as the first week of the NGO Forum '85 unfolded on the campus of the University of Nairobi. Twenty thousand women and some men milled around the central lawns of the main campus. Groups of women sprawled over the grass in deep conversation. Posters, workshop notices, bulletins and flags waved all around and the striped Peace Tent took centre stage at one end. In one corner of the lawns was a Prayer Tree that had been erected by an African-American woman wearing brightly colored skirts. She sat near the 'tree', strumming a ukelele and helping women place scraps of paper on which they had written their prayers. A lesbian research group was engaged in intense discussion with a growing number of Kenyan women dropping by curiously to find what that was all about.

The day before, there had been a tense situation at the Peace Tent as Dame Nita Barrow, the NGO Forum Convener from Barbados, had negotiated a settlement between the Kenyan authorities and the Film Festival organisers. One of the films to be shown was about Lebanese women and the authorities thought it was about lesbian women. The matter was resolved after much animated discussion and Nita's extensive negotiating skills.

Things were still tense in this first week, with the police expecting marches through the main streets of Nairobi and authorities on the lookout for any women stripping off their clothes in public. This fear was traced back to a false rumour that had been circulated in the weeks leading up to the NGO Forum regarding the previous NGO Forum in Copenhagen in 1980, where supposedly, women had stripped naked in public. Some women might have sunbathed in the parks of Copenhagen during the time of the Forum in 1980. That is perfectly acceptable in that country. But there were no naked demonstrations.

Given all these events and happenings, there was much uneasiness when word spread that the President of Kenya, Daniel Arap Moi, had expressed a desire to visit the NGO Forum. Initially, it was planned to completely clear the central campus of all questionable displays and groups, including the Prayer Tree, the lesbian research group, the posters, banners, flags, notices, etc. Then the women protested. This was their space and they didn't want it cleared.

So a plan was hatched by the Kenyan Organising Committee to bring the President of Kenya to the appropriate technology exhibition, Tech and Tools, on the University of Nairobi sports ground. In addition, he would visit the craft market put on by Mandeleo ya Wanawake, the national women's organisation of Kenya. These would represent the NGO Forum '85 and the chaotic scenes at the main campus could continue untroubled.

Tech and Tools was a collaborative effort between IWTC, the Appropriate Technology Advisory Committee (ATAC) of Kenya and the World YWCA. For months we had been planning how to stage what was to become an extraordinary display of ingenuity and technology that was appropriate to the needs of women. Joanne Sandler and I from IWTC went to Nairobi a couple of weeks before the Forum opened to work with ATAC and get everything finalised. This included the building of huts on the sports ground, each hut made from sustainable materials such as bamboo, wood, reeds and stones.

With a group of Kenyan workers, we had erected all the buildings in two weeks and outfitted them with equipment and materials for each of the technologies. I had hand-painted huge banners for each hut, naming the type of technology – health, water and sanitation, computers, solar energy, cooking, bee keeping, etc. Although it was a little distance from the main campus, many women had found their way to Tech and Tools and it had become something of a meeting place, particularly for those involved in rural activities. But we had not attracted the crowds that gathered in the other forum spaces.

That is, until the arrival of the President. On the morning of his visit, a team of men suddenly appeared and began to transform the previously simple, unadorned entrance. Down came the hand-painted banner announcing TECH AND TOOLS: IF IT'S NOT APPROPRIATE FOR WOMEN, IT'S NOT APPROPRIATE, and up went a professionally printed sign NGO FORUM. Flagpoles were erected on either side of the track leading to the entrance and the Kenyan flag was hoisted on each.

Then the soldiers arrived and formed a guard of honour. Finally, with much cheering and ceremony, a fleet of limousines came down the road and entered through the line of flags. The President stepped out of his limo and was greeted by members of the Kenyan Organising Committee. Then one by one, we were all introduced.

I had been asked to show the President around the various buildings illustrating each technology. Demonstrations were performed in each building. Women cooked using smokeless stoves, others used solar-powered computers. There were beekeepers hiding behind net masks and reaching into their beehives for honey, and women sanitation engineers illustrating water catchment and disposal technologies. Ruth Lechte and her YWCA team of women from Africa, Asia and the Pacific, Latin America and the Caribbean were building smokeless stoves out of mud. In a separate part of the sports grounds, Wangari Maathai and her Green Belt Movement women had planted trees to publicise that movement that has since planted tens of millions of trees across the country.

Wangari's work in environment and peace activities earned her a Nobel Prize for Peace in 2004. At the time of the visit of the President of Kenya to Tech and Tools in 1985 however, Wangari was being watched by the government as a troublemaker for her outspoken views on peace and democracy and her demands for more government support for the needs of women and the environment. It was therefore a small surprise for the President to find himself face to face with her, and an opportunity for Wangari to have a few words with him.

Finally the tour was over and we saw the President and his entourage off in their limousines. We were relieved that it had all gone off well and that the President seemed pleased with what he had observed. He believed, of course, that this was the NGO Forum itself and not just one small part of it all.

We were exhausted and looking forward to some calm the next day, but nothing could have been further from that. We arrived early to set up for the new day, and there at the entrance was a fleet of buses, loaded with village women. As we opened the front gates they came flooding through and as the day progressed, more buses arrived, more women, crowds of villagers all going from one building to the other. Everything was new and exciting. And we were giving away dozens of smokeless stoves, information pamphlets in Swahili, drawings on how to make things for themselves. We were astounded by the size of the crowds and most particularly by the distances some of them had travelled. How had this happened?

One of the Kenyan members of our team sat down with some of the women late in the day and asked them how they had heard about Tech and Tools. It was the President's visit the day before, which had been closely covered on the radio, in Swahili, and broadcast throughout Kenya. Descriptions of the technologies, the mud stoves, the beehives, the planted trees, the cooking demos, the solar-powered computers even, all had been broadcast far and wide. The women in the villagers had jumped on buses and headed for town and they were delighted and amazed at what they saw.

Tech and Tools gave quite a boost to the knowledge and use of appropriate technologies for women in Kenya and Africa in general. And for the publicity it gained on the day of the President's visit, we had to thank the Kenya Organising Committee and their efforts to save the NGO Forum central compound, with its seemingly outrageous displays and discussion groups on touchy subjects, from the earnest gaze of authority and the possibility of closure. And we had to thank the President himself, for spending a day with us at Tech and Tools and so clearly approving of the technologies and ideas there. His approval was broadcast around the country to great and ongoing effect.

Computer training for women in Zimbabwe Harare, 1988

At IWTC, we experienced a computer revolution in the early 1980s, transferring our extensive mailing list of 25,000 names and addresses representing women and groups in 125 countries onto a computerised database. The computer was large and bulky and the system complex.

So it was with much relief that we were introduced to the simplicity of the Macintosh computer in the late 80s with the donation of two Classic Macs by the United Methodist Global Women's Division in New York. Actually, by two great supporters of the work of IWTC, Rose Catchings and Doris Hess. Rose and Doris were veterans of the United Methodist Church and had worked with the Global Women's Division for many years. Doris had been a missionary in various parts of the world, most especially in the Philippines. They knew firsthand how important information and technical assistance in the development and production of print materials was for women in the Global South. We dedicated those first two Macs to them and named the hard drives Rosendoris.

Then in 1988, Rose and Doris came to us with a request. Would we go to Zimbabwe and train the people at the Harare United Methodist Church to be able to use a Mac computer system recently donated by the United Methodist Church of the USA? After much discussion and rearrangement of work programs, we agreed. I would be traveling with Angela, our young computer expert.

We began to make preparations for the workshop. This was

pre-email and fax and way before Skype, Twitter, Facebook, and even the World Wide Web. So preparations were done by snail mail. We were basically flying blind as to participants and the equipment available – other than the new Mac computer system.

A week before we were to fly to Zimbabwe, I decided to call the church in Harare on the phone, carefully estimating when there might be someone in the church office. A secretary answered, I introduced myself and she rushed off to get Rhodes, the church treasurer. I began to ask him about the participants. Who were they? What training did they have? What occupations? From the list of names we had been sent, I could not tell if there were any women in the group.

'Well no', said Rhodes. 'This is a computer course so of course there are no women amongst the participants.' 'Who were these men who would be taking part?' I asked. 'There's the minister', said Rhodes. 'And the choirmaster. And the organist. And the President of the church council.' And so the list went on.

'Rhodes', I said. 'Could you tell me who puts together the news bulletin each Sunday?' Why that would be the Bishop's secretary said Rhodes. 'Do you have any print materials for the Sunday School at the moment and who puts them together?' I asked. That would be the second secretary. 'And are there any people who type minutes for the church council meetings?' Yes was the response. They were all women who worked for the church.

Then we would want to have them all in the workshop group I said. Which may mean some of the current list might miss out because we didn't want more than ten participants, but if we were to train a group of people who could develop the print materials that the church wanted, we would most definitely need the women who were currently doing that. We would just be updating the equipment from typewriter, stencil and duplicator to a computer.

Rhodes admitted later in Harare, when we had met him and got to know him well, that he was somewhat shocked at the thought that the women of the church office would be part of the group. But he felt he had to comply with our wishes After all, computers were high tech and needed great intelligence and education, all of which clearly meant that the group had to be made up of men.

Suffice to say, at the end of the training week, it was the women who had picked up the skills needed and were by far the most competent and expert. They were also the most responsible and took on the job of security and care for the equipment, setting up each morning and locking the equipment away each night.

Some time after we had returned to New York, a parcel from Harare turned up. It contained the first of the new Sunday School materials, bulletins, newsletters and even a hymnal, all developed and produced by the women of the church office on their new Mac computer.

A letter from Rhodes confirmed what we had seen in the group we had left behind. He was amazed at the self-confidence amongst the women and how this short course in computer training had empowered and encouraged them to move into other activities and senior positions in the community.

And he was apologetic about the way he had not thought the women capable of tackling computers. It was mainly a misunderstanding of the skills needed, he said.

An Australian woman diplomat in Nepal Kathmandu, 1989

At the invitation of Worldview International, the inter-national media organisation headquartered in Sri Lanka, I had flown from Bangkok to Kathmandu to participate in the Worldview International AGM and afterwards, to run a low-cost media development workshop for women's organisations in Nepal.

I was booked into a beautiful hotel with views from my window of the mountains that surround Kathmandu, a city in a saucer as it's known, with the rim of the saucer the mighty Himalayas. If I'd been following world news more closely, I would have known of the tensions on the border between Nepal and India and the consequent cutting off of some essential food supplies. Then I would have stopped eating some of the meals earlier, meals that had been regenerated several times and not refrigerated. I came down with violent diarrhoea.

Luckily, my workshop was pretty well over by the time I was really ill. I took things easy and for a few days drank only lassi, the yoghurt concoction recommended to me, and delayed my departure back to Bangkok while I recovered.

It was in this space of time that I made several visits to various women's training centres and organisations and noticed the almost entire lack of training materials. I knew that many of the manuals and materials that we were producing at IWTC would be a great help in their work and decided to visit the Australian Embassy in Kathmandu to see if we could work out a way to ship the materials to the women.

Imagine my surprise on arriving at the Australian Embassy to find that the Ambassador was a woman. She welcomed me into her office warmly and we sat down for a cup of tea together. With my still sensitive, recovering stomach, I had to decline the delicious looking cupcakes and biscuits!

The Ambassador was Diane Johnstone, one of only seven women out of a total of 87 ambassadors representing Australia in overseas diplomatic missions. Appointed at age 36, she was the first full-time residential head of mission to Nepal. Diane was particularly interested to learn about the workshop for women's organisations in Nepal, on new low-cost techniques to develop and produce their own print materials. I could tell she was delighted with that. I then went on to talk with her about the extreme lack of visual training materials for both women and school children and she agreed. Then I showed her a couple of the manuals and bulletins I had brought with me from IWTC and she became quite excited.

'Of course we can help you to ship them and distribute them', she said. 'Just pack them up and call the Permanent Mission of Australia to the UN in New York and I will make sure someone comes by your office and collects them. And I will handle the rest.'

After more talk and some discussion about the needs of women in Nepal, I left. The next day I flew to Bangkok, where my friends there deposited me at a doctor's office and I was introduced to the wonders of Imodium.

On my return to New York, I packed up a good number of IWTC manuals on small business, issues of *The Tribune* on various women and development issues, IWTC posters on women and appropriate technology, women's rights, rights of the girl-child, and much more. We called the Australian Mission to the UN and sure enough, around came an official car with driver to pick up the packages.

A few weeks went by. Then the delighted messages from women's groups all over Nepal began to arrive. 'The Australian

Ambassador came in her car with the Australian flag flying and she brought us all kinds of wonderful materials from IWTC', the messages said. 'And she stayed for a cup of tea and talked with us about other assistance that Australia can give our village and group.' 'How did this happen?' 'We are all so thrilled!' And so the messages continued.

Later, I was able to make contact with the Ambassador to thank her for what she had done. She assured me it was of enormous benefit to her to be able to have a reason to sail off into villages in the official car and meet with women and villagers across Nepal without them being apprehensive. And the manuals and posters had been enormously popular, an added benefit that she felt she really didn't deserve.

I was once again reminded of the difference it makes to have a woman at the head of a diplomatic mission. How many men would have used some packages of materials from a small NGO in far-off New York as a basis for making journeys into the mountains to visit women and children and sit down for a chat?

Pacific women using space technology Vanuatu, 1989

A United Nations workshop on media was taking me back into the Pacific: a workshop to be held at the University of the South Pacific campus in Port Vila, Vanuatu. Organised by the Pacific regional office of UN ESCAP, it would bring together women communicators and media specialists from Fiji, Tonga, Solomon Islands, Niue, New Caledonia, Cook Islands, Federated States of Micronesia, Papua New Guinea, Samoa, Nauru, Kiribati, Tuvalu and of course Vanuatu. I was looking forward to meeting up with many old friends from my 11 years with the YWCA in Fiji from 1962–1972.

As the plane came in to land, I was struck again by the isolation and beauty of this part of the world. And later I was again taken by the ease with which the women picked up new skills. The workshop was a practical one and we spent many hours developing and producing single line drawings and lettering, pages cut and pasted for offset printing, and producing training materials and tools that the women could use back home.

One morning, I noticed a space during the morning had been set aside for a teleconference. It was not part of the workshop so I was intrigued. With a fellow trainer, from the USA, we followed the women into a meeting room with a large central table and microphones set up in front of each woman. We sat down to watch and listen.

Over a public address speaker hung high on the wall came a slight crackle and then the voice of the moderator. 'This is

Papua New Guinea, come in please'. Then, with ease, each woman began to talk in response to the moderator bringing in other women from islands flung across the Pacific Ocean. They managed with such incredible ease and confidence it was clear this was commonplace for them all. They discussed an upcoming meeting on several major women's concerns and made decisions on future actions.

We talked about the meeting with the women afterwards. They were utilising PeaceSat, the satellite left over by the US military many years before and loaned to the University of the South Pacific for its Extension Services work from the main campus in Suva. USP had allotted time each month to various community groups for discussions in the 'downlink' meeting rooms on each USP campus. These women were thoroughly used to talking to each other via satellite across the vast expanses of the Pacific.

This was long before fax machines, email, the World Wide Web, Skype, Twitter and Facebook. Yet here was an isolated and vast expanse of the world using space-age technology in the simplest of ways and building a close community of women, via satellite.

I could see the trainer from the US was impressed. We talked about the Pacific being a community that is much more accustomed to talking than writing and this was therefore perfect for the region. And how much better that PeaceSat should be used like this than as a military facility!

Discussing rights with a village woman Turkey, 1992

Another conference was finally over, this time the International Conference on Nutrition (Rome, 1992), where First Ladies from developing countries met to discuss a program to combat poverty in their countries. I participated to find more information for a special issue of IWTC *Tribune* newsletter and to meet some of the program leaders struggling with this major concern, particularly in Africa.

It had been a surrealistic meeting for me, held as it was in an extraordinary Italian palace, complete with marble floors, crystal chandeliers, satin drapes, exquisitely woven, enormously expensive tapestry-covered seats, and one sumptuous feast after another. The clash of this luxury with the stories of extreme poverty was difficult to comprehend.

With my head full of these thoughts, I set off to Istanbul where my brother Robert was spending a year teaching at the Semiha Sakir Experimental Secondary School. Robert was fluent in Turkish having spent time some years before teaching in a rural school in Turkey. He also had a number of Turkish friends in Melbourne, a city of many Turkish immigrants, and was familiar with the people and the country. I was looking forward to some 'down time' after the conference on poverty.

I arrived at the Istanbul Airport and was delighted to see Robert's head through the glass walls. After clearing customs we had a cup of coffee and proceeded to wait for the arrival of Ahdinal, Robert's foster son from Melbourne, returning home to Turkey for the first time since his parents had left, which was before he was born. Both parents were gone now, Ahdinal was 18, and there was a risk officials might take him off for compulsory military service. I felt sure they wouldn't do that as he didn't speak a word of Turkish and was holding an Australian passport. But I was wrong. Before our eyes, we watched them march Ahdinal off into the distance.

Some very anxious minutes later, suddenly there he was, smiling at us through the glass and heading for the exit. How had he escaped? Then he was with us and we hurried away before anyone changed their mind. Apparently, his total lack of Turkish had finally exasperated them and they gave him up. Amazing really as his name is Turkish and Turkish authorities don't usually care where you were born or what your passport is when it comes to military service.

Robert lived in a little white stone-walled apartment in Maltepe on the Asian side of the Bosphoros. We caught the airport bus to Sirkeci then the ferry across the Bosphoros to Kadikoy, an absolutely beautiful ride across that water with the shimmering city behind us. Then a mini-bus from Kadikoy to Maltepe. On the way we drove past huge stormwater drains piled by the road as part of roadworks. I remarked that such huge, solid pipes in New York would have homeless people living inside. Robert said that would never happen in Turkey because people looked after each other.

Robert had arranged for Ahdinal and I to travel south with him to visit friends in the township of Sultanhisar. So after a day in Maltepe we set off on the Pamukkale Express. We had a 4-bed sleeping unit and had brought food to eat on the train, after which we settled down for the night. And what a ride it was, full of strange unknown sounds from the countryside as we rattled by with much rocking and rolling. But we got some sleep and were up and about for the arrival many hours later in Denizli.

In Sultanhisar, a fair-sized town of several thousand, Robert's friends Yuksel and Nebahat Ozaydin met us and sat us down to a delightful meal. Their two children Ozge (8) and Ozgur (10) shyly showed us where we would be sleeping. I had picked up a brown-haired doll for Ozge at the airport in London at Robert's suggestion, and it was a big hit. It was her first doll and much treasured.

The next day, we set off walking around the town to get to know it a little and maybe meet some of the inhabitants. One elderly woman sitting on the side of the road hailed us and began to talk. She was the mother of the mayor of the town and initially, as I talked with her, her son did the translating. Robert, fluent in Turkish, was aware that some of the son's translation was not exactly what the woman was saying, so I was pleased when the son wandered away. Suddenly, with Robert translating, the woman became more eloquent, wanting to know who I was, what work I did.

I began to talk with her about my work with women worldwide, that it was mainly getting information on women and development issues to them, plus technical assistance and training in low-cost media skills when requested. As I talked, the woman stood and began hugging me. I told her that those of us working on these issues knew that it was women who did most of the work in the community, especially the growing and marketing of food, the bringing up of the children, health, education, and so on. She began to cry. I asked why she was crying. And out came a stream of words that Robert struggled to keep up with as he translated. 'We didn't know anything about this', she said. 'We believe that no-one in the world knows how hard we women work just to keep the family alive because it's only the men who go to the big meetings and have the chance to speak.'

I found it very moving, and kept assuring her that indeed we did know, that the world knew, and that there were so many things happening to try and get them the help they needed, plus some credit for all their work.

Has that woman been helped? I don't know. But I do know that many women in Turkey have worked tirelessly on behalf of women's human rights, some had been active participants in the UN Decade for Women and beyond, including some young Turkish women who worked as interns in our office for some months. Others interned with international organisations including the United Nations, and they had returned home to set up women's human rights organisations to fight for the empowerment of women. I would love to think that the woman sitting by the road that day, and all the other women that we met as we walked through Sultanhisar, are living better times now than they were before.

A 'comfort woman' tells her story Vienna, 1993

We came to Vienna from all parts of the world: women human rights activists, women who had been exploited and whose rights had been violated, women who had lost their husbands, brothers, sons, daughters. All were joined by one goal: to see women's human rights made an integral part of the final document that would come out of the UN International Conference on Human Rights.

At IWTC, we had worked with a group of fellow activists from international, regional and national women's rights organisations to put together a Rights Place for Women for the display of materials on women's human rights, and to provide a place for women to meet and discuss strategies for the future.

Also part of the NGO Forum was the Global Tribunal on Women's Human Rights. Led by the Center for Women's Global Leadership with a team that included many women's human rights groups, the Global Tribunal was to hear a selection of the cases of women whose rights had been violated, with a panel of experts who would respond. Testimonies were in five categories: human rights abuse in the family; war crimes against women; violations of bodily integrity; socio-economic rights; and political persecution and discrimination.

The judges who presided over the Tribunal were: Justice P.N. Bhagwati, former Chief Justice of the Supreme Court of India and Chair of the Asian human rights NGO AWARE; the Honorable Ed Broadbent, a former Canadian MP and President of the International Centre for Human Rights and

Development in Montreal; the Honorable Gertrude Mongella, Secretary-General of the UN 1995 Fourth World Conference on Women and former Tanzanian High Commissioner to India; and the Honorable Elizabeth Odio, Minister for Justice in Costa Rica and a member of the UN Committee Against Torture. The judges worked in consultation with an advisory committee of women lawyers from several countries.

The women who were to testify were from every world region. They were all briefed beforehand and had a very clear understanding that if they did not want to be photographed or videoed with the spotlights on at any time, we would have the lights and cameras stopped immediately. We were taping the whole tribunal for posterity but of more importance were the women themselves, their confidence and wellbeing.

My job, after briefing the women, was to work the slide machine. Not all the women had brought slides or other visual material but many had. So I was positioned at the back of the hall organising the slides and making sure the testimonials and the visuals were synchronised. The Global Tribunal ran for many hours. Delegates came and went from the upstairs official conference as word spread about the stories being told. Hundreds of people were crushed into the hall; it was standing room only.

One after the other, the women spoke, many with translators by their side. Some broke down and the cameras and lights were turned off. When and if they regained their composure, the testimony would proceed. Searing stories of extreme violations of human rights, humiliation, emotional, physical and mental violence were told.

Then onto the platform mid-morning came a small, elderly, dignified woman from Korea, dressed in a magnificent traditional costume of iridescent green with a wide sash around her waist. She wore a traditional headpiece in her intricately waved hair and on her feet wore silk socks and traditional platform sandals. Her name was Kim Bok-Dong.

By her side was a young woman student to translate.

She began her story very quietly and with enormous dignity. She told of being a young woman of 16 living in her village of Yang San, in the Nam Bu Dong area of Korea, with her mother and one younger sister. Her older sisters were already married as it made them safe from being taken by the Japanese to work in factories. It was 1941 and World War II was underway. Her mother thought Kim Bok-Dong was too young to be taken and so let her roam freely around the village.

But her mother was wrong. An official came one day with a Japanese person and began asking for her. He demanded that her mother stamp some document. In those days, women could not read so her mother conceded to the demand, believing what she was told – that her 16 year-old daughter would have to work in a factory and would be free after three years.

From Yang San, Kim Bok-Dong was taken to Pusan where there were 20 other young girls her age. They all thought they were going to work in a factory. They were taken to a big storeroom with mats on the floor and told to stay there. After a few days they were moved to Shimonosekki in Japan where they stayed for about a week. Then they were taken to Taiwan where they stayed for three months. They were kept under lock and key.

The girls thought that the people who were keeping them were waiting for a contact to be made with a military uniform factory and assumed the decision on what district they would be going to had not been finalised.

From Taiwan, the group was taken to Guandong. There they were met by military doctors and were ordered to strip and expose 'previously unexposed parts of their bodies' in front of these unknown medical men. Everyone was very afraid. None of them had ever exposed themselves like this before, or had any knowledge of sex. They could not imagine why they were being treated this way and were quite terrified and outraged. It was a venereal disease check as it turned out, but none of that meant anything to them and they continued to protest loudly. This very quiet, dignified woman told us of how she kicked and struggled while they forcibly removed her clothes and spread her legs, several men holding her down.

After the examination, very scared and afraid, she was taken with the others to an empty 15-storey building. On the first floor were soldiers and on the second floor was the 'Comfort House'.

Kim Bok-Dong then began to describe in the most straightforward way what happened next. Each girl was placed in a cell just wide enough to lie down in on her back, her body touching the wooden wall on both sides. None of the girls had ever had sex before. In fact, she said, they did not even know what it was all about. In Korea, young women found out about such things on their wedding night.

Then the horror began. Long lines of Japanese soldiers lined up outside each cell and systematically, one by one, raped the girls. At first Kim Bok-Dung resisted forcefully. For this she was beaten brutally and given no food. She could not continue to refuse. So she gave in and decided to do what she was told. She could not initially endure the pain. Her internal sexual organs were torn and swollen. She told us she could not describe the suffering and even speaking about it was humiliating. Her only thought was to escape but she could not. She continued to sustain many injuries and when that happened, she was allowed to rest until she recovered and then was sent back to receive soldiers again.

It was impossible for her to remember how many soldiers came and went each day. It was tens of soldiers, she said, maybe fifty. Each soldier carried a ticket and a condom. In the evening, the women took the tickets to the administrator and he would check them off. Then they would get food, sometimes clothing and cosmetics. They were lied to even about this, she said. They did not know they were supposed to get money, in fact were told they would be paid lots of money at the end of the war.

During the rare rest times, all the young girls gathered and sat together and cried. They prayed for a Japanese victory soon, thinking that then they could go home. Once a week, they were checked for venereal disease.

After two years in Guangdong, the women were sent to Hong Kong and then on to Singapore. The Singapore 'Comfort House' was a long building partitioned off into small rooms. It was extremely hot. Many of the women fainted after servicing long lines of Japanese soldiers hour after hour.

They were kept in one place for about two months, and then transferred to another, following the battle. Usually the front line fighting was only about eight kilometres from them and they could hear the gunfire. Sometimes they had to go up into the mountains in groups of ten to service the soldiers for one week at a time. Each time they were moved by ship, they were crammed into the decks below the soldiers. Wherever the soldiers went, they followed behind.

By now, there was not a sound in the Global Tribunal hall. Hundreds of people had come in from all over the conference centre as word spread about this woman's story. People were standing, kneeling, wherever they could find a space. I was in tears, how could one not be? Yet this incredible woman was speaking on in a low voice, almost monotonous, emotionless, stoic, steady, without tears.

And then, she said, Liberation was announced. Japan had lost the war and they could now go home. This came from the Japanese soldiers and they had no way of knowing if it was the truth. They also did not know where they were and how to get home. They were taken to a military hospital by the Japanese commander. The Japanese needed nurses and cleaners and the women were taught these skills.

While at the hospital, a miracle happened for Kim Bok-Dong. Her cousin's husband came and found her, carrying a photograph of her given to him by her mother. When he was drafted to the South Pacific in the supplies division, her mother had told him to check every place he came across where there were Korean women, to search for her and bring her home. She didn't know the man but when she saw the photo she had sent her mother so long ago, before the first 'Comfort Home', she knew it must be right.

Her cousin's husband took her to the receiving centre, where the women were processed before going home. At the centre there were more than 200 women. And, as she described them, there were tall people with large noses. That was the first time she had ever seen American soldiers. All the women's bags were emptied and anything of any value removed. She spent one year at that receiving centre before boarding a boat for the journey home. There were almost 3,000 people on board, hundreds of women, hundreds of men. Many of the women had been 'Comfort Women'.

On the journey, one person died of suspected cholera so they were not allowed off in Pusan where the boat sat for a week. Investigations found it was not cholera that had caused the death and everyone was allowed ashore. It was night-time. They were sent into a room and told to hand over all the money they had from any country. The investigators were Korean and American. The women gave them everything they had and in return were each given a train ticket and 1000 Korean won.

On finally arriving home at her village, Kim Bok-Dong was 23 years old. She had been gone for eight years. Only her mother was left in the family home in Yang San. After she had been taken, many others were taken away. Everyone said they had been working in factories. No one said they had been 'Comfort Women'. In fact, Kim Bok-Dong said that she had been working as a nurse at a military hospital all the time.

Fearful of what her mother and family would think of her, she decided not to tell anyone what had really happened. She tried to settle back into her old life. But her mother, overjoyed to have her daughter back after so many years of believing her dead, was anxious for her to get married and to start a family. Arrangements were made for her to be married to a man in the village.

All this time, this woman telling her terrible story had been calm and dignified. There didn't seem to be anything more that could possibly hurt her as badly as she had been hurt already. But she suddenly began to tremble uncontrollably.

Trying to keep her composure, she began to speak of how she decided to tell her mother what had happened to her during those years. But she couldn't contain herself any longer and suddenly broke down. One of the Tribunal team stepped forward and offered to have the cameras and lights turned off as had been promised. She shot up her head and straightened her back immediately and shouted 'No! Keep the cameras and the lights on. I have waited 50 years to tell my story and I'm not going to be stopped now!'

'I was so ashamed of what had happened and did not want my mother to know. But my body was destroyed and there was no way I would ever sleep with another man. I had to tell her,' she sobbed. Only then did her mother stop trying to get her married.

I can't begin to describe the stillness in that room that day. This incredibly courageous woman had told us a most horrific story that none of us could really imagine, and had related it all with a calmness and dignity that was inspiring. Yet at the memory of having to tell her mother the whole story she broke down and sobbed uncontrollably.

When she had regained her composure, she continued her story. There were girls from her 'Comfort Women' group in the region where she lived. Many of them could not get jobs so in desperation became prostitutes. She started up a drinking house because, she said, this was all she could do and she was definitely not going to work as a prostitute. But it was difficult to run this small business on her own. After a while, she met an older man whose marriage had failed and they got married. He helped her with the business and was a kind and gentle man.

But she never told him her story and he died without ever knowing what she had gone through. She told us how sorry she felt for him because she could not bear children and he died without an heir. She said she went to the hospital to find out why she couldn't have children and they said there was nothing wrong with her. She never told any of the doctors her story.

She continued running the drinking house by herself until the building was pulled down. With the money she gained in compensation for the building, she bought herself a small apartment and was now living in that. She was looking for a job, she said. And she wanted compensation from the Japanese for what she had lived through.

After the Tribunal in Vienna, Kim Bok-Dong became part of an ever-diminishing group of 'Comfort Women' who then spent years telling their story to the world. It was a story taken up by Japanese and other feminists who finally got it to the highest levels of justice in Japan. Years later, the 'Comfort Women' did receive an official apology from the Japanese government. To my knowledge, there has never been any financial compensation.

A personal friend in Nepal Washington, DC, 1994

The Association for Women's Rights in Development, founded in 1981 at a meeting in Wisconsin in which I participated, held an international conference for women every four years.

The 1994 meeting in Washington DC was focused on women and media and I was on a panel of about eight women, my specific subject being women's media networks worldwide. Because of the popularity of the topic, we had been allocated a large room that seated around 200 people. It was packed. At the conclusion of the meeting, the floor was opened to questions.

Midway down the room sat a young woman dressed in a sari that covered her head and fell full-length to the floor. She stood up and began to wave at me. 'Anne, Anne', she called out, jumping up and down with excitement. 'It's me!' Then she called out her name. 'You know! I'm the one you send a fax to every week with all the news about women! That's why I'm here!'

I was startled. It was true; we had started a Global FaxNet recently, in an effort to keep women's organisations in touch with the plans and programs of the NGO Forum coming up in 1995 in Beijing. Fax machines were fairly new and we had put together a fax list of about 500 groups and organisations and sent a one-page bulletin off each week.

But here was a young woman who thought it was just coming direct from me to her. I waved back and smiled. Then I asked her if the news in the fax each week was useful to her. And she began to talk about how her life in Nepal had changed since she had invested in a small fax machine to be able to receive this faxed bulletin.

'People knock on my door every day asking me if it has arrived yet', she said. 'I have to tell them no until finally it arrives. Then we translate it into Hindi and write it by hand onto a large poster and take it into the middle of town where there is a news wall. We tape it up on the news wall and crowds of women gather to read it, or listen as it is read out to them. It makes us feel as though we are part of the world and it has changed our lives!'

She went on. 'Now I'm a journalist for the local paper too. I take some of the news and I write articles that they print in the paper. And they pay me. So I've already paid off the loan for the fax machine. And it's all because I wrote to you in New York and now you write to me every week by fax!'

The whole room broke into applause. The young woman sat down suddenly in embarrassment. She had talked as though there were just the two of us and had somehow forgotten she was in a large room surrounded by people.

I jumped down from the platform on which the panel was seated. We hugged each other. She was in tears and so was I. I thanked her for what she had said, telling her how important it was for me to know that someone like her was making such good use of the information. And I promised we would keep sending her the bulletins for as long as we could.

I often thought about this young woman, a true feminist and activist, able to take information and make best use of it for the benefit of everyone around her. Such women are the hope of the future.

Scary stories in Beijing
Huairou to Beijing, 1995

The NGO Forum at the Fourth World Conference on Women had originally been scheduled as a parallel event in the same city as the UN conference, as had been the case at each of the previous three NGO forums – Mexico City 1975, Copenhagen 1980 and Nairobi 1985. But with less than three months to go, the Chinese government had decided that this was going to be a troublesome meeting of wild women, and had moved the entire forum 50 miles out of town to Huairou, a regional town on Beijing's outskirts. With not much time to prepare, the government had sent in an army of construction people and equipment and had rapidly tried to transform a totally unsuitable area into a meeting place for 35,000. There were a few halls and open spaces to begin with and they tried valiantly to add large covered areas for exhibitions, training and workshop spaces, but largely failed. There was just not enough time.

So we arrived to find half-finished structures, seas of mud, footpaths and roads only partly completed, and a cordon of military police stationed at every entry point. We were searched from top to toe each day as we arrived. In fact, the IWTC team was followed by authorities from the time we reached the Beijing airport. IWTC had sent out faxes and emails to women's groups throughout the world in the preceding months, keeping everyone up to date with the changing plans and preparations for the forum and assisting where possible with visas and accommodation. We had also unsuccessfully lobbied the delegates to the final

UN Commission on the Status of Women in a vain attempt to stop the forum from being moved from the Workers Stadium in Beijing out to Huairou. The Chinese authorities had their eyes on us as possible troublemakers from the very beginning!

But now all that was in the past. The NGO Forum was over. For two weeks, 35,000 women from all parts of the world had met and mingled, learnt from each other and from the world at large, and coped as best we could with the mud, tight security and makeshift meeting arrangements. Those of us who had lasted the full two weeks (and we were in a minority) cleaned up our various pavilions and work places in Huairou, waved at the buses loaded with Chinese tourists passing through the empty forum site, and piled into our own buses and taxis and headed for the big city. I was looking forward to a room of my own at a hotel and a hot shower. The next day I would be off to the main UN conference to join the other non-governmental representatives who were lobbying for various resolutions yet to be passed and made part of the final Platform for Action, the document that the Member States of the UN were to sign, and then implement.

There were four of us in the taxi as we left Huairou on the long journey to Beijing. On either side of the road were families going back to Huairou: the town's people had been told to vacate their houses and shops while we were there. One of our group in the taxi was Chinese American and could speak Mandarin. She greeted the taxi driver and explained where we each needed to be dropped off in Beijing. He was surprised to find that someone spoke Mandarin and almost drove off the road with excitement.

'Are you all from the women's meeting in Huairou?' he asked. Yes we responded through our translator. 'But you look like nice people!' he said, and we laughed. Was he expecting something else we asked? 'Why yes. We were told many terrible things were going to happen while all these

Western women were here and many of us ran away to the country to stay with friends and relatives. Only bus and taxi drivers, hotel personnel and food workers were supposed to stay. Plus the police and the military for security.'

'Was it the rain that stopped you from running naked through the streets?' the driver continued. 'We taxi drivers were all issued with white sheets that we carried around in the trunk of our taxis. They were to be used as covers to throw over naked women as they hailed taxis to travel to planned demonstrations in Tiananmen Square. Hotel porters were also issued with white sheets so they could toss them over naked women as they left the hotels. What happened? Was it too cold for you?'

We started to laugh. Then we couldn't stop laughing. The driver joined in. 'We were also told you were all lesbians and would be kissing and hugging and things like that in the street. We were all very scared. And we were told you would be going to wild nightclubs in the bad part of town and some clubs closed down for the duration because they didn't want their places to be trashed!'

How sad, we said. We must have been terribly boring for you when you were expecting so much more. Our driver grinned broadly and admitted that the men were really looking forward to much more excitement.

Yet for us, after the laughter had gone, it was sad indeed to think so many people had gone away to the countryside so they wouldn't accidentally bump into any of us. Another opportunity lost for friendships to develop and better understanding to grow.

Muslim and Christian women come together Huairou, 1995

After the NGO Forum, some of us were to stay for the final week of the United Nations Fourth World Conference on Women in the clean streets of Beijing. I was one of them and would be driving in a taxi from Huairou to Beijing the following day

But first, we had a birthday to celebrate. One of our team from the Once and Future Pavilion was turning 30 and after the turmoil and chaos of the past two weeks in the mud, rain and tight security of the Huairou forum construction site, we felt we all deserved a bit of partying. We had earlier found a pleasant restaurant in a quiet street in the town of Huairou and a room situated one side of the central courtyard had been booked.

We gathered around the table laden with Chinese delicacies and bottles of sweet cordial and tea. After a wonderful shared meal, the restaurant staff carried in a cake loaded with candles. We all joined in with the cake in singing Happy Birthday.

From the next room, a group of women suddenly appeared. I recognised one of them as a friend from the Women in Black movement in Serbia. She stepped forward and said that they would also like to sing Happy Birthday to our team member. Then they sang. There were several languages involved. They were women from Serbia, Croatia, Bosnia and Herzegovina. In their home countries, their fathers, brothers, sons and uncles were locked in battle, killing each other and causing mass mayhem as their countries fought out a murderous campaign. Yet here were the women singing Happy Birthday together as a sign of goodwill and love for others participating in this extraordinary international meeting.

They had been dining together, discussing ways of making peace in their countries, of mending ancient wounds, of planning a future together. And they wanted to share all of this with us along with the birthday celebration. There were many tears that evening. It was hard to know what to say.

Then as we left the restaurant and walked back down the deserted streets of Huairou, children began to creep out of their houses and walk beside us. Then more doors opened and women began to join us, walking beside us down the darkened streets. One of our team spoke Mandarin and she started a conversation with the growing group of followers. They erupted with questions. Where were we from? Was the meeting over? They had been told that we were to be feared and that they were to either leave town or shut themselves up inside their houses because they might get hurt. How could we hurt them? we asked. What was there to fear from women getting together to talk about peace, non-violence, the environment and other important issues?

What a night it had been! Beginning as a birthday party, progressing into an emotional reconciliation between warring neighbors and finishing with meeting the lost people of Huairou, of whom there had not been a trace in the streets for two weeks.

Strange ideas
Nakaseke, 1999

When the project was first brought to us at IWTC in New York, we were not sure we could do it. Here was a Canadian research group (IDRC) asking us to develop and produce a computer program for rural women in Uganda, women who could in most cases neither read nor write, but who had access to rural telecentres being built across Uganda by various multinational organisations.

We had never developed and produced material for computers, or, as in this case, CD-ROMs containing highly visual, simple language information that the women could access on computers with minimal literacy skills. Yet we knew that small children were accessing programs of this kind and felt we had to research the possibilities and see what could be done.

As a member of the International Board of Directors for Isis-WICCE (Women's International Cross-Cultural Exchange) in Kampala, Uganda, I was about to set off for Uganda from New York for the annual meeting of the Board. So I agreed to research the possibilities while I was there. Plans were made for me to stay an extra day in Uganda and contact had been made with women in an outlying village called Nakaseke.

The Executive Director of Isis-WICCE, Ruth Ojiambo Ochieng, and the Program Director, Jessica Nkuye, knew of the plans and had arranged for me to be driven to Nakaseke in their 4-wheel drive van by their driver Samuel. Ruth and Jessica were rather dubious about the idea of computer programs for the women. After all, the women of Nakaseke were farmers and market women who had little time apart from working in the fields and providing for their families. But they still supported the plan for me to visit Nakaseke and provided me with the means to make the journey. I appreciated their help enormously.

The Board meeting was long and I couldn't get away until early afternoon. A phone call was made to Nakaseke early morning advising that I would be there to meet with the women at 4 pm. The first part of the journey was on sealed roads. Then we cut off the main road and started across country on increasingly bumpy, muddy, sloping roads that set the van spinning in all directions. As I held on to the side of the van, Samuel began to speak. He was a shy young man of limited English and with a distinct stammer. I struggled to hear him over the racket of bumps and slides: 'Why are you going to this village to talk to these women about a computer program when they need so many other things more?' he asked.

I replied that I wasn't sure about the idea either and that was the reason why I needed to talk with them. He continued: 'They need floors in their huts, money for school uniforms, water taps, proper lavatories. Why on earth do they need computers?'

Again, I responded that I agreed with him that their needs were probably very much what he had listed and if they also felt that way, the computer plans would go no further. We would try to develop other ways of getting information to them on whatever issues they requested.

'And if they do learn to use the computers (which they will never be able to anyway because they're women and can't read or write) and spend time at the telecentre,' said Samuel, 'their husbands will probably beat them up because they won't want them wasting their time on such things when they should be working in the gardens growing barley and vegetables and looking after the family.'

By now, I was becoming concerned, not least because I was seriously wondering whether this seemingly gentle young man was in fact very angry with a foreigner coming to a village such as Nakaseke to introduce strange ideas to the women. Again I responded to his concerns by making it as clear as I could that I just wanted to talk with the women and get their feelings about such a project. If they in any way did not think it was a good idea, then of course we would not go ahead with it. Besides, we didn't know how to do such programs ourselves yet.

Added to all this, I was not at all sure we would arrive at Nakaseke in one piece! Although the day was unbearably hot and humid, recent rains had washed most of the track away and there were times when our (thankfully) 4-wheel drive small truck was hanging sideways, sliding down into ditches and small streamlets coursing along the muddy edge. I wanted the driver to focus on his driving. Was this where my final chapter would be written – upside down in a truck on a muddy road in Uganda?

I did not expect more than one or two women to be gathered in the village as plans had been hurriedly made on my arrival in Kampala via a phone call and not much had been explained to them. In fact, I think they only knew that a white woman from New York was coming to talk with them about using the computers at the telecentre. Nothing more. My expectations were low.

Imagine my surprise on arriving at the telecentre to find a crowd of more than 20 women gathered there waiting for our arrival. Not only this but it transpired that they had been waiting for six hours in their very best traditional outfits including head gear and full length dresses, and were not permitted to wait inside the telecentre but instead had waited outside in the blazing sun.

How could they have been given the wrong time for our meeting? It was to be some time before I got an answer to that.

My two great-nieces, Sarah and Melanie Bird, studied Swahili when they moved to Kenya with their medical missionary parents. I later learned from them that Swahili and Luganda languages have many similarities and one of these is time telling. The day starts at 6am and time begins then. So four hours later (or 4 o'clock) is 10 am. And the women of Nakaseke had been told the time of my arrival in the Luganda language.

I was deeply impressed that their interest in the project was so strong that they had waited for hours in such heat. We went immediately into the telecentre and began the discussion. It was long and intense. Everything had to be translated. I took notes carefully of everything being said. The women were mainly small farmers, some had market stands, some were cleaners, most were mothers and grandmothers and almost all lived during the week without their husbands, brothers, fathers, who worked in Kampala and came home only at weekends. These women were responsible for their family's food, health, wellbeing and for almost everything that made the village a functional community.

There was such excitement at the thought that they would finally be able to use these shiny new computers. And they were delighted that their village had been chosen for a telecentre. Yet it took almost an hour to get them to say what they themselves wanted from it all. Their husbands might want such and such information, their sons would like such and such, their school-aged children would want help with their studies, and so on. But the programs I was discussing with them would be for them, the women, I would say. What information did they want?

Finally they understood. Pure disbelief showed on their faces. Computer programs for them? Was I crazy? No, I responded through the translator. We at IWTC worked with and for women and this project was for them.

Suddenly ideas began to run freely. They wanted information on food processing, small business and marketing, how to bring up children, agricultural problems, how to care for cows and, most troubling, why were some of them getting sick when they didn't sleep with anyone other than their husband?

The list grew. I explained that IWTC first had to work out how to develop a program that would suit them, one that they could use easily by themselves without having to know how to read and write. Once we had worked out how to do such a program, we would find the requisite specialists in the subject area they had chosen and begin to develop it.

Finally the group decided on a first program dedicated to ideas for making money, using what they had available to them in their village. We agreed that IWTC would begin work on that issue and would get back to them when there was something to field-test. Then I told the women that, before I left, I wanted to discuss some other things that I had been told would be a problem if indeed we were able to develop a computer program for them. I did not tell them where this information had come from and I saw Samuel at the back of the room breathe more easily. I made it clear that I took these problems very seriously.

First problem: 'Why was I coming to this village to talk to these women about a computer program when they needed so many other things more? They needed floors in their huts, water in their homes, lavatories and money for school uniforms much more than computers.'

There was a moment's silence following the translation into Luganda. I waited nervously. Then to my utter surprise, laughter broke out. Before long, the room was shaking with mirth until finally one brave woman stood to respond on behalf of the others.

Was I really as stupid as that? she asked me through the translator. Did I imagine that these development agencies (she actually said big white men in hats who visited the village occasionally) came to the village with wads of money in their hands and handed the money around to the women and said they could spend it on anything they wanted? (Gales of laughter). No, that never happened. But what had happened out of the blue was that a telecentre had been built in their village, with computers, printers, fax machines, a telephone, and they wanted very much to be able to use it.

Second problem, and one that I told the women I was particularly worried about: 'If the women do learn to use the computers and spend time at the telecentre, their husbands or fathers will beat them up because they won't want them wasting their time on such things when they should be working in the gardens growing barley and vegetables and looking after the family.'

Again a moment's silence after the translator repeated my question. And again, gales of laughter!

I was more than amazed. I put my pen down and stared at my notes. I must have looked a bit perplexed. Then the brave woman again stood and gently said I was not to worry about things like that, they were strong women and could handle their men. Yes, she admitted, there was violence in their homes and they regretted that. But no man in that village was going to stop them learning how to use these computers.

I ventured a further suggestion, saying that maybe we could include the men in the program and the women could show them what they were learning as we went along. To which the woman said 'No way!' This was their program and too bad about the men.

I left the meeting exhausted late that afternoon, and sat quietly in the truck beside the driver for the long, bumpy journey back to Kampala. Samuel was as taken aback as I was by the responses and struggled to tell me how wrong he had been. I assured him I was also surprised and had much to think about in the next months as we began working on the project.

Arriving back with something to show Nakaseke, 2001

Many months had passed since that first trip to Nakaseke village and IWTC had struggled to come up with a way to develop a CD-ROM program for the women to use on the computers at the Nakaseke Community Telecentre.

Our expertise was in highly visual, simple language print materials, not computer programs that could be accessed easily by rural women who could not read or write. But we were determined to find a way to make the project happen and had worked on several ideas. We had also been in discussion with IDRC, the Canadian research group with an office in Nairobi, Kenya, who had asked us to develop the program. We needed a Program Director based in Uganda and they had someone they thought would fit the bill. Rita Mijumbi was keen to take on the position and I had met and talked with her about ways to proceed.

We had discussed content with women experts in small business and marketing. Maggie Range and Suzanne Kindervatter had developed small business marketing materials for women in the Global South and agreed to help. Maggie came up to New York from Washington for a few days to work with us in laying out a process for the materials. Peg Snyder, first Director of UNIFEM, had written a book on small business women in Uganda which gave us some excellent case studies to use.

At IWTC, we had worked out a way to develop the program as a computer book, using Quark Xpress page layout software in the same way as we did when developing print materials. This was a breakthrough and suddenly, the project looked possible.

Finally, we enlisted the help of a computer programmer who could take the text and visuals for each page and digitise them so that a click with the mouse would activate a voice. We taped the voice of an IWTC staff member from Sierra Leone, Isha Dyfan, as narrator, and two women from Uganda working in New York to be the voices of other women featured. We completed the first five pages of the experimental program and were ready to field-test them in Nakaseke.

Well, not quite. The women of Nakaseke spoke Luganda, one of several Ugandan languages. We needed to reproduce these first five pages using Luganda text, and Lugandan voices. With Rita's help, we contacted Agnes Nakibuuka in Kampala, who had set up a media business producing videos and computer programs. Rita had also made contact with a woman professor at Makerere University in Kampala who had agreed to help with translating the English text into Luganda.

I went to Kampala to meet with Rita, Agnes, and the professor. First we took my English version of the five pages to the professor. She was initially uncertain about the project but soon became one of our greatest allies. She translated the first pages for us and I took the translated text back to my hotel to reproduce the pages on my laptop. It was essential that each page look as colourful as it did in the English version.

The next day, Rita and I took the new pages to Agnes. She had brought in her sister to record the text and her brothers to help with digitising the visuals on each page. Cutting and pasting, they put together the first five pages of our new program.

In February 2001 I was driven again to Nakaseke village to meet with the women of the village to actually field-test the first pages of the new program in the Luganda language. This time the van belonged to Agnes and her media group. Would the women of Nakaseke remember me and the project?

As the 4-wheel drive wagon ground to a stop outside the telecentre a small group of women awaited our arrival. They broke into smiles and clapping as we got out of the van. They couldn't believe I had returned. So many times, they said, development people (again they said big white men in hats) came and promised all kinds of things for their telecentre and then were never seen again. They had begun to think that I would be the same. But instead, here I was, and they were overjoyed and full of excitement.

I pointed out that we only had five computer pages to test with them and they may not be what they wanted. But it didn't matter, the main fact was I had returned.

So we began the field-test. The three young men who ran the centre pleaded to be able to watch. They had laughed at the women on my previous visit and told me they didn't think women could do anything on a computer. I was doubtful they would keep quiet as they observed this very first test. So I said they could sit on the side but I would ask them to leave if there was any laughter or any derogatory comments directed at the women. They assured me they would do no such thing.

The women sat facing the computer. The first page came up. Rita asked for a volunteer to step forward and try using the mouse. No one moved. Then the oldest of the women, Anastasia aged 70, small and shrunken from decades working in the fields, stepped up and sat before the strange machine. There was a snigger from one of the men. Rita instructed Anastasia to put her hand on the mouse. Then she told her to move it around and to watch the little arrow on the screen move upwards towards the picture of the narrator in the top corner, then to click and hear the narrator talk (in Luganda).

Anastasia picked up the mouse and waved it through the air. A guffaw of laughs broke out from the young men. I asked Rita and Anastasia to stop for a minute and told the men to leave. There was a startled silence. They stared at me, not moving. I insisted. Slowly they got up and walked out. Once the door was closed behind them, the women jumped to their feet and started cheering and waving their hands above their heads. Such delight! I was not feeling so good and began to apologise. But the women assured me they were delighted and there was much hugging and laughter. We returned to the testing.

Anastasia slowly moved the mouse on the mouse pad and the arrow moved up the screen to the drawing of the narrator. She clicked the mouse – and the narrator began to speak. That moment will live in my mind forever. The look on the faces of those women as they realised they could do this easily. The mystery of the computer was not a mystery at all. That first movement of the mouse and the click that brought on the first words in Luganda became the only training those women ever needed. From that moment on, they taught each other how to use the program.

The following months saw a lot of back and forth between Kampala and New York via email and telephone as we gradually developed more pages for the program. Mistakes were rectified, case studies changed around, photographs and video bits were changed to single line drawings, music was added then removed, and each section was carefully field-tested before being finalised.

But it was that first day of testing that will always stay in my memory. It was the day the women realised they could use the computer and could have a say in the kind of information and the way it was presented. From that day, they grew in stature and confidence around computers and became recognised by the community as competent and assured. They had such great ideas for further programs too, and developed a plan for a Women's Folder to be placed on the desktops of all the computers that would contain lots of different programs based on the methodology of that first CD-ROM. They said: 'That way no-one can steal our stuff and it can't be burned.'

How prophetic of them! Because in later years, the telecentre was burned down by a gang of young men who climbed through the window one night to steal things and accidentally dropped a match into a box of papers.

A fire at the telecentre Nakaseke, 2001

It took us some months at IWTC to develop the final CD-ROM package for the Nakaseke women but at last it was completed. It was called *Rural Women in Africa: Ideas for Earning Money*. Field-testing had been done for a portion of each new section to make sure it was what the women wanted. The result was a program that the women of Nakaseke village regarded as their very own, made by them for their use in their telecentre.

When they were completed in August 2001, I carried the CDs back to Uganda and presented a copy to each of the women who had taken part in the field-testing, along with copies for Rita Mijumbi, IWTC's Program Manager in Kampala, and Agnes Nakibuuka, our Kampala media developer. There were also copies for some of the groups in Kampala who had helped us with information and other types of support.

So it was with enormous regret that I received a phone call late in 2002 from Rita telling me that the telecentre had been burnt to the ground. What had happened? Was anyone hurt? And was this in any way a kind of payback for the work we had been doing with the women? Rita didn't know but said she would drive out to Nakaseke the next day and find out what she could.

I was anxious. I guess at the back of my mind I had always been a little wary of any possible expressions of anger, particularly from some of the men in the village. Samuel, the Isis-WICCE driver had warned me of such a possibility in 1999 on that first visit to Nakaseke.

Rita called me back the next day. She had arrived at the village to find all the women gathered in one of their houses, terribly upset with many of them crying. She sat down with them and began asking questions. What had happened? Was anyone hurt? Was the telecentre a complete loss?

The women looked at Rita with some confusion. Why was she asking those kinds of questions? No-one was hurt. Two boys had climbed in a window in the middle of the night looking for money and had accidentally dropped the lighted stick they were carrying as a light source into a box of paper and the whole place went up in flames. And yes, it was burnt to the ground but the men were already busy rebuilding it. None of that was the problem.

'What is the problem then?' asked Rita. 'Why are you all crying?'

'The computers are gone'. The women wailed. 'Our program was on the computer and it's been burnt up. We've lost it. What will we do?'

Rita began to talk in a calm and soothing voice. They were initially inconsolable, until she took the CD-ROM in its packet out of her pocket and held it up. 'Here's the program', she told them. 'It can be loaded onto any computer, anywhere. It doesn't have to be those particular computers. The computers might be destroyed but the program is on this CD and we can use it anywhere we like.'

There was a stunned silence, then the smiles and laughter started. Pure joy, Rita said. They were so relieved and excited. They had not realised that the CD they each had was the program on the desktop. Our fault really, for not having them upload the program for themselves in the first place.

The problem of replacing the destroyed computers did not seem to faze them at all. I tried to find out from Rita how they would do that but she was unsure.

She returned to Nakaseke a couple of months later and was surprised to find the women using the program on two new computers. 'Where did you get the computers from?' she asked. Oh we managed to find them they said.

Apparently they made a request to an agency in Kampala for the computers and then just camped out the front of the agency until the people inside gave in and came through with the computers!

I've not been able to verify all the details of this, but it seems a possibility. The women of Nakaseke village are extremely persuasive and very determined. And they were not going to live without their program.

Anastasia Nakaseke, 1999–2007

A story within the story of the CD-ROM and its development is the story of Anastasia, the 70-year-old farmer who had stepped forward to try out the program at the first field test in Nakaseke in 1999.

In October 2001, IWTC brought Anastasia to New York with Rita Mijumbi, our Program Officer in Kampala and Agnes Nakibuuka, the head of the media group who had transferred the English version of the CD-ROM program into the Luganda version. It was barely a month after the destruction of the World Trade Centre towers in Lower Manhattan and JFK Airport was on full alert, as was the whole of New York City. We had to move heaven and earth to get visas for the three women, in the end asking for assistance from friends at the US Mission to the UN.

It was a relief to see them walking through the arrival gates at JFK. Anastasia broke free and ran across the empty space cordoned off by the security guards and flung herself at me with a great embrace. And she produced a sentence in English! I was a little taken aback as one of the reasons for bringing her to New York was to show people how the Luganda language version of the program could be used by a woman who spoke only Luganda and could not read or write. But she had learned just the one sentence from the nuns at Nakaseke, 'I am so pleased to see you again'. And that was that. I was very touched that she had made the effort.

We invited UN officials, other international agencies, funders and supporters to the official opening ceremony, where Anastasia demonstrated how to use the program. There was nothing we could have done that was more effective than having her work her way through the program with such ease and enjoyment, talking all the time, waving her hands at the audience as she explained things and offering her assistance with getting started in a small business.

Anastasia had never been away from Uganda before and it was a brave and somewhat scary trip for her. She slept on the floor beside her bed at the hotel where the three of them stayed, and spent most of her time in the hotel room watching TV. When we did do some walking around the streets of Manhattan, she became very upset at seeing homeless people, particularly if they were African American, and would go over to talk to them, in Luganda, telling them to go back to Uganda. She clearly thought they were from home and should go back. We kept her pockets full of quarters for her to hand around.

On Anastasia's return to Nakaseke, we sent the money for a laptop computer and gave her a laminated card to wear around her neck that named her as an IWTC trainer. With a small stipend that Rita administered on our behalf, Anastasia began to travel around the countryside showing women in their huts and villages how to use the program. Many times, the young men at the telecentre would seat her on their motor scooter and drive her to some far away hut where a woman waited for her arrival.

If need be, Anastasia would offer these women a chicken from her farm to get them started earning money. In late 2002, we asked her and Rita to demonstrate how to use the program at an international women's conference in Kampala and, with Rita translating, Anastasia offered these women from around the world a duck or chicken to get them started!

In fact, she gave me a duck on one of my trips and insisted I take it home with me. The problem with air travel did not seem to trouble her a bit. I gave the duck to Rita's mother who was very pleased to have it and started to raise some ducks herself. Anastasia's influence is everywhere.

Some years later, a team of Dutch women film makers tracked Anastasia down and filmed her on her rounds as she visited villages showing women how to use the program. That film is probably available somewhere on the internet.

While in New York, Anastasia saved some of her money and when she returned she started, with Rita's help, to construct a new house. Rita's family in Uganda and my partner and I in Australia gave some additional money towards the construction and in 2006, Anastasia completed her new house. It was meant to replace the dilapidated little hut in which she was living. We also replaced the worn-out laptop. Anastasia kept it charged using power from a local Catholic church where the nuns were extremely kind and generous with their support.

In 2007 however, when Elizabeth Carew-Reid (Lade) and I visited Anastasia at Nakaseke village after attending a World YWCA International Women's Summit on Women and HIV/AIDS in Nairobi, we found her still living in the original hut with the brand new solid little house standing alongside. She had ducks and chickens living with her in the hut and a fire in the middle to keep everyone warm and dry. She explained thar she couldn't have a fire in the middle in the new place and was still working out an alternative system. She was also used to sleeping on the ground and was not used to a floor.

Rita subsequently informed us that Anastasia had moved into the new house. She had a pot-bellied stove for warmth and a bed to sleep on. The new house kept out the torrential rain that Uganda often experienced and it wouldn't be as easily blown away as had happened regularly to the original hut. I imagined the ducks and chickens were with her inside when it was cold.

Anastasia is still working on her farm and whenever possible, showing women how to use the CD program. Being well over 80 years old now, she has slowed down a bit and doesn't do as much walking over the hills and through the valleys to find isolated women and help them earn money for survival. But she has convinced herself that she has to stay alive so that she can keep doing that. It is her main mission in life and she won't give it up easily.

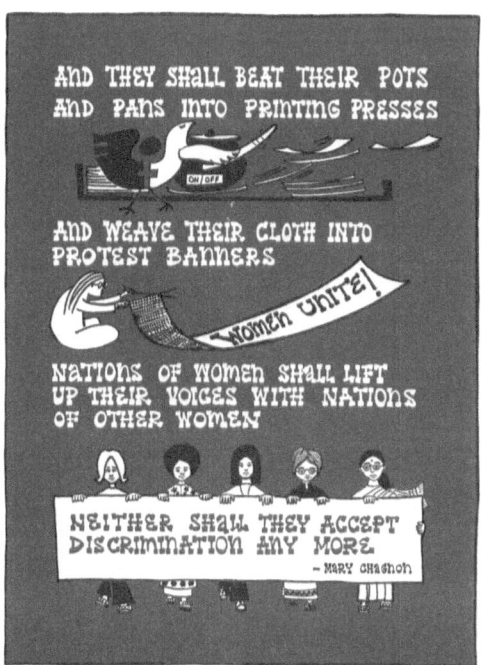

INTERNATIONAL WOMEN'S TRIBUNE CENTRE, 777 United Nations Plaza, New York, N.Y. 10017, U.S.A.   Artist: Anne S. Walker

Appendix

Letters and messages from women worldwide to the International Women's Tribune Centre when Anne S Walker retired as Executive Director, December 2002

I think I met Anne first in Copenhagen at the UN Second World Conference on Women in 1980. We both were active in popular education and I was drawn to her free-flowing creativity and how she was using that creativity to enable women around the world to find their voices and mobilize their collective power. More than twenty years later, Anne continues to use her unique talents, always in original ways, to advance women's rights globally.

Anne's imprimatur is part and parcel of the global women's movement. Her simple yet 'true' black and white illustrations of village women and girls can be seen in learning materials and in newsletters around the world. Then, as technology changed, so did Anne's work. I remember her doing amazing things on her Mac computer before I'd figured out how to even use my PC. And, more recently, she's been working to enable women in communities overseas to harness the power of ICTs.

I've always felt that being with Anne is the equivalent of entering into a right brain portal! Regardless of how many months may have passed, Anne would always swoop me up into whatever creative process was percolating within her at the moment: look at this on my computer … here's what I'm thinking about that … did you see our latest newsletter … Anne's energy and enthusiasm have always been catching and invigorating.

I am grateful for all the times that Anne and I have crossed paths and made common cause over the years.

Suzanne Kindervatter
InterAction, Washington, DC

***

My most happy memory was drifting around Port Vila Harbour, Vanuatu, on a catamaran on beautiful afternoon, with Anne. It was one of those glorious, sunny, blue Pacific days, and we just lapped up the tranquility, the beautiful environment and yarned away. Our real reason for being in Vanuatu was to work with Pacific women who were setting up information networks and we had a marvelous week with a bunch of very diverse and fabulous women from all around Oceania. I'm sure we learned at least as much as they did!

My other main association with Anne was the UN women's conferences, where she and IWTC made such a huge impact, especially at Nairobi with Tech and Tools. What a fabulous exhibition it was! I still have the lovely posters too. I mounted them and kept them on the walls of my office in Canberra when I was Director of the ACFOA, so that the messages got across to everyone who walked in to see them. No women's conference would have been complete without Anne, whose constant presence reminded us of our global sisters at the grassroots. Amazing how a woman based in New York of all places, could be so connected to the most isolated rural women on any continent!

Janet Hunt
International Women's Development Agency,
Melbourne, Australia

***

Dear Anne,

An invitation to reminisce brings to mind your arrival at IWTC in the summer of 1976. You will remember that our quarters were the spacious but abandoned offices at the corner of 46th and UN Plaza that had been lent to us in the spring of 1974 to organize the IWY Tribune in Mexico City, June 1975. Our two staff members and part time secretary had long gone. The walls were bare and spotty where pictures had once hung. The raucous din of frequent anti-Vietnam protests below on Dag Hammarskjold Plaza echoed through the empty rooms. Ros Harris and I were working in one end of the complex trying to compile the list of participants from the IWY Tribune in Mexico and to answer their enquiries.

Your arrival changed everything. Assessing the dreary environment with your artists' eye, you made lavish use of poster board, colored markers and transparent tape. Overnight we were working in an atmosphere crackling with energy that projected the spirit of optimism, excitement, gaiety and humor that you were to infuse into IWTC's worldwide communications. Immediately you set about creating the first IWTC newsletter, demonstrating the possibilities of professionally produced low-cost media and eliminating our laborious efforts to respond to individuals' questions about International Women's Year follow-up. You designed compatible letterhead, envelopes and business cards to enhance the message.

One of your finest achievements was to bring on Vicki Semler. When we could move into a nearby loft building at a rent we could afford, together you and Vicki transformed a former industrial site into a wonderland of creative, colorful (and low-cost) furniture, tropical plants and stunning posters. Was the huge fern you hung over my desk chair some kind of a sword of Damocles?

You had sense enough to decline an invitation to organize

the NGO Forum at the next of the UN world conferences on women. Instead, you put IWTC's resources and verve into VIVENCIA!, another wonderland of art and energy and excitement that hosted programs in a large wing of the university in Copenhagen provided for the Forum. As the times and opportunities demanded, you and your dedicated and accomplished team continues to bring enormous creativity and surprise to subsequent NGO Forums at UN world conferences on women in Nairobi and Beijing.

Anne, you are the most talented photographer I know. Your beautiful and sensitive pictures from your travels and the four slide-tape sets from the women's conferences that you and Vicki made with those photos are a precious pre-video record of women's way of advancing their own, their sisters' and as a consequence, the human family's status in the world. Despite political obstacles and backlash, may you continue to find opportunities to use your gifts in the service of the goals we have all worked so hard to make part of life. I wish you Godspeed

Mildred Persinger
Convenor of IWY Tribune, Mexico City 1975,
World YWCA UN Representative,
First President of IWTC Board of Director

***

To think of IWTC without Anne is like thinking of New York without IWTC! Anne's legacy is not just that, with Vicki, she created this wonderful resource centre following the IWY Tribune in Mexico City, 1975, but that she created a 'home away from home' in NYC for countless women from around the world.

Anne was also part of my history in this movement. We have worked together since the 1970s when I was involved in setting up programmes in the Caribbean, first the Jamaican Women's Bureau and later the Women and Development Unit (WAND)

at the University of the West Indies in Barbados. When I was setting up WAND it was Anne who came to Barbados for several weeks to help design WAND's logo, stationery and communications strategy (and a very special birthday card for my daughter Alison). WAND's image has always borne the imprint of Anne's style. And Anne with her team at IWTC produced our first regional resource kit, bringing together all the women's organizations, projects, resources, publications and funding possibilities for the Caribbean. That was a major asset in growing our Caribbean women's network.

Later, Anne and IWTC were the people who introduced WAND to the new communications technology that has changed the way we communicate and organize. WAND was one of the networks included in IWTC's programme to introduce first fax machines, then computers into the work of women's networks and projects. The IWTC strategy of bringing women together from the regions to do their computer training and orientation in New York served multiple purposes, including establishing the basis for ongoing networking between the groups and between these groups and IWTC. IWTC prompted the first 'networking among networks'!

But it was as a 'home away from home' in NYC that I will especially treasure IWTC and Anne. For me, no visit was complete without a call at the Centre. In the early days, and probably still, the unsuspecting traveller from warm parts of the world would sometimes be stunned by the cold of winter, and at IWTC they could always find a spare coat, gloves or pair of boots. The welcoming smiles and helpful hands were always there, even as the technology advanced.

I know that 'retirement' for Anne will be like 'retirement' has been for me: you continue to do much the same kinds of things that you always did, but without being paid for them. That's what happens when you love your work! Good luck Anne. You know that you take the love and best wishes of countless women around the world with you when you return to Australia.

Peggy Antrobus
former Director of Women and Development Unit,
University of the West Indies, Barbados, W.I.

***

Anne has been and will remain someone enormously special to me, as a feminist activist and as a dear friend.

I am thankful our paths crossed at the beginning of the eighties, when I was launching the Latin American women's media network Fempress. At the time, I clearly had a lot more panache than knowledge of how to go about the business of building international networks and IWTC was already in full bloom. Twenty years have passed, only to help me see how rare the spirit and generosity of that organization is: how much it has reflected the qualities Anne brought with her from Fiji as she planted the first seed in 1976; and as she led the place through thick and thin. I have yet to encounter a more genuine talent that Anne's for team building and team playing, and for giving wholehearted support where others drown in rivalries...

In those early beginnings, Fempress had its first pamphlet drawn by Anne with graphics that hardly needed a signature. She helped write the budgets, spell-checked reports, introduced us to funders, showcased our work in The Tribune newsletter and invited two of us from our Santiago office to workshops where we learned our first steps in computing. This alone changed our whole publication production systems and tuned us all into Mac computer addicts! In later years, Anne helped us to raise miraculous funds at the last moment to finance a stadium where the women of Chile organized their greatest and most creative rally against Pinochet.

Anne had the stamina and humour to contribute her media skills hands on to the Third Latin American Encuentro Feminista in Lima Peru in 1983. She turned up in the midst of that crowd of 800 Latinas with a giant bag full of media tools and, without knowing two words of Spanish, she put us to work on banners, billboards and pamphlets and then humbly buried herself in a screening room where she single handedly exhibited dozens of films and videos brought by the participants.

Yes, Anne and Vicki and their team of workers at IWTC have built an organization where thousands of women have come to find information, support but mostly good energies with the kind of warmth that makes life worthwhile.

Adriana Santa Cruz
Director, Fempress, Santiago, Chile

Speech by Charlotte Bunch at IWTC farewell, 9 December 2002

I want to focus tonight on how important a role Anne and IWTC have played in building a global women's movement because not enough has been said about how vital they have been to what has happened these past few decades.

I first met Anne in 1979 soon after I moved to NYC 'to do global feminism.' Everyone I asked – from Elizabeth Reid of the Aussie feminist UN mafia to Peggy Antrobus at WAND in Barbados to folks at Ms. Magazine – all said talk to Anne and Vicki at IWTC.

It was the most valuable advice I received. They welcomed me and gave me a home base in NYC as they have to so many women from around the world. At IWTC I met women from every world region, housed a few projects of my dreams, and with Anne and Vicki, collaborated on many joint ventures, such as:

- The 1980 Stony Point International Feminist Workshop and the World Feminists video, in preparation for the Second GO Forum and UN world conference on women in Copenhagen, 1980.

- The International Feminist Networking section of the NGO Forum in Copenhagen. Isis International was also part of that collaboration. There, as in other places at the Form, women debated if they could work across North-South lines. Anne quietly just did it!
- The first Global Feminist Workshop Against Trafficking in Women in The Netherlands in 1983. IWTC gave Shirley Castley, Mallika Dutt and me a home and their full support to work on this project.

And certainly, many of us would never have found a place to sleep in Nairobi at the Third UN world conference on women and NGO Forum in 1985 without IWTC fighting to keep our beds at the hotel we had all booked that were about to be given to government delegates!

But my experience is not unique. IWTC has been a home away from home-a place of our own in NYC – for women from around the world for almost three decades. It is the first stop on many a feminist's trek to NYC whether to get assistance and a helping hand in approaching funders or to learn the ropes of getting around the UN.

IWTC has provided road maps for women not only here but also around the world, whether through their publications, postcards, newsletters, FaxNets and now the IWTC Women's GlobalNet. And it had helped many women enter the world of ICTs. In fact Roxanna Carrillo and I first learned how to use computers and email through IWTC in the mid-1980s.

Anne has provided this assistance not only in NYC but also around the world. I remember her on the floor with markers at the Third Latin American Encuentro Feminista in Lima Peru in 1983, preparing posters and instructions in a language both of us were struggling to speak! Always there has been Anne's helpful guidance and her graphics ... those birds (from the UN Decade for Women logo) and women marching into history!!!

When the history of the global women's movement is told ... Anne and IWTC should be recorded as one of the most important behind the scene forces – assisting women's dreams and visions to become real. Through laughter and tears, with paint and posters, they are always in the picture and taking pictures.

As some of us moved into working for women's rights as human rights, again Anne and IWTC were there – providing information like the manual on Rights of Women – first in the 1980s and updated in the 1990s ... and creating posters and postcards to celebrate the occasion.

They helped us launch the 16 Days of Activism Against Gender Violence Campaign – which ends tomorrow – Human Rights Day – as one of the original co-sponsors of the worldwide petition that we cooked up together here in this office – in our fight to get women's human rights centre stage at the United Nations.

They worked with the Global Campaign for Women's Human Rights in preparing for the World Human Rights Conference in Vienna in 1993, – both the Global Tribunal on Women's Human Rights and the amazing Rights Place for Women. Anne is pictured on the video of the Tribunal, briefing the women testifiers and helping them before they give their testimony.

It is impossible to say enough about how Anne and IWTC have contributed to building the global women's movement – especially at the grassroots – making it all accessible and real for women worldwide.

Let me just say thank you to Anne from thousands of women around the world. We simply cannot imagine you not being here in that corner desk, but we wish you the best Down Under and we know that you will still be with us from there and that we will see you back here for many years to come. Thank you, Anne.

Charlotte Bunch
Director, Center for Women's Global Leadership, Rutgers University, NJ, US

Acknowledgements

There is no way in which I could thank everyone with whom I have lived and worked all these many years. Many of you appear within the pages of this book. Others are too numerous to mention. However, I am deeply indebted to the late Ruth Lechte and Amelia Rokotuivuna for our years working together in Fiji, to Mildred Persinger and Rosalind Harris for their support in establishing the International Women's Tribune Centre in New York, and to my fellow long-time IWTC staff members, most especially Vicki Semler, the late Martita Midence, Alice Quinn, Vanessa Davis, Vicky Mejia and Joanne Sandler.

Importantly, I would like to express appreciation to the tens of thousands of women who continue to put their lives on the line every day in the fight for women's human rights who we at IWTC were fortunate enough to learn from and support, and to the many donors who supported the work of IWTC over more than three decades of activism.

A number of people have encouraged me over the past few years to write about my life and work. Some of them have read through early drafts of the book, made suggestions and generally given the kind of support that has spurred me on. Foremost among these would be my friend and partner Elizabeth Carew-Reid and her wonderful family who have made me feel so much part of their lives since my arrival home to Melbourne after 44 years living and working overseas. Elizabeth put me in touch with writers Iola Matthews and Joan Grant who read through an early draft and urged me to find an editor and publisher as soon as possible. Subsequently, I met Bev Roberts who became my editor and wise counsel for many months. I could not have completed the book without her.

And then there is my own family, all of whom have always supported my work with children and women's human rights, even though it meant I was rarely home. I regret that our mother and father, Ethel and Roy Walker, are no longer alive as they would have particularly enjoyed the stories from the early years at Box Hill Grammar School, the only home we eight children ever knew growing up.

Within my family, special thanks go to Robert and Frances, who read through early drafts and made important suggestions. Jean and Evan were major supporters of this book and I have felt their loss keenly. I wish they could both have been around to see the final result. Jean especially loved me reading stories from the book to her in her final weeks and would laugh out loud at some of the memories. Evan's wife Judith has likewise been a great supporter of the book. And my love and thanks to Mavis, Kath and Ruth, pillars of the family, always there when help and encouragement are needed.

Thanks to you all.

Index

Abzug, Bella 166
Adi Cakobau School (ACS), Fiji 66, 73, 78
Africa Regional Conference, Lusaka 241, 246
African Mothers 153
Africa Platform for Action 241
Africa Resource Kit for Women 249–50
Africa Training and Research Centre for Women (UN/ATRCW), Addis Ababa 130–2
Africa Women, Law and Development Network (AWLD) 130
Amager University, Copenhagen 135, 251–2
Anastasia, *see* Namisongo, Anastasia
Angelou, Maya 125
Anthony, James 75
Antrobus, Peggy 123, 125–6, 318
Asia and Pacific Centre for Women and Development (APCWD), Teheran 127
Asia and Pacific Women, Law and Development Network (APWLD) 150, 215
Asia Pacific Development Centre/Gender and Development Unit (APDC/GDU), Kuala Lumpur 130
Association for Progressive Communications/Women's Network Support Programme (APC/WNSP) 173
Association for Women in Development (AWID) 141, 167, 182–4
Australian Council for Overseas Agencies (ACFOA) 162, 165
Australian Embassy in Kathmandu 271–2
Australian International Development Assistance Bureau (AIDAB) 140, 165
Australian Woman Diplomat in Kathmandu, Nepal 271
Avecilla, Carminia 174
Awori, Thelma 132, 241–3

Backer, John 104
Bangkok Declaration: Women Empowering Communications 174
Bangkok, Thailand 130, 133, 159–60, 164, 174, 215, 236, 271–2
Banuelos, Stephanie 174
Barrios de Chungarra, Domitilla 136–7
Barrow, Dame Nita 145, 148, 182, 263
Barrow, Lesley 126, 139
Bazinet, Jean-Michel 97
Beijing Platform for Action, 1995

174, 180, 188, 191, 211, 213
Beijing Plus Five 187, 189–90, 211
Beijing Plus Five Special Session, June 2000 189, 211
Belize Committee on Women and Development 139
Bellagio Conference Center, Lake Como, Italy 152
Beneath Paradise 178
Bhagwati, Justice P.N. 280
Bird, Melanie and Sarah 297
Bishop, Karen 174
Bok-Dong, Kim ('Comfort Woman') 281–5, 287
Boutros-Ghali, Boutros (UN Secretary Genera) 183
Box Hill City Baths 22
Box Hill City Library 9
Box Hill Girls' Technical College 28
Box Hill Grammar School (BHGS) 3–4, 16, 30, 99–100, 323
Box Hill Methodist Youth Fellowship (MYF) 37–8
Bread for the World, Germany 95
Breakthrough, New York and India 141
Broadbent, Hon. Ed. 280
Brown, Father Stan 215
Brown, Noel 113
Bunch, Charlotte 134, 168, 319, 321
Buresova, Nina 83

Camp Walker, Rosebud/Balnarring/Wilson's Prom 19
Canadian International Development Agency (CIDA) 125, 146, 157
Canto Grande, Lima, Peru 258–9
Carew-Reid (Lade), Elizabeth 73, 311, 322
Caribbean Resource Kit for Women 125, 127, 246
Caribbean Sub-Regional Meeting, Jamaica, 1979 123
Carnegie Building, New York 122, 130, 214
Carter, Rosalynn 125
Castley, Shirley 134, 320
Catchings, Rose 156, 168, 268
CD-ROM: Rural Women in Africa: Ideas for Making Money 192, 194–5, 295, 301, 304, 306–7, 309
Center for Women's Global Leadership (CWGL) 169, 170–1, 280, 321
Centre for Documentation and Information on Women, Jakarta 163
Cheddie, Charlotte 77
Chicago, Judy 118
Chileshe, Beatrice 154
China Organizing Committee for Beijing, 1995 175
Church Center at the United Nations (CCUN) 143, 145, 148, 169, 189, 200, 214
Church Women United 104
Clarke, Marion 30
Colonial War Memorial Hospital (CWM), Suva 73
Comfort Women 285–7
Communicating Appropriate Technologies with Rural Women 161
Communications Consortium Media Centre (CCMC) 189

Conference of Non Governmental Organisations in Consultative Status with the United Nations (CONGO) 122
Convention on the Elimination of Discrimination Against Women (CEDAW) 137–8
Cottingham, Jane 185
Cox, Elizabeth (Sabet) 162

Danielsen, Bengt 143
Danielsen, Marie-Therese 143
Davis, Vanessa 131, 135, 142, 185, 322
DAWN, Development Alternatives with Women in a New Era 150, 167
DAWN/IWTC Meeting of women's media networks, Barbados, 1993 173
Developing Strategies for the Future: A Feminist Perspective 134
Douglas, Laurel 130, 174
Dutt, Mallika 147, 320
Dyfan, Isha 302

East-West Communications Institute, University of Hawaii 118
Ellis, Zoila 139
Encuentro Feminista, Peru, 1983 164, 258, 318, 320
ESCAP UN Economic and Social Commission for Asia and the Pacific 159, 162, 215
ESCAP Pacific Operations Centre (ESCAP/POC) 162, 215, 274
Fairfield Infectious Diseases Hospital 13
Feminist Forum, Stony Point, NY 134
femLink Pacific, Suva 102
FemPress, Santiago 143, 152, 318–19
Fiji Arts Club 71, 73, 81, 96
Fiji National Youth Council (FNYC) 84
Fiji Women's Rights Movement (FWRM) 102
Fiji YMCA 102
Fiji Youth Training Programme 84
Fiji YWCA 83–4, 86, 95, 100, 111–12, 116, 120, 136, 145, 226
Finland Ministry of Development Cooperation (FINNIDA) 158, 216
Flora Tristan, Lima 258
Ford Foundation 144, 162
Ford, Betty 125
Forward Looking Strategies for the Advancement of Women to the Year 2000 (FLS), Nairobi, 1985 151, 155
Foundation for People's of the South Pacific (FPSP) 215
Fraser, Arvonne 150
Friedan, Betty 115, 137
Friedrich Ebert Foundation 157

Gachukia, Eddah 145
Global Media Project 189
Global Tribunal on Women's Human Rights, Vienna, 1993 171–2, 280–1, 284, 321
Gorodé, Dewe 112
Grand Tour, USA, 1961 56
Grant, Kathy 92–3

GRECMU, Montevideo 154
Green Belt Movement for Women, Kenya 143, 265
Greenpeace 85
Griffin, Vanessa 112

Haddawi, Dr, Bloomington Indiana, USA 106
Hague Appeal for Peace Gender Task Force 186
Hansen, Annelise 136, 251
Harris, Rosalind 122, 131, 183, 322
Hatiye-Atwater, Yolande 185
Hess, Doris 156, 268
Heyser, Noeleen 215
Heyward, Carter 118
Himmelstrand, Karin 146
Hirshon, Tea 112
Hollis, Miss (Holly) 61
Huairou, China 175–8, 290–1, 293–4
Hull, Elmyria 96
Hume, George 55–6
Hunt, Janet 162, 314
If It's Not Appropriate for Women, It's Not Appropriate, Nairobi, Kenya, 1985 263, 265
Illkaracan, Ipek 164
Indiana University 25, 101–2, 104, 113, 117, 122, 124, 170, 214, 220, 225–6
Information, Communication and Networking Forum (INCONET) 134
Intermediate Technology Development Group (ITDG), London 151, 177
International Alert (UK) 186

International Archives for the Women's Movement (IIAV), Amsterdam 185
International Board of Directors of Isis WICCE, Kampala 193, 295
International Board of Directors, Isis International, Manila 184
International Conference on Nutrition, Rome, 1992 169, 276
International Council on Adult Education 157
International Development Research Centre (IDRC), Canada and Kenya 146, 192
International Policy Action Committee (IPAC) 140, 166
International Research and Training Institute for the Advancement of Women (INSTRAW) 115, 140
International Telecommunications Union (ITU) Gender Task Force, Geneva 205
International Training Institute, USA YWCA, New York 74, 87–8, 105
International Women's Day (IWD) 155, 160
International Women's Day, Santiago, Chile, 1983 254
International Women's Rights Action Network (IWRAW) 150
International Women's Tribune Centre (IWTC) 122, 126, 140, 202, 223, 313, 322
International Women's Year

(IWY) Tribune, Mexico City, 1975 111–13, 115–16, 121–4, 134, 137, 140, 192, 225, 227–8, 315–16
Isis Internacional, Santiago 152, 185
Isis International, Manila 154, 172, 174, 184–5, 188, 320
Isis Women's International Cross Cultural Exchange (Isis WICCE), Kampala 154, 164, 184–5, 193–4, 295, 306
It's Our Move Now, IWTC publication 155
IU Mathematics Education Audio Visual Unit 109
IWTC Board of Directors 131, 212
IWTC CSW Book of Days 187
IWTC Women's Global FaxNet 170, 175–8, 288, 320
IWTC Women's GlobalNet 178, 180–1, 201, 203, 208, 320
IWY Tribune Project Newsletter 124
IWY Tribune, Mexico City, 1975, *see* International Women's Year Tribune

Jackson and Walker 96
Jackson, Dorothy (Dot) 136
Janeway, Sir Derek 76
Japanese International Cooperation Agency (JICA) 164–5
Jennings, Miss (Jenny), Suva 61
Johnson, Ellen Sirleaf 244
Johnson, Lady Bird 129
Johnstone, Diane 272
Jorgensen, Tina 174
Jung, Grace 130, 153

Kalapurakal, Rosemary 173
Karl, Marilee 185
Katz, Jane (Garland Summer) 216
Kenya Appropriate Technology Advisory Committee 145, 148, 197
Kenya NGO Forum Organizing Committee 145
Kindergarten Training College, Kew 30, 73
Kindervatter, Suzanne 301, 314
Kingsley Hall, Bromley-By-Bow, UK 38–9, 44–5, 51
Kingswood College, Box Hill 29, 100
Kiribati 97, 101, 128, 274
Know How Conference on Women's Knowledge 185
Kuala Lumpur 130, 160, 215, 236
Kwok, Chi 174

Lade, Elizabeth, *see* Carew-Reid, Elizabeth
Lady Northcote Free Kindergarten, Montague, Melbourne 34
Lal, Brij V. 75, 79
Laucala Bay Air Force Base, Suva 70, 85
Lechte, Ruth 37–60, 63–70, 74–5, 83–4, 86, 95, 98–9, 102, 111–12, 128, 145, 149, 226, 265, 322
Lester, Doris 38
Lester, Muriel 38
Liberia 131, 240, 244–5
London 38–41, 44, 46–7, 50–1, 55, 95, 151, 174
Lord, Doreen 24
Lyon, Heather 73

Maathai, Wangari 149, 265–6
MacBride, Seán 113, 226
McNeur, Lynda (Wismer) 93, 217
Maddocks, Lady Elinor 58–9, 62
Maddocks, Sir Kenneth 8, 75
Maendeleo Ya Wanawake, Kenya 261
Mair, Lucille 83–4, 137
Manila YWCA, see YWCA Manila
Marketing Strategies 195
Mastrangelo, 166, 174
Mathare, Kenya Water Project 237–8
Media and Communications Centre 178
Media One (Kampala) 194
Mehta, Monica 174
Mejia, Vicky 131, 135, 138, 142, 153–4, 164, 322
Methodist Ladies' College 6, 73
Midence, Martita 123–4, 126, 130, 136, 142, 155, 322
Mijumbi, Rita 301, 306, 309
Mills, Sonia 147
Mok, Duncan 201
Molinero Roldan, Maria Angeles 174
Molisa, Grace Mera 112
Mongella, Hon. Gertrude 175, 181
Moore, Elizabeth Luce 91
Mount Kosciusko 25
Movilazando la Mujer 139
Murrell, Katie 24–5
Mururoa Atoll 85, 226
Museum of Modern Art, Oil Painting Classes 88
Muslim and Christian Women Come Together, Huairou 273

Nadarivatu YWCA Camp, Fiji 72
Nakaseke Community Telecentre, Uganda 193–5, 295–8, 301–3, 306–11,
Nakibuuka, Agnes 302, 306–7
Namisongo, Anastasia 303–4, 309–11
National Congress of Neighborhood Women, NY 157
National Council of Churches of the USA 101, 104
Negroni, Maria 164, 174
Nepal, Kathmandu 159, 215, 245, 271–3, 288
Netherlands Ministry of Development Cooperation 147
New York State Women's Meeting, Albany, 1977 124
New York Under Attack: 11 September 2001 199
NGO CSW Planning Committee for the NGO Forum, Beijing 1995 151
NGO Forum '85, Nairobi, 1985 263, 264
NGO Forum, Beijing, 1995 173–8,
NGO Forum, Copenhagen, 1980 134–7, 251, 316
NGO Status of Women Task Force on Women and Armed Conflict 186
NGO Women's Global Communications Network 188
NGO Working Group on Women, Peace and Security 186, 196

Nkuye, Jessica 295–6
Norfolk Island 25–7
Norway Ministry of Development Cooperation 146
Nuclear Free and Independent Pacific Conference 111
Nuclear Free Pacific Movement 102, 111–12, 225–6

Ochieng, Ruth Ojiambo 295
Odio, Hon. Elizabeth 281
Okwenje, Elizabeth 131, 241
Once and Future Action Network (OFAN) 209
Once and Future Pavilion, Huairou 173, 177–8, 293
Onsa, Pauline 141
Organisation for Economic Co-operation and Development, Development Assistance Committee, Women and Development Expert Group (OECD/DAC/WDEG), Paris 147, 157
Overseas Education Fund (OEF) 195

Pacific Conference of Churches 101, 108
Pacific Regional YWCA 166
Pacific Women's Regional Network (PAWORNET) 166
Palmer, Elizabeth 74, 135–6, 251
Pan Pacific South-East Asia Women's Association (PPSEAWA) 62, 64
Panapasa, Raijeli 83
Papua New Guinea 5, 80–1, 128, 152, 183, 274–5
Parkinson, Susan 99

Patel, A.D., Fiji 76
Peace Corps 84, 136
Peace Tent 148
Peacesat satellite 275
Persinger, Mildred 112, 116, 121–2, 124, 126, 131, 183, 316, 322
Pett, Dr Denny 105, 111
Plaxton, Jean 89
Princess Ashraf, Iran 127, 232

Qionibaravi, Anaseini 77, 88
Quinn, Alice 147, 166, 185, 200, 322

Ramacake, Ana 81
Ramrakha, K.C. 80
Range, Maggie 301
Rathgeber, Eva 192
Reid, Elizabeth 127, 129, 160, 215, 231, 236, 319
Rights of Women 111, 136, 155, 161, 321
Rights Place for Women 171, 172
Rockefeller, Mary 91
Rokotuivuna, Amelia 66–9, 71, 77, 86, 96, 102, 111–14, 116, 143, 225–7, 322
Ross Frankson, Joan 173, 175
Rubeiro, Shamila 164
Rural Women in Africa: Ideas for Earning Money, IWTC CD-ROM, *see* CD-ROM
Russell, Fanny Dontoh 125

SAKHI, *see* South Asian Women's Support Group 167
Samuel Rubin Foundation 200
Sandler, Joanne 130, 135, 138, 142, 148, 154, 163–4, 219, 264, 322

Santa Cruz, Adriana 143, 319
Santiago, Chile 107, 143–4, 152, 172, 185, 254–5, 318
Santiago, Irene 151
Saran, Sima 174
School for International Training, Vermont 157
Semiha Sakir Experimental Secondary School, Istanbul, Turkey 276
Semler, Vicki 107, 112–18, 120, 123–5, 130, 134–5, 138, 142–4, 160, 163, 170–1, 185, 200, 209–10, 214, 216–17, 220, 225–6, 228–9, 315–16, 319, 322
Shahani, Leticia 151
Silverstein, Betty 215
Silverstein, Maurice 215
Silverstein, Pam 216
Singh, Meera 164, 172, 174
Siwatibau, Suliana 77
Slatter, Claire 112
Snyder, Margaret (Peg) 140, 194, 244, 301
Sookmyung Women's University, Seoul, Korea 188
South Africa 195, 219
South Asian Women's Support Group (SAKHI) 167
South Pacific Arts Festival 100
South Pacific Commission (SPC) 85–6, 97, 108, 138, 143
South Pacific Commission Community Education Training Centre (SPC/CETC) 138
South Pacific Games 79
Starkey, Jacqui 134, 217
Steinem, Gloria 118
Stewart, Marjorie 83–4
Sultanhisar, Turkey 170, 277–9

Sutherland, Joan 39, 217
Suva City Council 65, 95
Suva Multiracial Women's Basketball Association 69
Suva Primary School 82
Suva Tennis Club 69
Suva Town Hall 63, 66, 102
Suva Women's Basketball Association 69
Suva Women's Crisis Centre 102
Suva Women's Hockey Association 69
Sweden International Development Authority (SIDA) 146, 204

Tadesse, Mary 131–2, 247
Tamesis, Pauline 173
Taylor, Michele 71
Tech and Tools 145–50, 197, 264–7, 314
Tech and Tools Book 151, 161
Teheran, Iran 127–9, 160, 231–5
Toganivalu, Adi Davila (Uluilakeba) 73, 81–2, 96
Toganivalu, Ratu David 117
Tora, Apisai 75–6
Tora, Seniloli 71
Toy, Judy 38, 39
Tribune, The 124, 135, 139, 145, 152, 154, 159, 161, 163–4, 167, 175, 181, 237, 258, 261–2, 272
Tuvalu 97, 101, 274
Twelve Critical Areas of Concern 180, 211

Uberoi, Yasna 200, 220
Uganda Council for Economic Empowerment of Women 194

Uganda National Council for Science and Technology 194
Uganda YWCA 194
Uganda: From Boardroom to Burning Sun: Interviews with 75 Successful Entrepreneurs in Uganda, Margaret Snyder 194
Uganda: Isis WICCE, *see* Isis Women's International Cross Cultural Exchange
Uganda: Media One, *see* Media One
Uganda: Rural Women in Africa: Ideas for Making Money, IWTC CD-ROM for the women of Uganda, *see* CD-ROM
Uluilakeba, Adi Davila, *see* Toganivalu
UN Association of Australia 16
UN Commission on the Status of Women (UN/CSW) 138, 144, 186, 191, 210, 291
UN Conference on Environment and Development (UNCED), Rio de Janeiro, 1992 168
UN Convention on the Elimination of All Forms of Discrimination Against Women (CEDAW) 137
UN Decade for Women 133, 146, 148, 227, 279, 320
UN Department of Public Information (UNDPI) 156, 183
UN Development Fund for Women (UNIFEM) 115, 140–1, 153, 155, 157, 164, 166, 186, 249, 301
UN Development Programme (UNDP) 132, 234–5, 244, 247, 249
UN Division for the Advancement of Women (UNDAW) 115, 183
UN Economic and Social Commission for Asia and the Pacific (UN/ESCAP) 159, 162, 215, 274
UN ESCAP Pacific Operations Centre, Port Vila 159, 162, 215, 274
UN Economic Commission for Africa (UNECA) 248
UN Fourth World Conference on Women, Beijing, 1995 174–5, 177, 211
UN Group on Equal Rights for Women 160
UN International Conference on Human Rights, Vienna, 1993 170–2, 280
UN International Research and Training Institute (INSTRAW) 115, 140
UN International Women's Year World Conference, Mexico City, 1975 127, 140
UN Millennium Development Goals 207
UN Secretary General 170, 175, 183
UN Security Council Resolution 1325: Women, Peace and Security 187, 196, 207, 212
UN Special Session on Africa 153
UN World Conference on Women, Copenhagen, 1980 174–5, 177, 211

UN World Conference on Women, Nairobi, 1985 142, 144, 146, 155, 320
UNESCO Toronto Platform on Women and the Media, 1993 174
United Methodist Church, Board of Global Ministries, Women's Division 156–7, 268
University of Nairobi 148–9, 263–4
University of the South Pacific (USP) 84, 100, 108, 118, 136, 162, 274, 276
US Peace Corps 84, 136
USA International Women's Year Conference, Houston, 1977 124–5, 228
USA National Plan of Action 12, 229–30
USP Campus, Port Vila, Vanuatu 275

Vakalala, Dr Anarieta 77
Vakalala, Esiteri 77
Vakatale, Taufa 77
Van den Assum, Laetitia 147
Van Hussen, Jose 147
Vasquez, Lourdes 174
Veron, Kaye 139
VIVENCIA, NGO Forum, Copenhagen, 1980 135–7, 251, 316

Walker, Charles Fitzroy (Roy) (Dad) 3–29, 38, 59–60, 99–100, 322
Walker, Chris 88
Walker, Ethel (Mum) 3–19, 23, 29, 163, 322
Walker, Evan 4, 23, 26–7, 29, 38, 51, 55–6, 88, 210, 323
Walker, Frances (Millar) 4, 6, 8, 18–21, 27, 29, 163, 322–3
Walker, Jean (Provan) 4, 6, 38–9, 44, 90, 97
Walker, Judith 88, 323
Walker, Kathleen (Beanland) 4, 29, 323
Walker, Mavis (Chappell) 4, 29, 323
Walker, Robert 3–4, 8, 10, 22, 27, 29, 145, 170, 201, 276–8, 322–3
Walker, Ruth (Bartle) 4, 8, 20–1, 26–7, 29, 323
We The Peoples: 50 Communities Award 181
Weiss, Cora 200
Wellesley College Women and Development Conference, 1976 118–19
White, Eirene 75, 77–9
Wiener, Leonora 184
Williams, Dr Esther 58, 61–2
Wilson, Nancy 14
Wismer, Lynda, *see* McNeur, Lynda
WNYC 199
Women and Development Unit of the University of the West Indies (WAND) 125–6, 130, 133, 139, 316, 318
Women and Media Conference, Monrovia, 1979 132
Women and New Technologies Workshop, Netherlands 163
Women Empowering Communications conference, Bangkok, 1993 174

Women for a Healthy Planet conference, Miami, 1991 167
Women in Black 293
Women, Environment and Development Organization (WEDO) 167
Women, Ink. 166, 173, 178, 182–3, 185, 197–8
Women, Law and Development International (WLDI) 150
Women's Bureau, Jamaica 123, 316
Women's Division of the United Methodist Church in the USA 156, 268
Women's Global NGO Communications Plan of Action 185
Women's Information Network for Asia and the Pacific (WINAP) 159
Women's Institute for Freedom of the Press (WIFP) 141
Women's International League for Peace and Freedom (WILPF) 141
Women's Network Support Programme (WNSP) 188
WomenAction 2000 (WA2000) 187, 189
Wong, Mary 200
Woodward, Jimmie 88
World Trade Center, New York 199–201, 204–5, 219, 309
World YWCA 74, 87, 95, 108, 111–12, 123–4, 128, 136, 145, 148–9, 163, 177, 195, 251, 264, 316
Worldview International Foundation (WIF), Oslo 159

Worldview International, Sri Lanka 271

Yee, Joan 136
Yokohama Women's Centre 165
Youth Ideas for the South Pacific 98, 128
YWCA Kindergarten, Fiji 63, 67, 72–3, 95–6, 100
YWCA Mutual Relations Committee, USA 91
YWCA of the USA 87, 96, 104, 108
YWCA, Manila 128
YWCA, Fiji. *see* Fiji YWCA
YWCA, Pacific Regional, *see* Pacific Regional YWCA

Zambia 131–2, 152, 154, 164
Zambia YWCA 132
Zimbabwe 141, 157, 197, 268–9
Zimbabwe International Book Fair 182, 197
Zimbabwe Office of UNIFEM 157
Zimbabwe Women's Resource Centre 157
Zimbabwe YWCA 157
Zimmer, Layton 136
Zimmer, Nan 136

www.ingramcontent.com/pod-product-compliance
Lightning Source LLC
Chambersburg PA
CBHW030850170426
43193CB00009BA/553